Kentucky Super

Daniel Lindsey Thomas,

Lucy Blayney Thomas

Alpha Editions

This edition published in 2020

ISBN : 9789354036309

Design and Setting By
Alpha Editions
www.alphaedis.com
email - alphaedis@gmail.com

KENTUCKY SUPERSTITIONS

BY

DANIEL LINDSEY THOMAS, Ph.D.

LATE PROFESSOR OF ENGLISH AT CENTRE COLLEGE,
AND FOUNDER AND PRESIDENT OF THE KENTUCKY
BRANCH OF THE AMERICAN FOLK-LORE SOCIETY.

AND

LUCY BLAYNEY THOMAS, M.A.

TEACHER OF ENGLISH AT WARD-BELMONT SCHOOL, NASHVILLE, TENNESSEE.

PRINCETON UNIVERSITY PRESS
PRINCETON N. J.
LONDON: HUMPHREY MILFORD
OXFORD UNIVERSITY PRESS

1920

PREFACE

To bring together odd beliefs for the possible amusement of the curious is not the object of a research in the field of folk superstitions such as we have attempted. The end sought is not humor or satire; our hope is rather that such value as is present will be serious. The study of superstitious survivals throws light on what the working of the human mind was in the early stages of its evolution. Eccentric and illogical beliefs of today were accepted principles of life centuries ago. A collection of superstitions, in so far as it has scholarly value, is a partial record of what men have thought and believed. It is, therefore, our hope that this collection may be in a real, though perhaps small, sense, a contribution both to history and to psychology. In Kentucky and elsewhere, the folk superstitions are gradually passing away; many of them are already irrecoverably lost. For purposes of permanent record, it would seem worth while to preserve in print all that can be saved from loss.

In the collection of the materials for this volume, we have received assistance from many people. For example, teachers and students of eight or ten colleges and sixty or seventy high schools, grade schools, and district schools have made contributions, small or great. Many other men and women, white and colored, in the mountains and in the lowlands of the State, have sent us items. It is impossible to mention all to whom we wish to offer our grateful acknowledgments. Those who have sent us the largest number of usable folk superstitions are Miss Louise Kelly, of Lebanon, Reverend and Mrs. Lucien Waggener and Mr. C. M. Fackler, of Danville, Mr. Josiah H. Combs, of Hindman, Rev. G. S. Watson, of Booneville, Miss Stella Nolan, of Harlan County, Mr. Joseph Hart, of Buckhorn, Professors L. L. Dantzler, of the University of Kentucky, B. N. Daniel, of Georgetown College, C. C. Freeman, of Transylvania College, John F. Smith, of Berea College, Thos. A. Hendricks, of Hamilton College for Women, Miss Mary Shaw, of Kentucky College for Women, Miss Ada G. Croft, of Cumberland College, Miss Mattye Reid, of the Western Kentucky Normal School, Dean Kirke Smith, of Lincoln Institute (colored), and Professors W. O. Hopper, of the Mt. Sterling High School, M. E. Ligon, of the Lexington High School, G. W. Colvin, of the Springfield High School, J. T. Norris, of the Augusta High School, J. H. Addams, of the Franklin High School, J. W. Welch, of the Henderson High School, J. H. Risley, of the Owensboro High School, and J. S. Cotter, of the Coleridge Taylor School (colored), of Louisville. We wish to express our very great gratitude to Professor George Lyman Kittredge for advice and encouragement in the production of this collection.

KENTUCKY SUPERSTITIONS

CONTENTS

INTRODUCTION

Superstitious beliefs are more persistent and more wide-spread than most people would suspect. We have all been fully aware that they swayed the minds of people in earlier centuries. We know, also, that they are sprinkled through our earlier literature; for example, the folk superstitions of Shakespeare fill a volume of generous size,[1] and instances are no less common in the writings of his contemporaries and are perhaps even more common in the works of Chaucer. Their potent presence, however, in the minds of people of our own time may reasonably cause surprise. In 1907,[2] Mr. Fletcher B. Dresslar, of the University of California, asked almost nine hundred normal-school students of the University to write down superstitions that they knew and to indicate frankly their belief or disbelief in them. As a result, 7,176 slips were handed in, each containing a superstition. Of these, 3,951 were accompanied with expressions of disbelief, 2,132 of partial belief, and 1,093 of full belief. Thus 44.9 per cent of the superstitions that were noted were shown to command complete or partial credence. The ones mentioned by the largest number of those engaged in the research were the superstitions associated with Friday, the number thirteen, the dropping of a knife, a fork, or a spoon, the picking up of a pin, the first sight of the new moon, the breaking of a

---

[1] T. F. Thistleton-Dyer: "Folk-lore of Shakespeare." London, 1884. 8vo. 515 pages.

[2] Quoted by H. Addington Bruce in an article entitled "Our Superstitions," in *The Outlook*, 1911, vol. 98, pp. 999-1006.

1

mirror, the presenting of a knife to a friend, the potency of the horseshoe, the burning of the ear, the passing of two companions on the opposite sides of a post, the howl of a dog, the presence of a bird in the house, the opening of an umbrella in the house, and the turning back after one has started anywhere. - Mr. Bruce, from whose article the results just quoted were taken, gives also the results of a canvass of believers in superstition among the professors, instructors, and assistants of Harvard University. This investigation showed that only 26.6 per cent of the Harvard teachers questioned could say that they believed that they were entirely free from superstition. A large number of the 73.4 per cent who confessed belief denied at first that they were in any degree superstitious, but under close questioning, they showed that they were not entirely innocent. Professor Edwin M. Fogel, whose volume of superstitions[3] contains the largest collection hitherto published in America, has listed 2,083 separate superstitions that are current among Pennsylvania Germans. The authors of the present volume have found almost 4,000 superstitions in Kentucky. As Pennsylvania Germans and Kentuckians are in general probably much more conservative than the average of Americans, inherited beliefs doubtless persist with exceptional strength among them; yet superstitions, it may safely be said, have disappeared entirely from no community in our country.

The origin of all superstition may probably be traced to the desire of mankind to propitiate fate, to avert evil, and to dispel the mystery of life and of the universe. Primitive man, in his fear of evils that he did not under-

[3] Edwin Miller Fogel: "Beliefs and Superstitions of the Pennsylvania Germans," 1915.

stand, sought to avoid disaster by any means that he could find. In his ignorance of logic, he often accepted a co-incidence as a cause. Francis Bacon well says:[4]

"That hath given them [coincidences] grace, and some credit, consisteth in three things. First, that men mark when they hit, and never when they miss; as they do, gen-erally, also of dreams. The second is, that probable con-jectures, or obscure traditions, many times turn themselves into prophecies; while the nature of man, which coveteth divination, thinks it no peril to foretell that which indeed they do but collect.—The third and last (which is the great one), is, that almost all of them, being infinite in number, have been impostures, and, by idle and crafty brains, merely contrived and figured, after the event past."

The reasons for the survival of superstition from a more primitive age into our own are that people are slow to surrender beliefs that they have inherited, that many of them are still ignorant and timorous, and that in spite of the explanations of both science and religion they con-tinue to find life and the universe largely inexplicable.

Search for the origins of individual superstitions has enlisted the energies of many folk-lore scholars. Their researches have led them to trace various folk practices to starting-points in the Bible (often misinterpreted and modified by tradition), in pagan mythology, in plant and animal worship, and in sun or moon worship, and to other sources. In as much, however, as the beginnings of folk-lore lie in nearly all instances far back in the most primi-tive periods of the human race, conjecture is often the only means of seeking them. The results of research have therefore been marred by uncertainty and guess-work,

[4] Francis Bacon: "Of Prophecies," 1625.

and scholars have frequently not arrived at agreement. For these reasons, it has seemed best in connection with this folk-lore collection, to refrain from an attempt to record the genesis of the various separate items. Readers who are interested will find in the bibliographical list at the close of the introduction the names of several works in which the attempt is made to trace superstitious survivals to their sources.

In consideration of the distribution of folk-lore in Kentucky, it may as well be remembered that there are three somewhat different classes of people within the State: the mountain whites, originally from Virginia and the Carolinas; the lowland whites, originally from Virginia, the Carolinas, Pennsylvania, and Maryland; and the lowland negroes. The first and the third of these classes have been less influenced either by immigration or by education than the second; even the lowland whites have been less affected by the coming in of people from outside the State than have the inhabitants of most parts of our country. Most Kentucky superstitions are common to all three classes of the people, because the negroes originally obtained most of their superstitions from the whites, and because the superstitions of Kentucky are in almost all cases not recent inventions but old survivals from a time when they were generally accepted by all Germanic peoples and even by all Indo-Europeans.

The only class of original contributions made by the negroes to our stock of superstitions is that of the voodoo or hoodoo signs, which were brought from Africa by the ancestors of the present colored people of America. These have taken only slight root in the Caucasian mind. On the arrival of the negro in America, his child-like mind

4

was readily receptive to the white man's superstitions. Reciprocally the black slaves and servants in Kentucky and elsewhere in the South have frequently been the agents through which the minds of white children have been sown with these supernatural beliefs, some of which have remained permanently with them. Nearly all classes of superstitions find acceptance among the negroes. The most widely prevalent are beliefs concerning haunted houses, weather signs, bad-luck and good-luck signs, "charm" cures, and hoodoo signs. In particular, the negroes' belief that the date of the planting of vegetables should be determined by the phases of the moon, is unshakeable, and the fear, especially of the older negroes, is ever-present that an enemy will impose a hoodoo upon them. With increase of travel, with somewhat broader and more active industrial life, and with improved chances for education, the Kentucky negroes appear to be slowly, though very slowly, losing their superstitious beliefs. Even in the very good negro schools of Louisville and Lexington, however, most of the students, older ones as well as younger, have thus far progressed but little in this direction.

Until the past decade, the life in much of the mountain region of Kentucky has been isolated and primitive. Before that time, not only were there no railroads in the heart of the mountains, but even roads were surprisingly scarce. The beds of small streams served, and in many places still serve, as ready, if not satisfactory, substitutes. Along with feuds, illicit stills, emotional religion, and genuine hospitality, which are characteristics of the pinched life in the mountain fastnesses, folk superstitions have survived with great tenacity. Of late, however, a transformation has begun in this once remote section. Railroads have entered from several directions to open up the coal, oil, and lumber fields. At present, with a fuller industrial life, newcomers have arrived, old families have been scattered, schools have become better and more numerous, and the life of the old communities has entered upon a process of change. The superstitious beliefs still retained by the old-type mountaineers are in general those that were brought to Kentucky by their English and Scotch-Irish ancestors. Many are concerned with good and bad luck signs, which are more or less similar to those that have survived in other places. The chief difference is that these survivals are more widely accepted in the conservative fastnesses of the mountaineers than elsewhere among the white people of Kentucky. Folk remedies and medicines are, also, very widely trusted by the highlanders; for example, many folk practices are customary in connection with child-birth. Men and women who are thought to accomplish cures by incantations, or "ceremonies," and physicians who reinforce more or less legitimate medical practice with charm cures are only gradually becoming less numerous and less influential. One of the most remarkable classes of folk-lore survivals in the mountains of Kentucky is that of witch lore. Perhaps there is at this time no other place in the English-speaking parts of the world where superstitions concerning witches receive so much credence. The supposed activity of these malevolent beings is now, however, as one may judge from the data of later pages in this volume, confined mainly to the bewitching of cows and rarely to the "spelling" of a dog, a horse, or a person. The mountain witch stories are slowly passing into the same class with fairy tales. At present,

6

the witches are few, and the witch and charm doctors are chiefly old men and women, who, when they die, will in many cases leave no successors. Yet so instinctive and deep-rooted is superstition that education and the interests of an increasingly more conventional life in the Kentucky mountains combat it with but slow success.

As the lowland whites of Kentucky are more numerous, more varied, and geographically more widely spread than either the negroes of the Blue Grass and the western parts of the State or the white people of the mountains, probably as many individual superstitions may be gleaned among them as among either the negroes or the mountaineers. Naturally they are more fully current in small towns and in country districts than in cities, and more fully among children and illiterates than among educated adults. In a small Kentucky town, life changes less rapidly than in many other places. As it is still in some measure similar to the life in a typical town of a border-Southern State such as Mark Twain reproduces in Tom Sawyer and Huckleberry Finn, it is not surprising that every folk superstition mentioned in those two books is to be found in the following pages.

A larger percentage of the negroes than of the mountaineers are strongly swayed by folk signs, and a larger proportion of the mountaineers than of the lowland Caucasians. Of this collection of almost four thousand separate items, the majority may be found among both lowlanders and highlanders and among both negroes and whites. In the presence of improved and more accessible educational advantages and of increasing complexity of life, superstitions are very gradually dying out in Kentucky.

BOOKS TREATING FOLK SUPERSTITIONS

COLLECTIONS OF SUPERSTITIONS

V. S. Lean: Lean's Collectanea. 1902-1904.

Cora Linn Daniels and C. M. Stevans: Encyclopaedia of Superstitions, Folklore and the Occult Sciences of the World. 3 vols. 1903.

J. G. Frazer: The Golden Bough. 14 vols. 1914.

S. Baring-Gould: Curious Myths of the Middle Ages. 2nd Edit., 2 vols. 1868.

T. F. Thistleton-Dyer: The Folk-Lore of Plants. 1889.

Fanny D. Bergen: Current Superstitions culled from the oral tradition of English speaking folk, with introduction by Wm. Wells Newell. 1896.

Fanny D. Bergen: Animal and Plant Lore. Memoirs of the American Folk-Lore Society. 1899.

Clifton Johnson: What they say in New England. (This volume contains several hundred New-England superstitions.)

Edwin Miller Fogel: Beliefs and Superstitions of the Pennsylvania Germans. 1915. (This volume contains 2083 separate superstitions).

PERIODICAL PUBLICATIONS

Folk-Lore. A quarterly review. London. 1893-
The Journal of American Folk-Lore. 1888-

BOOKS ON SOURCES OF FOLK SUPERSTITIONS

J. G. Frazer: The Golden Bough. 14 vols. 1914.

John Fiske: Myths and Mythmakers. 1873.

John Brand: Observations on Popular Antiquities. A new edition with the additions of Sir Henry Ellis. 1900.

KENTUCKY SUPERSTITIONS

Charles Hardwick: Traditions, Superstitions, and Folk-lore (chiefly Lancashire and North of England); their Eastern Origin and Mythical Significance. 1872.

Robert Means Lawrence: The Magic of the Horseshoe, with other Fold-lore. 1898.

William George Black: Folk Medicine. 1883.

Thomas Sharper Knowlson: The Origins of Popular Superstitions and Customs. 1910.

Frank W. Nicolson: The Saliva Superstition in Classical Literature. Harvard Studies in Classical Philology, vol. 8. 1897.

BIRTH AND CHILD LIFE

(The notation of a section of Kentucky in connection with a superstition shows that it has been reported only from that section. The absence of localization indicates that the superstition is general. The attribution to definite localities is necessarily somewhat loose.)

1. A woman in travail should hold salt clenched in her two outstretched hands..............Mountains
2. In a case of child labor, place an axe edge up under the bed of the mother...............Mountains
3. If an expectant mother places her hand upon her body, the child will have a birthmark at the position on its body that she presses...........Mountains
4. An expectant mother should not have her teeth filled.
5. In a case of child labor, cross hazel twigs, put them across an open Bible, and place them under the pillow ....:...........Mountains
6. Wine is necessary to women with child. At communion a pregnant woman, whether a church member or not, may receive the communion wine.,....
.... Mountains

9

7. To drain a woman at child-birth, the physician places his shoes on the woman and makes her walk about in them until the time of the after-birth; then he places his hat on her head............Mountains
8. To hasten child-delivery, give a woman a drink of which another woman has partaken....Blue Grass
9. To hasten child-delivery, beat a rattlesnake's rattles fine and give the powder to the one that is in labor ....Blue Grass
10. The number of balls on the naval string of the first child shows the number of children that a woman will have ....Mountains
11. Children are brought by a stork.
12. A child born with a caul, that is, with the birth membranes unruptured, will have second sight.
13. If a green veil shrouds the face of a new-born child, the child is gifted with prophecy.......Mountains
14. If an enemy, at the birth of a child, can get possession of the baby's after-birth, he can control the child's fate for evil ever afterwards.
15. If you visit a new boy baby and kiss it, you will have good luck..............North-eastern Kentucky
16. If you make fun of a little baby, you will have the thing that you ridicule in it....................
..................Central Kentucky Negroes
17. If one finds a baby-pacifier, there is going to be an addition to the family.
18. When a baby smiles in its sleep, angels are talking to it.
19. A child that is born on Christmas Day can understand the speech of animals..........Mountains
20. A baby's crying at christening is a good-luck sign.

21. If a child's ear runs into the cheek without a crease at the lobe, it will have criminal tendencies.
22. Bald-headed babies are from fine stock.
23. If a child's hair is long and heavy, the child will not grow, as all its strength will go into its hair......
............................Central Kentucky
24. If a baby is born with an unusually large amount of hair, it will have very little at maturity..........
............................Central Kentucky
25. If a baby is born with no hair or but little, it will have a great deal at maturity.......Central Kentucky
26. If a child has a large mouth, it will be a good singer
............................Central Kentucky
27. If a baby has early teething, there will be a new baby in the family soon...................Mountains
28. It brings bad luck to put a new-born baby on a table.
29. If you take a baby down the hill before you take it up the hill, it will go down hill in life...Mountains
30. Carry your baby upstairs before you do downstairs, so that it will rise in the world.
31. If a child sings in bed, it will wet the bed..Mountains
32. If you crack the first louse found in a child's head on the bottom of a tin cup, the child will make a good singer ....Mountains
33. When a boy baby is taken for the first time on a call, its disposition will be affected by that of the man of the house...............Southern Kentucky
34. When a girl baby is taken for the first time on a call, its disposition will be affected by that of the woman of the house.........Southern Kentucky
35. If a child is homely when it is small, it will be good-looking when it is grown.

11

36. If a child is good-looking when it is small, it will be homely when it is grown.
37. A beautiful girl will not be nervous when she is a woman.
38. If an infant clutches a coin that is put into its hands, it will love money.
39. If an infant does not clutch a coin that is put into its hands, it will be a spendthrift.
40. If a baby's fist closes over money that is put into its hands, it will be prosperous when it is grown.
41. If a baby's fist does not close over money that is put into his hands, it will be poor when it is grown.
42. Place a child on the floor with a Bible, a dollar, and a deck of cards. The one that he chooses first indicates his future as a preacher, financier, or gambler.
43. If the hand of a new-born baby is closed tight, it will be close or saving.
44. If the hand of a new-born baby is open, it will be of a generous disposition.
45. If a child cries a great deal when it is an infant, it will make a good man or woman.
46. It brings bad luck to change a baby's name.
47. If in dressing the baby for the first time you put its right arm into its dress first, it will be right-handed.
48. If on the first time that a baby is dressed the left arm is put into the dress before the right arm, the baby will be left-handed.
49. It causes bad luck to put a baby's dress on over its head before it is one year old.
50. Pull the baby's clothes on over its feet instead of over its head, or it will never grow.

51. Do not cut the baby's nails until it is one month old. It will be light-fingered if you do.
52. If you bite a baby's finger nails, it will steal when it grows up.
53. If you cut off a baby's finger nails, it will die before it is six years old.
54. Anyone except a mother may cut a baby's nails without damage.
55. If you place a hat on a baby's head before it is a year old, it will not grow any more.
56. You must not put a hat on a baby's head, for, if you do so, you will cause bad teething.
57. Make a baby cut teeth by putting a hat on its head before it is six months old.
58. It brings bad luck to cut a baby's hair before it is a year old. The child will die.
59. To keep a person from growing, take three hairs from the back of his neck and three from each temple, make a hole in a Columbia poplar at the person's height, put the hairs into the hole, and drive in a peg..........................Mountains
60. It is bad luck to let the baby look into a mirror before it is one year old.
61. Do not let the baby look into a mirror before it teethes. This act will make teething hard.
62. If a baby looks into a mirror, it will be small.
63. If a baby looks into a mirror before it is one year old, it will die.
64. If a baby looks into a mirror before it is a year old, it will die before it is two years old.
65. If you show a baby itself in a mirror before it is six months old, it will die before it is a year old.

13

66. If you measure a child on the day that it is two years of age, it will be half as tall as it ever will be......
..........................Louisville Negroes
67. It causes bad luck for a child to be put under a bed on its ninth birthday, for it will never grow any more ....Mountains
68. It brings bad luck to count a baby's teeth.
69. If a child puts its tooth under its pillow at night, it will become a five-cent piece by morning.
70. If a baby's first tooth grows into the gum above, it will be a thief.
71. If you tickle a baby, you will cause it to stutter.
72. If a child is prematurely wise, he will not live long.
73. The good die young.
74. If a baby does not fall off the bed, it will never be reared.
75. If a young child marks the furniture, it will soon die. "It is marking itself out of the world.".........
.... Western Kentucky
76. Unless a baby crawls before it walks, it will crawl in after life.....................Central Kentucky
77. A baby's sneezing at the table is a sign of death.
78. If a baby talks before it walks, its tongue will ruin it.........................Central Kentucky
79. If the teakettle boils in a room where there is a little baby, the baby will have colic...Central Kentucky
80. Never carry a baby in a funeral procession before it is a year old; if you do, it will die..............
....................Central Kentucky Negroes
81. If you think too much of a child, he will die. (2nd Commandment.) ....Mountains
82. The third son has the brains of the family.Mountains

14

83. If any one steps over you, you will not grow any more.

84. When a baby sticks out its tongue, it wants something that it has not.

85. When a baby sweeps a floor, the act is the sign of someone coming.

86. If a child blows all the fluff from the dandelion in one blow, his mother wishes him very much; in two blows, not so much; in three blows, not enough to cease play ....Mountains

87. Blow the seed-ball from a dandelion and then count the seeds left; the number you count will indicate the number of days until you will get a whipping.

88. The boy that steps on another boy's foot is his worst enemy; but if a girl does so, she is his best friend. .
............................Louisville Negroes

89. If a child drops his school book and picks it up, he will miss his lesson in it. He can avert the disaster by kissing his book.

90. If a child drops his book and does not stamp it before picking it up, he will miss his lesson........
............................Louisville Negroes

91. If some one picks up for a child a book that he has dropped, the former and not the latter will miss the lesson.

92. A girl who drops her school books may avert bad luck or a missed lesson by walking around each article and putting her foot on it.

93. To keep from missing his lesson, a child should step on his books........................Blue Grass

94. If a child sleeps with his text book under his head at night, he will know his lesson next day.

95. If a child goes for a switch for the punishment of another child, the former will himself be whipped.
96. On a child's birthday, he should receive a blow with a switch or other instrument of pain for each year of his life. Each blow should be accompanied by the pronouncing of a line of the following or a similar incantation, adapted to fit the age of the child:

> One to live on;
> One to grow on;
> One to eat on;
> One to be happy on;
> One to get married on.

FAMILY RELATIONS

97. A poor man is sure to have many children ("A fool for luck and a poor man for children").
98. If there is strong family resemblance between parent and child, the child will outlive the parent.
99. If a daughter resembles her father, she is born for good luck.
100. If a boy is born like his mother, he is born for good luck.
101. It is unlucky to be named for your mother . . . . Mountains
102. Step on a crack,
Break your mother's back.
103. If you are walking backwards, you are cursing your parents.
104. If you walk backwards and look over your left shoulder, you curse your mother . . . . . Central Kentucky
105. One in each family can locate water or veins of water

by taking a peach-tree fork and turning it upside down like this—V—. The fork will turn down in the neighborhood of water underground.

LOST ARTICLES

106. To find which way the cows have gone, catch a daddy-long-legs by the hind legs, and he will point with one of his front legs.

107. Count a hundred stars without repetition; then you will find something lost.

108. If you secretly bury a marble and go back in three days, all the marbles that you have ever lost will be there.............................Blue Grass

109. Find a marble or other lost article by throwing another one and watching where it goes.

110. In order to find anything lost, shut your eyes and turn around several times. Then throw something at random. The way it goes is the way toward the lost article.........................Blue Grass

111. To find a lost article, spit into your hand, strike the saliva with your other hand, and watch the direction of the splash.

112. If you have lost a ball, spit into the palm of your hand and say, "Spit, spat, where is the ball at?" While you are repeating these words, take the other hand with two fingers and strike the saliva. It will fly in the direction of the ball.............
..........................Central Kentucky

113. If a person loses a needle and someone else asks if there was a thread in it, the loser of the needle will find it.................North-eastern Kentucky

114. If you lose anything, you will find it seven days later at the same time that you lost it, provided you do not look before....................Blue Grass

115. Shut your eyes and throw a piece of gravel. After a week, try to find it. If you succeed, you will have good luck.

116. To find a ring that has been lost, carry a peach switch gripped tightly. It will turn down when you reach the place where the ring is lost.

117. To find gold that is lost, place a dime in the end of a forked cherry or peach switch and proceed as in the last given superstition.

118. You may recover lost money by kissing a negro.

119. If you find that you are lost, go in the opposite direction, and you will come to your destination.

120. If you are lost, throw a knife over your back. The way the blade points is the way to take.

WISHES

121. A wish made on the new moon will come to pass.

122. Make a wish on a new moon; if you do not look at the moon until it is new again, your wish will come true.............................Blue Grass

123. When you see the new moon, turn a piece of money over and make a wish; the wish will come true....
.... Mountains

124. If you see the new moon over the left shoulder, any wish you make will come true..Western Kentucky

125. If you see the moon over your right shoulder and make a wish, it will come true........Mountains

126. Make a wish when you see the first star and do not

speak until you see another. The wish will come true.

127. Put a ring on the finger at the sight of the first star in the evening. Your wish will come true.......
.... Mountains

128. If when you see a meteor you can make a wish before it disappears, your wish will come true.

129. When you see a shooting star, if you say "Money" three times you will have a full pocket book......
.... Mountains

130. If you see a bluebird and make a wish before it flies away, the wish will come to pass.

131. If you see a crow flying through the air, make a wish. If he does not flap his wings before he goes out of sight, the wish will come true. If he does flap his wings, look away, and if you do not see him again your wish will come true.

132. Your wish will be realized if you make it when the first turtle-dove of the spring coos....Blue Grass

133. Make a wish when you see a redbird.

134. If you throw a kiss at a redbird and make a wish, it will come true.

135. Make a wish when you see a redbird. If it flies to the right, the wish will come to pass.

136. After you have made a wish at the sight of a redbird, the wish will come to pass if the bird flies upward
...........................Western Kentucky

137. Name a redbird. If you make a wish before the bird flies, it will come true.

138. If you see a redbird, make a wish and spit at it three times before it gets out of sight. Under these conditions the wish will come true........Mountains

19

139. If you make a wish when you see a lone turkey-buzzard and do not look at it again, it will come true
..........................Central Kentucky

140. A wish made on the first whippoorwill in spring and kept secret will come to pass..........Mountains

141. When you hear the first whippoorwill of the year, walk three steps back, pick up whatever is under your left heel, spit on it, and make a wish.

142. If you see a flock of birds, make a wish, and do not look at the birds again..............Mountains

143. If you see a flock of blackbirds, name them and make a wish...........................Mountains

144. When you see a gray cat, look at its fore feet and make a wish. If you see it again, the wish will come to pass......................Mountains

145. If you see a spotted horse and make a wish, it will come true, provided you do not see it again.

146. Make a wish at the sight of a white horse.

147. If you spit over your little finger when you see a white horse, your wish will come true..........
.........................Western Kentucky

148. If you find a horseshoe with the toe towards you, throw it over your right shoulder and make a wish
.... Mountains

149. Put a horseshoe above a door. The first one that passes under it must make a wish.

150. Spit on a horseshoe and throw it over your head. If the outside remains up, your greatest desire will be realized ....Southern Kentucky

151. You can avert ill luck from the passing of a double horse or mule wagon by running across the road and making a wish. The wish will come true.

152. When you see a gray mule, make a wish, wet your thumb, and stamp your hand.........Mountains

153. If you find a nail, hammer it into something, and at the same time make a wish. The wish will come true ....Mountains

154. Two people may each make a wish and then break a wishbone between them. The one that gets the shorter piece will be married first, and the other will obtain his wish.

155. If you make a wish before you go up a hill and do not look back, your wish will come true. Mountains

156. Make a wish and throw a piece of wish vine over your right shoulder into the weeds. If it grows, your wish will come true............Mountains

157. Make a wish on a grain of corn that you have found and bury the corn. The wish will come to pass....
..........................Southern Kentucky

158. If you find a four-leaved clover, hold it above the head and make a wish...............Mountains

159. Put a four-leaved clover into your shoe. Make a wish. When it is lost out, the wish will come true.

160. Share a double almond with some one. Let each make a wish. When you two next meet, the first that says "Philippino" will get his wish.

161. Make a wish at the sight of a hay wagon.

162. When you see a wagon of hay, make a wish. Count thirteen while you look, then turn away, and do not see the wagon of hay again. The wish will come true. If the hay is baled, the wish will not come true until the bales are broken.

163. If you pass a loaded wagon, make a wish. If you

pass it a second time, the wish will not come true
and you will have bad luck.

164. It brings bad luck to pass a hay wagon without making a wish. A serious sickness in the family or
death will ensue.

165. Make a wish at the sight of a freight-train. Count
"yes, no, maybe so," to find whether the wish will
come to pass........................Blue Grass

166. Whenever a yellow railroad car passes, make a wish.
If you do not look at the car again, the wish will
come true.

167. Make a wish when you cross a new bridge.........
.........................Southern Kentucky

168. When you pass over a railroad bridge, you may make
a wish, and if you do not speak until you have
passed over the bridge the wish will come true.

169. If you spit over a bridge-railing into the water and
then do not speak until you are off the bridge, your
wish will come to pass.

170. If you count twelve while you cross a bridge and
make a wish, the wish will come true...Blue Grass

171. Always go the end of the walk, hang your left foot
over, and make a wish. The wish will come true.
If you do not follow this plan precisely, you will
have bad luck.

172. If on the first time you go into a new house you make
a wish, it will come to pass.

173. Upon entering a strange house go to the kitchen and
make a wish. It will come true.

174. A wish made in a bed never before slept in will come
true.

175. When an eyelash falls out, make a wish and blow the

lash from the back of your hand; if the lash falls off, the wish will come true, but if it sticks to the back of the hand, the wish will not come true.

176. If you find a loose eyelash on another person, put it on your left hand, make a wish, and blow the eyelash over your right shoulder. Your wish will come true.

177. Make a wish while untangling your hair.

178. If when you find a pin pointed toward you you make a wish, it will surely come to pass.

179. Find a pin, stick it on your left shoulder with your right hand, make a wish, and pass it on.

180. When you find a pin, make a wish, put the pin on your shoulder, and do not glance at it again. Your wish will come true. Variant: if you lose it without knowing when, the wish will come true.

181. Make a wish when you put a ring on some one's finger.

182. If you turn another person's ring around eighteen times and make a wish, it will come true.

183. If you make a wish and then look over your left shoulder (not looking through trees at the new moon), your wish will come true......Blue Grass

184. A girl may make a wish if her skirt turns up.

185. If you must change a garment accidentally put on wrong side out, make a wish while doing so. This act will avert bad luck, and your wish will come true.

186. If a point of scissors that you drop sticks into the floor, make a wish. It will come to pass.

187. Find a hairpin, make a wish, and hang the hairpin up.

188. If you bend the ends of a found hairpin while mak-

ing a wish, and throw the hairpin away, the wish will come true.

189. If you find a hairpin, bend each prong with someone, make a wish, and then throw it over the left shoulder.

190. If you drop a comb, you may turn the teeth down and make a wish.

191. If you drop a comb, put your foot on it and make a wish.

192. When two persons speak the same word at the same time, they should join their little fingers and make a wish.

193. If two people say the same thing at the same time, they must lock their little fingers and say alternately: Red, blue (or other color); needles, pins; Shakespeare, Longfellow (or other poets). Then each may make a wish.

194. If two people say the same thing at the same time, they should make wishes, touch wood, and touch blue, and their wishes will come true.

195. Make a wish and open the Bible. If anywhere on the page these words occur, "And it will come to pass," the wish will come true.

196. When you look into a well for the first time, any wish you make will come to pass..........Mountains

197. If you drop a dish cloth, step over it and make a wish ....Mountains

198. If you eat the point of a piece of pie last and make a wish on it, the wish will come to pass.

199. If you forget something and come back for it, sit down and make a wish before going on.

DIVINATIONS CONCERNING LOVE

200. If you hold an apple in your armpit until it is warm and then eat it, your sweetheart will love you.....
...................................Southern Kentucky

201. If you can break an apple in two, you can get any one you choose for your life partner............
...........................North-eastern Kentucky

202. If you can break an apple in two after some one has named it, the one named loves you....Blue Grass

203. An apple peeling that has been removed from the fruit without a break may be thrown over the left shoulder to form the initial of the person that one will marry.

204. Count apple-seeds with the use of this formula: "one, I love, two, I love; three, I love, I say; four, I love with all my heart; five, I cast away; six, he loves; seven, she loves; eight, both love; nine, he comes; ten, he tarries; eleven, he courts; twelve, they marry."

205. As many fresh apple seeds as stick to the forehead when pressed against it, so many days will it be until you see your sweetheart.........Mountains

206. Shoot an apple seed up; your sweetheart lives in the direction that it goes...............Mountains

207. Name apple seeds and shoot them at the ceiling. The one that hits the ceiling shows which one loves you best.

208. Put an apple seed on each eye. Name each seed. The first that falls shows which one loves you the more.

209. Put five seeds on your face and name them. The first to fall off shows which one you will marry.

210. Place apple seeds on the grate. Name them. The ones that jump show which ones love you.

211. Count apple seeds to learn the number of children you will have......................Mountains

212. If you can eat a crab apple without frowning, you can get the person you desire.........Mountains

213. If a girl's apron comes unpinned, her sweetheart has been taken.

214. If a girl's apron becomes unfastened and drops off, her lover is thinking of her.

215. If your apron slips off, your sweetheart is talking about you.

216. Make a string of beans and throw it down. The initial that it forms will be that of your future mate.

217. Name each corner bed post when you retire. The post that you have your hand on in the morning indicates the one you will marry.

218. Rub each post of the bed with the peeling of two lemons which you have carried all day. The person who offers you two lemons in your dream is your future partner in life.

219. Name the corners of the bed-room. The one that you look at first in the morning will show which person loves you best.

220. If you look under the bed, you will never marry.

221. Make up a bed with some one and do not speak while you are doing it. You will marry the first person with whom you shake hands afterward.

222. If you cannot make a bed well, you will marry a worthless man.

223. To eat beets is a sign that you are in love. Mountains
224. If you can touch with your finger a piece of soot (a so-called beauty spot) on your face, your sweetheart loves you.........North-eastern Kentucky
225. If you sleep with a Bible under your head three successive nights, you will dream whom you shall marry ....Mountains
226. Before you go to bed at night, get the Bible, select a chapter that has as many verses as your sweetheart is years old, memorize the last one, repeat it two or three times, put the Bible under your pillow, and go to sleep. If you dream of the person, you will marry him or her, as the case may be...Blue Grass
227. If uninvited you take the last portion from a dish, you will not be married that year. Leave it for fairies.
228. If you take the last portion on a dish at the invitation of someone, you will have a handsome husband or wife.
229. If you take the last biscuit on the plate, a rich young widower or widow is your fate.
230. If you take the next to the last biscuit on the plate, you will never marry.
231. If you take the next to the last biscuit or the like, you will have a handsome husband.
232. If a bird flies into the house, the one who discovers it will be married before the year is out. His spouse will be from the region from which the bird came; for example, a robin represents a town person and a meadow lark a country person.
233. If you find a bird's nest empty, you will never marry. If it has one egg in it, you will marry within one

year; if two eggs, two years; et cetera..Mountains

234. If you stick your finger, put three drops of blood on a piece of cloth and leave it by your bedside. Your future husband's or wife's initials will be written on it in the morning.....North-eastern Kentucky

235. If you burn your bread, your sweetheart is angry with you.

236. If a girl allows the bread to burn while baking it, she will never be married.

237. If a girl burns bread while baking it, her married life will be unhappy........Southern Kentucky

238. If you kill the "British lady" (the red-winged black-bird), you will marry the next man you meet....
.... Mountains

239. If you can jump over a broom placed on the seats of two chairs, you will marry within a year......
.... Mountains

240. If you step in front of a broom with which some one is sweeping, you will not be married that year....
.... Mountains

241. If you cut first into a cake of butter, you will be an old maid....................Western Kentucky

242. If a butterfly settles on you, you will get a new sweetheart ....Mountains

243. To learn your future husband's profession count your buttons, saying:

"Rich man, poor man, beggar man, thief,
Doctor, merchant, lawyer, chief."

244. If you take the piece that is on top of the cake, you will never marry.............Central Kentucky

245. Light a candle and leave it. Your intended mate will blow it out.

246. Blow out the candles of a birthday cake. If you extinguish all at once, you will be married within a year.

247. The number of birthday candles left unextinguished after you have blown once shows how many years your wedding is off.

248. Get a bow of ribbon out of a boy's cap and put it into your locket. The first boy that you cross water with thereafter will be the one you are to marry..
.........................Southern Kentucky

249. In the telling of fortunes, the cards have the significations shown below:

Hearts.
ace—house or home.
two—kiss.
three—short space of time: 3 hours, 3 days, etc.
four—pleasant crowd: dining, dance, extreme
and "mushy" social pleasure.
five—marriage.
six—love.
seven—jealousy.
eight—large number of love affairs.
nine—you get your wish.
ten—extreme love pleasures.
king—somewhat gray elderly man.
queen—rather blond woman.
jack—rather blond young man.

Clubs.
ace—introduction.
two—new things in your life.
three—space of time longer than in hearts.

four—crowd: smaller or quieter than in hearts.
five—ring at bell, knock at door, etc.
six—ride in carriage, motor, etc.
seven—journey on water.
eight—business transaction.
nine—sure luck (best in deck).
ten—long journey.
king—elderly rather dark man.
queen—rather dark woman.
jack—rather dark man.

Diamonds.
ace—a letter.
two—very good luck.
three—three pieces of good fortune together.
four—pleasant crowd, less extremely so than
    in hearts.
five—diamond ring.
six—money.
seven—conversation.
eight—more money than six.
nine—disappointment.
ten—more money than eight.
king—elderly, very white-haired man.
queen—extremely blond woman.
jack—young blond man.

Spades.
ace—a strange bed.
two—trouble: lie, angry words, etc.
three—long period of time: three years or
    more.
four—crowd or sorrow: at accident, fire, etc.

five—sickness.

six—funeral, death.

seven—tears.

eight—strong drink, d.t.'s.

nine—disaster. Worst card in deck.

ten—loss (not necessarily extreme like other
   tens).

king—elderly, extremely dark man.

queen—extremely dark woman.

jack—extremely dark young man.

250. Fortunes told with cards should involve the use of
a new deck.

251. A woman that loves a cat will be an old maid.

252. If you give a black cat a piece of pickle and it eats it,
the first man the cat goes to you will marry.

253. To meet a black cat with green eyes is a sign that
your sweetheart is likely to quarrel with you......
   ....Western Kentucky

254. If you tie a knot in a cedar limb and name it and it
grows, the person it is named for loves you......
   ....Western Kentucky

255. If you walk across a cellar door or a cellar grating
you will never be married.

256. The falling back of a chair as you leave it means that
you will not marry within a year.

257. If when you turn a chair over you let it lie until you
count thirty, you will marry twice.....Mountains

258. If you turn over a chair in rising, begin to say the
alphabet. The letter you pick it up on is the initial
of your future life partner.

259. If you knock a chair over and some one begins to
count, the number counted before you pick the

chair up is the number of years before you will marry.

260. Bathe your hands, feet, and face in some water in which you have placed charcoal. You will find a lock of your husband's hair in one piece of the charcoal.................Western Kentucky

261. If your cheeks burn, your sweetheart is talking about you.

262. Name the chestnuts on a grate. The first one to jump shows which person loves you most.

263. If a girl soaks her bread or cake in her coffee, she will be an old maid.

264. If you look into a coffee pot, you will be an old maid.

265. In the grounds of a coffee cup the small lines that form a heart shape means a letter, a snake shape an enemy, a coffin a death, and a straight line peace and happiness.

266. If you find a four-leaved clover, put it into the bottom of your shoe. The first man you meet while carrying this clover in your shoe will be your husband.

267. "If a maid finds a four-leaf clover,
    On that day she will meet her lover.
    She will know him by her beating heart,
    For love is of each life a part.".......Mountains

268. Put a four-leaved clover into your shoe, go to sleep, and you will see the one you are to marry........
    ....Southern Kentucky

269. If you find a four-leaved clover and place it in your left shoe, and then shake hands first with a person of your sex, you will never marry; if first with one

of the other sex, that person is destined to be your mate .... Blue Grass

270. If one finds three four-leaved clovers inside of three hours, the third person he will see will be his future mate .... Blue Grass

271. Different colors, such as red, blue, and the like, indicate the different states of love, for example bad, true, and so forth.

272. If a blue vein shows plainly on your nose when you are a baby, you will never see your wedding clothes .... Blue Grass

273. If you see a blue-eyed dog, your next sweetheart will be whiteheaded .... Mountains

274. If you wear red, you will never wed.... Blue Grass

275. If you see a hen flying with a red tail, you will marry the next person that sees her......... Mountains

276. If you find a red ear of corn, you will be married within a year.

277. Count a hundred red ties; the man who has the one-hundredth on will be your husband.

278. After you have counted a hundred boys with red neckties, the first boy you see with a blue tie on, you will marry; and the first boy you see with a white one on, you will love first.

279. If a girl meets a team of white horses and then names ten different colors of ties, the last color she sees will be the one on the man that she is going to marry.

280. Count one hundred white horses. The first man you see thereafter with a red necktie you will marry.

281. Count one hundred gray horses; you will marry on the day you count the last one.

282. If you count one hundred white horses, you will marry before the year is out.

283. Stamp ten white horses; then the first man you see with a red necktie on is the man you will marry.

284. After you have counted forty gray horses, the next man you meet with a red necktie will be your life mate.

285. After you have counted a hundred grey horses, name a color; the first man you meet wearing a tie of the same color will be your future husband.

286. Count one hundred white horses and one white mule. The next man you meet will be your life partner.

287. Count ninety-nine horses and a white mule; the first person you shake hands with thereafter you will marry.

288. When you are counting a hundred gray horses, one gray mule will be equivalent to ten of that number.

289. If the first corn silk that you see in any season is red, you will soon attend a wedding. (Cf. the sign that if the first corn silk is white you will go to a funeral.)

290. If the first butterfly of the season is a white one, you will go to a wedding before the season is over.....
..........................Central Kentucky

291. If you wear a yellow flower, you are jealous.

292. If you shake hands across the communion table, you will marry ....Mountains

293. If you find an even number of grains on an ear of corn, you will marry once and have a happy marriage.

294. If you find an odd number of grains on an ear of corn, you will marry twice, both times unhappily.

295. Cut seven initials on the ground, put a grain of corn into every one, and turn a hen loose. The one she picks up first shows whom you will marry.

296. If your cornbread is rough, your husband's face will be rough.

297. If you cross a street corner diagonally, you will not be married this year.

298. If you have two crowns, you will cross the water and marry twice.

299. A curly-headed individual can get anybody he wants .... Mountains

300. Pluck the petals from a daisy, repeating as you do so: "He loves me, loves me not." The words on which the last petal is plucked reveal the fortune.

301. It is lucky to receive a proposal at a dance and refuse it........................Western Kentucky

302. Blow a dandelion ball. The number of seeds left indicates the number of children you will have.

303. Blow a dandelion ball. If you drive away all of the seeds in one exhalation, you will be married.

304. The number of seeds left on a dandelion ball when you have blown it once will be the number of years before you are married.

305. If in early spring, a young woman will sit on the ground, reach behind her, and pick up a handful of dirt, she will find in it a hair the color of her future husband's.

306. If you drop your dish cloth, your sweetheart is coming.

307. If a girl allows dish-water to come to the boiling point, she will not marry that year.

308. If a dog follows you, encourage him, as he will bring you a handsome husband.....Western Kentucky
309. If you go in one door and out another, you will catch a new sweetheart............Central Kentucky
310. The direction of the first turtle-dove which you hear in the spring is the direction of your sweetheart...
...............................Mountains
311. If when you hear the first turtle-dove of the season you turn around three times on your heel and then look into the heel of your stocking, you will find a hair the color of your future mate's....Mountains
312. If you are the first to sleep under a new quilt, the hero or heroine of your dream will be your partner in matrimony...............Southern Kentucky
313. If you dream of a coffin, you will marry rich but die soon after.
314. If you dream that you cry, you will be married within a year.
315. To dream of dates is a sign that you will break your betrothal.
316. A dream of death is a sign of a wedding.
317. If with the dream bone of a hog under your pillow you dream of a person of the opposite sex, you will marry him.
318. To dream of a horse is a sign that you are loved by one person alone....................Mountains
319. If you dream that you kiss somebody, you will be disappointed in love.
320. If you dream that a log (or a plank) falls out of your house, you will lose your married partner. If you dream that some one puts or helps put it back, you will marry that person..............Mountains

321. If a girl dreams in church that she nods towards the minister, she will marry a young parson..........
.........................Western Kentucky

322. To dream of money is a sign of marriage.

323. If a girl dreams that she eats a pickle, an old bachelor will kiss her.................Western Kentucky

324. If a young man dreams that he eats a pickle, he will be beloved by a woman older than he is and of a sour temper.................Western Kentucky

325. If you dream of old shoes, someone will take your sweetheart away from you............Mountains

326. If you dream of a wedding, you will never marry.

327. If you get the front of your dress wet while washing your clothes, your husband will be a drunkard.

328. If your dress is turned up on the right side, your sweetheart loves you.................Mountains

329. If your dress is turned up on the left side, your beloved dislikes you....................Mountains

330. If you swallow a wild duck's heart, you will get the person that you desire.

331. If your ears burn, name each one for people of the opposite sex; the one which ceases to burn first shows the one who loves you the better...........
......................North-eastern Kentucky

332. If your left ear burns, your lover is thinking of you ....North-eastern Kentucky

333. If you boil an egg, remove the yolk, fill it with salt, and eat it just before going to sleep, the man that brings you a cup of water in your dream you will marry. If the cup is of gold, you will be wealthy; if of tin, very poor.

334. Place an egg in front of an open fire at night and sit

in front of it without speaking. Your future mate will come in and turn the egg when it is hot.

335. If someone tells you his right eye itches and you do not pass the statement on, you will never marry.. ....Western Kentucky

336. A quivering or twitching of the eye is a sign that your lover is thinking of you.

337. Take an eyelash, name your lover, and then blow the lash away. If you do not see the eyelash any more, your sweetheart loves you.

338. Pull an eyelash out and hold it between the thumb and the first finger. Let one person name the thumb and another the finger. Open them. The one that the eyelash sticks to has the name of the one that loves you.

339. If you go to the joining place of three farms, you will meet the person you are to marry..Mountains

340. If you find a crooked feather in your hair, your husband will be a humpback.............Mountains

341. If you crook your little finger while holding a cup, you will never be married.

342. The number of times you can pop your fingers shows the number of sweethearts that you will have..... ....Central Kentucky

343. Anyone who can make the first and fourth fingers touch over the backs of the others may marry anyone he chooses.

344. If you can cross your forefinger and little finger over your other fingers, you can get whom you please and please whom you get.

345. Name a lighted fire. If it burns, the person named loves you.

346. If you can make a good fire, you will make a good husband or wife.

347. The man or woman that can not make a good fire will not get a good wife or husband.

348. If your fire fails to burn, your lover is not busy.

349. If a fire that a girl makes goes out, her sweetheart is thinking of her.

350. If a girl builds a good fire, her sweetheart loves her.

351. If the first of a family to marry marries well, the rest will marry well, but if the first marriage is a poor one the rest will be poor.

352. While you are fishing, name the worm. If you catch a fish, your lover is true.

353. If a girl spills flour while she is baking, her husband will be a drunkard.

354. In pinning a bouquet on, if you put the flowers accidentally upside down, you wish to be married.

355. If you wear a flower with the stem up, you are engaged ....Blue Grass

356. When a boy wears a flower to school, he is hunting a girl.

357. Certain crosses of stone, found in the Kentucky mountains, are thought to have been tears shed by the fairies when they learned of Christ's crucifixion. The cross brings good luck, especially for lovers.. .... Mountains

358. If two forks are placed at your plate, you will hear of a wedding......................Mountains

359. If a woman gets two forks at her plate, she will have two husbands.

360. If you have two forks at your plate, someone will take your girl away from you.........Mountains

361. Put the web of a goose's foot into the beverage of a girl whom you would have love you....Mountains

362. If a child is held down by a hair across his nose, the first word he says will be the first word he will say after his marriage.

363. Pull a hair through the fingers. It will curl. In whatever direction the hair points, your sweetheart lives......................Western Kentucky

364. If a man to whom you give a hair from your head holds it between his thumb and his first finger, the first word he says will be the first word that he utters to his wife....................Mountains

365. A hair found in the heel of your stocking will have the color of that of your future husband.

366. If you pull a hair out of a girl's head, she will love you.

367. Pull a hair from the head of a boy whom you wish to love you. If you bury his hair along with one of yours, he will love you forever.

368. If you sew a lock of your hair in the hem of a bride's dress, you will be married before a year has passed.

369. If you wear a lock of your sweetheart's hair in your hat, he will love no other.

370. If someone takes the combings from the comb after you have combed your hair, she will get your sweetheart.

371. To find a hairpin is a sign that you will find a lover.

372. When you find a hairpin, hang it up and name it a color. The first boy you pass wearing a tie of this color will be your husband..........Blue Grass

373. Hang up a hairpin which you have found and name

it for a friend. If anyone takes it before the
week-end, she takes the friend........Blue Grass

374. If you wear in your shoe a hairpin which you have
found in the road, the first man you meet with a
red tie on will be your future husband.

375. If a girl finds a hairpin and keeps it six months, she
will have a proposal at the end of that time.

376. On Hallowe'en name an apple that hangs by a string.
If you can bite it, you are beloved by the person
that you have named.

377. On Hallowe'en, he who can bite an apple by bobbing
for it will marry.

378. If you walk in a grave-yard on Hallowe'en, you will
see your future husband or wife.

379. Look into a mirror at midnight on Hallowe'en to
see your intended.

380. On Hallowe'en look into a mirror on the cellar steps
to see the person that you are to marry.

381. Make a lover's knot of a handkerchief and pull the
ends. The end that stays in most tightly shows the
one that loves you the most.........Blue Grass

382. The accidental crossing of hands as four people shake
hands means that one of them will marry soon.

383. If four people cross hands, the youngest will marry
first.

384. If you have the letter M in your hand, you will marry
rich..................North-eastern Kentucky

385. If you hear a hawk calling, your sweetheart is near
.... Mountains

386. If a girl puts on a man's hat at night when she hears
a mocking-bird, she will marry that year and have
good luck..............North-eastern Kentucky

387. If you stand on your right heel and turn around three times, you may find in the hole a hair like that of your future mate............Mountains

388. If anyone steps on the heel of your shoe, the person doing this is trying to get your sweetheart.

389. If anyone steps on your heel, you will not be married for seven years.

390. If you step upon a person's heel unwittingly, you will dance at that person's wedding.

391. If you can turn a hoecake without breaking it, you are ready to marry.................Mountains

392. Name two hog bristles on a hot shovel. If they turn toward each other, the persons named will marry each other.

393. Name holly leaves that you throw into the fire. The one that pops first has the name of the one that loves you best......................Mountains

394. The number of nails in a horseshoe which you pick up will be the number of years before you will be married...........................Blue Grass

395. The number of years before you marry may be reckoned by the number of nails that remain in a horseshoe after you have thrown it over your left shoulder ....Blue Grass

396. Go to a deserted house at midnight and light a candle; then place a pin in the candle. When the pin falls out, your future husband will appear.......
.... Mountains

397. If you accidentally eat an insect, you will marry within a year.....................Mountains

398. If an insect lights on you, your sweetheart is talking unkindly about you.................Mountains

399. If you kiss your sweetheart over the back gate, you never will kiss him again.

400. An upsidedown kiss (that is, a kiss in which one leans over the chair in which the other is seated) is unlucky.

401. If you kiss a girl on the nose, you will cause trouble ....Western Kentucky

402. Never kiss a girl behind the ear; it brings bad luck ....Northern Kentucky

403. Do not let your beau kiss you in a buggy, for horses carry tails (tales).

404. If you find two knives at your seat, there will be a wedding within a week.

405. If a man gets two knives at his plate, he is going to have two wives.

406. If someone climbs a ladder and cannot go farther count the number of steps ahead; that will be the number of years until he marries.

407. Write the names of a boy and a girl. Strike out the common letters. Name over the words "love" and "marriage," on the remaining letters.

408. Write the names of a boy and of a girl. Strike out the common letters. Name over the words, "love," "friendship," "hatred," "marriage," on the remaining letters.

409. If you find a lilac blossom with five petals and swallow it, you can marry anyone that you desire.... ....Western Kentucky

410. Put a love vine on a bush and name it. If it grows, the person loves you.................Mountains

411. If you can tie a love vine, your sweetheart is thinking of you........................Mountains

412. A maid says, "If I'm not going to marry anybody, knock, Death, knock." If she hears nothing she says, "If I'm going to marry a young man, whistle, bird, whistle!" If her appeal remains unanswered, she says, "If I'm going to marry an old man, hoot, owl, hoot!"........................Mountains

413. Burn a match on one end and hold the burnt end down, catch it, and let the other end burn. If the match does not break, your sweetheart loves you.

414. Name a lighted match. If it burns to the end without breaking, the person loves you. If it breaks in the middle, you will marry him.

415. Light a match and put the end of it on a stove or something similar. When it burns out, the direction in which it falls is the direction of your lover .... Mountains

416. If you find a four-leaved clover on May first, you can get whatever you want....Western Kentucky

417. If one goes fishing on the first day of May, the number of fish caught will be the number of sweethearts one will have........................Mountains

418. Hold a mirror over a spring early in the morning of the first of May; you will see your future sweetheart's face reflected in the water.

419. If on the first morning in May you take a mirror and look down into a spring whose branch flows east, you can see your fated husband or wife..... .... Mountains

420. On the first day of May, if you lean over a well and hold a mirror so that you can see the bottom of the well in it, you will see your future lover's face.

421. On May first, look into an inverted mirror over a

well, to see your future husband or your casket; if
you see your casket, you will never marry at all.

422. On the first morning in May, if a girl goes out walking and finds a snail within its shell, she will marry
a man with a house. If she sees a snail crawling,
she will marry a man without a house.

423. If you find a snail on the first day of May, put it on
a plank in the sun; the letter it makes will be the
initial of your future husband's name.

424. If you find a snail before sunrise on May first, and
place it on a plate of flour or meal, it will write your
lover's name or initials.

425. If you look into a well on May Day you will see
either a coffin or the picture of the man you will
marry.

426. If on May Day at sunrise, you look into an open
well, you will see the reflection of your prospective
wife or husband.

427. Arise before breakfast without speaking a word on
the first day of May, get a bridle from the barn,
go to the spring, and say: "Here is a bridle; where
is the horse and rider?" Repeat this three times.
Then there will appear a man riding a horse without a bridle. This will be your destined husband.

428. On the first morning of May, place a tumbler of
water in a window at the rising of the sun; let it
remain all day. At sunset, look into the water.
If you are to die an old maid or bachelor, a coffin
will appear in the water.............Blue Grass

429. If you walk around a wheat field on the first day of
May, you will meet your fate.

430. If you walk down steps backwards looking into a

45

mirror, you will see your prospective husband or wife.

431. If you look at a mirror over someone else's shoulder, you will get a sweetheart.

432. Sleep with a mirror under your pillow, to see your future husband.

433. If you sleep with a mirror under your head for three consecutive nights, on the third night you will dream of the one you will marry.

434. If you count nine stars every night for nine nights and put a mirror under your pillow the last night, you will see in a dream the one that you are to marry .... Mountains

435. Name one leaf each of mistletoe for a boy and a girl. Place the leaves on a warm stove. If they hop towards each other, the two will marry; if they do not, there will be no marriage.

436. Put some mistletoe over a door. The first man that walks under it will marry the daughter of the house.

437. Hang a bunch of mistletoe over a door; the first person of the opposite sex who pauses under it will be your life partner.

438. On the first night of a new moon, take nine steps backward; then reach behind you and pick up a handful of grass or anything that happens to be there, and put it under your pillow that night. The next morning there will be a hair there the color of your lover's hair.

439. "New moon, true moon,
    Star in the stream,
    Pray tell my fortune in my dream".... Mountains

440. "New moon, true moon, a franklin free,

If he be a true lover, send him unto me.
May I know the color of his hair and of his eyes,
And whether he be witless or whether he be wise" . .
. . . . Blue Grass

441. Look at a new moon over your left shoulder and make this wish:

> "New moon, new moon, let me see
> Who my future husband is to be;
> The color of his hair,
> The clothes he is to wear,
> And the happy day he is to wed me". . . . .
> . . . . Western Kentucky

442. Bend a mullein stalk in the direction of your sweetheart's home. If the stalk grows straight again, he loves you.

443. White specks on the finger nails show the number of presents you will receive.

444. If you have a white mark on your little finger nail, you have a sweetheart.

445. You have as many sweethearts as there are white spots on your finger nails.

446. If you cut your nails on Saturday, you will see your sweetheart on Sunday.

447. If you cut your finger nails on Sunday, you will see your sweetheart before Monday.

448. Cut your finger nails for nine straight Sundays. On the ninth Sunday you will eat dinner with the one you are going to marry.

449. If you cut your nails for nine Sundays, you will marry whom you desire.

450. The first initial you pick up when eating noodle-soup is the initial of your married partner.

451. If your nose bleeds, you are in love.

452. If there is an old maid in the family, there will be one in the next generation.

453. If you eat onions on Saturday, you will not see your sweetheart on Sunday.

454. Fortunes are told by palmistry.

455. Before retiring, place under your pillow slips containing the names of three boys. Throw one slip out when you get into bed and another the next morning. The one left under the pillow will contain the name of your destined mate.

456. Before you go to bed at night, put some water in a pan, put each letter of the alphabet on a piece of paper into it, and place it under the bed. The next day the first letter on top shows the one you will marry.

457. Write the names of admirers on slips of paper and put them into a basin of water. The one that comes to the top of the water first will contain the name of the person that you will marry.

458. Write the names of three boys (or girls) on three pieces of paper, wrap them in bread crumbs, and drop them into a glass of water. The one that rises to the top first you will marry.

459. Write on separate pieces of paper the names of eleven boys, put these names into separate balls of mud, and put also one blank piece into a ball. Drop the balls into a bucket of water. The first one containing a name that comes to the top you will know to be the name of the person that you are to marry. If the blank piece comes to the top, you will not marry.

460. Write the names of certain persons on slips of paper, roll them up, and drop them into a pan of water. The slip that remains rolled up in the morning contains the name of the one that you will marry.

461. If you do not touch the end of the sidewalk in your walk, you will never be married......Blue Grass

462. Put the first pea that you find over the door. The first one who comes in, provided he is not a relative, will be the one that you will marry....Mountains

463. In order to learn when one will marry, let the individual take a pea pod with nine peas in it and place it over the door. The first person of the opposite sex and unmarried who enters, the individual will marry within that year...............Mountains

464. If the first letter from a boy to a girl happens to be written with a pencil, they will not be married to each other.

465. If a person eats pickles, he is in love.

466. If a girl in love craves pickles, her love is returned..
.........................Louisville Negroes

467. Your sweetheart will love you if you will sleep with his photograph under your pillow.

468. If you bury the photograph of a person whom you wish to love you, along with his hair, he will love you.

469. If you eat the point of a piece of pie first, you will be an old maid.

470. If a piece of pie is placed before you at the table with the crust toward you, you will be an old maid.....
.........................Western Kentucky

471. If you take the last piece of pie on a plate, you will get a handsome husband or a beautiful wife.

472. Push the corners of a sofa-pillow in. Name each
corner. Strike the center of the pillow sharply
with your fist. The corners that remain crushed in
indicate which of the people love you.

473. If you pick up a pin pointed toward you, you will
see your sweetheart that day.

474. If you pick up a pin lying at an angle, you will be
kissed by your sweetheart......Central Kentucky

475. If you pick up a pin with its side toward you, you
will see your sweetheart that day.

476. If a pin that is barely sticking into your dress is
struck on the saying of the letters of the alphabet,
the letter on which it falls out is the initial of your
intended.

477. If while you are trying on a dress, a pin is caught to
your petticoat, you will not marry that year......
...............................Blue Grass

478. Open all the doors and windows; stick nine pins in
a row in the floor; pour water over them. If a cat
comes in and licks up the water, and then if a man
dressed in white or a woman passes the door, you
will marry before you die. If a white coffin passes
in front of the door you will die unmarried.

479. After you have taken a newly made quilt from the
frame, toss a cat into it to make the quilt puff out.
The girl that the cat goes towards will be married
first ....Mountains

480. At a party throw a cat into the middle of a quilt.
The girl toward whom it goes will be an old maid.

481. If you can walk seven railroad rails without falling
off, you can marry anyone that you desire.

482. If you walk seven railroad rails without speaking, you will marry the first man you meet.
483. After you have walked ten railroad rails, the first girl you see with eyes of which the color is opposite to your own will be your future wife.
484. If you walk eleven rails of a railroad track without falling off, you will marry the first person of the opposite sex whom you meet.
485. If you walk eighteen rails on a railroad track without stepping off, you can get any man that you wish.
486. Walk twenty-one rails of a railroad track. Under the twenty-first will be a hair of the same color as that of your destined husband or wife.
487. Count the number of drops of rain from a roof or the like, to learn the number of years before you will marry.
488. If it is raining, walk backward nine steps; then under your heel you will find a hair. It will be the color of the hair of the one that you will marry.......
............................Southern Kentucky
489. If it rains while the sun is shining, turn over a stone, to find a hair the color of that of your destined mate.
490. When you find sunshine, rain, and rainbow together, look under a stone, to find a hair like that of your wife or husband.
491. If anyone fails to recognize you, you will be married.
492. Put names of girls (or boys) in the corners and in the middle of a rectangle. Let some one write on the reverse side these words, "love," "hate," "court," "kiss," "marry."

493. If you throw a kiss to a redbird, he will take it to your sweetheart.

494. If you see a redbird, you will see your sweetheart soon.

495. To hear a redbird singing is a sure sign that you will see your sweetheart before the end of the week....
.........................Western Kentucky

496. After you see a redbird, the next person that you see will be your sweetheart.

497. If you eat nine redbuds in nine days, the ninth boy or girl that you meet will be your fate..Mountains

498. "Make a rhyme,
You'll see your fellow before half-past nine."

499. If you say something that rhymes or hear someone else say it, kiss your hand, and you will see your sweetheart in twenty-four hours.

500. When you accidentally make a rhyme in talking, count the words in the two rhyming lines. The resulting number is the number of the letter of the alphabet forming the initial letter of your destined mate's last name.

501. After you have accidentally made a rhyme and obtained the initial of your mate, count "first, last," to learn whether it is the initial of the Christian name or of the surname.

502. To put on any one's engagement ring is a sure sign that you will never have one of your own........
................................Blue Grass

503. Put a ring on a horsehair and start it knocking. The number of clear knocks denotes the year and the unclear knocks the months and days before you will be married.

504. Get a glass half full of water. Hold a gold ring over it with a hair. As many times as the ring strikes the glass, so many years will it be until you marry.

505. Put a ring on your finger and think of a color. The first man you meet with that color of tie on is your future husband.

506. If you sleep in a ring that someone has given you, you love that person better than God.

507. If you turn nine set rings and two signet rings, the first man you meet wearing a tie the color of the stone in the last ring turned will be your future husband.

508. After you have turned ten signet rings and one diamond ring, the first boy with a red tie on who tips his hat or cap to you is your future husband.

509. Turn sixteen diamond rings and one signet ring. The first person you meet and speak to thereafter will be your future lover.

510. After you have turned nineteen signet rings, the first boy you meet with a red necktie on you will marry.

511. Turn twenty rings on people's fingers, and notice the color of the last stone. The next boy you see with a tie on of that color is the boy that you will marry.

512. After you have turned a hundred set rings, the boy that you meet with a tie the color of the last stone is your destined mate.

513. When you see the first robin of spring, sit down on a rock, take off your left stocking, and if you find a hair in it, your sweetheart will call to see you. . . .
. . . . Western Kentucky

53

514. If you run around the house three times and touch the same rock every time, you will see your future husband's hair.....................Mountains

515. Take a rose petal and name your sweetheart. If you can make it pop, he loves you........Blue Grass

516. Wear the image of St. Joseph around your neck. As he is the patron saint of marriage, you will marry soon. The charm will not work unless the image is given you.

517. One who turns salt over on the table will not marry within a year.

518. Eat a thimbleful of salt and go to bed backwards without drinking. You will dream of your sweetheart's handing you a drink.

519. Mix a teaspoonful of meal and a teaspoonful of water, then fry the mixture on the shovel, and eat it. Go to bed backwards. The person you dream about is your future husband or wife...Mountains

520. To shiver without apparent cause is a sign that one is in love.

521. It causes bad luck for a young man to give his sweetheart a pair of shoes, as she will walk away from him......................Louisville Negroes

522. If at bed-time you place your shoes in the shape of T and do not speak again before falling asleep, you will see the one that you are to marry.

523. Sleep with your right shoe under your head for three nights; on the last night you will dream of your future husband or wife..............Mountains

524. Put your right shoe and stocking under your head and say:

"My right shoe and stocking

I put under my head,
To dream to-night of whom I am to wed,
The color of his eyes, the color of his hair,
And his every day clothes I wish him to wear."
The one that you dream of will be your husband.
If you are not to marry, you will dream of a burial ....Mountains

525. If your shoe-string comes untied, your sweetheart is thinking of you.

526. If your shoe-string comes untied, you are thinking of your sweetheart.............Louisville Negro

527. If your shoe-string comes untied, your sweetheart is angry with you....................Mountains

528. If your shoe-string comes untied, your girl loves you .... Mountains

529. If your shoe-string comes untied and you step on it, you will see your sweetheart that day..Mountains

530. If your skirt turns up, your sweetheart is thinking of you.

531. If the hem turns up when you put on your skirt, you will have a new sweetheart soon.

532. If in walking, a girl's skirt catches on a branch of a shrub or a bush, the number of limbs from the bottom to where it catches is the number of the initial letter of the beau's name whom she will "catch."

533. If a briar catches in your skirt, your beau still loves you.

534. If a bramble catches on a girl's dress, a widower is in love with her...........North-eastern Kentucky

535. If a briar catches your skirt, your sweetheart is thinking of you.

536. Take a skirt, fold it, place it under your left arm, walk backward to the bed, and repeat:
"This is Friday (or any other night) I go to bed
With my skirt under my head.
I'll dream of the living and the dead
And of the one I am to wed."
In silence place the skirt under the pillow, and as you dream so shall it be..............Mountains

537. Three rings of smoke in one day are a sign of a secret marriage ....Mountains

538. To see two snakes at once is a sign of a wedding...
.... Mountains

539. To sneeze before breakfast is a sign that you will see your sweetheart before Saturday night.

540. "Sneeze before you eat,
See your sweetheart before you sleep."

541. To sneeze three times in succession is a sign that you will never be married.

542. A spider on the neck means that you have a secret lover......................Western Kentucky

543. To spit on yourself is a sign that you will not be married ....Mountains

544. If you spit on a piece of burning wood that falls down and name it for your sweetheart when you replace it, he will come before it burns out.......
..........................Western Kentucky

545. If two spoons are accidentally put into a cup, a wedding will result.

546. To drop a table-spoon is prophetic of your sweetheart's coming.

547. If a girl goes to a spring that she has never visited before and puts a rock from the spring into the

hem of her dress, she will marry the first boy that
she crosses water with........Southern Kentucky

548. Get a rock from a spring where you have never been
before; the one over whose head you can throw the
rock directly is the one that you will marry......
.... Mountains

549. Kneel at a spring on any night at nine o'clock, with
your back to it and repeat:
"If I marry in the spring, let me hear a bird sing"—
pause.
"If I marry in the fall, let me hear a cow bawl."—
pause.
"If I don't marry at all, let me hear my coffin
knock."
One of these requests will come true............
.........................Western Kentucky

550. The star under which a person is born influences his
life.

551. If a star falls, one of your family will be married
soon.

552. Name three stars in a row; the one you dream about
shows your fate..............Western Kentucky

553. If you see the morning star first over your right
shoulder for seven mornings in succession, you will
dream about your future husband or wife.

554. If you count seven stars for seven nights, the first
person of the opposite sex that you then shake
hands with will be your future husband or wife..
.... Mountains

555. Count seven stars each night for seven nights; on
the seventh night you will dream of your future
husband....................Western Kentucky

556. If you count nine stars for nine nights, the first boy you shake hands with will be the one that you will marry.....................Southern Kentucky

557. Count thirteen stars for thirteen nights. On the thirteenth night, the person that you dream of is your future wife or husband..........Blue Grass

558. If you steal something to eat and get caught, you will beg after your marriage.

559. If you fall up steps, you will not marry that year.

560. If you bump into a stranger, you will marry someone whom you have never met........Blue Grass

561. If you stumble up the steps, you will not be married for seven years.

562. You can tell your fortune by naming the corners of a lump of sugar just before putting it slowly into your coffee.........................Blue Grass

563. "Silent supper." Several girls make a fire and prepare a supper together, not speaking, and always walking backwards. They place a pan of water on the doorstep and hang a towel near. They sit at the table but do not eat anything. If these conditions are observed, the future husbands of the girls will come, wash, sit opposite them, and finally disappear.

564. After you prepare your supper as in 563, leave it and go; then look back through a crack. You will see your future husband at the table.

565. If anyone sweeps under you, you will never be married.

566. If you sweep under anyone, you will never be married.

567. Burn nine different kinds of switches. When the last one burns, your future husband will come in.

568. To sit on a table is a sign that you wish to marry.

569. "Sit on a table,
Marry when you are able."

570. If you sit on a kitchen table, you will never be married.

571. The one that remains at table longest will be married first.

572. If you sit on a table with a person of the opposite sex, you will marry that person.......Blue Grass

573. If you sit on a table under a joist in the loft, you will never be married...............Mountains

574. Fortunes may be told by interpreting the meaning of the tea-leaves left in a cup.

575. The presence of tea-leaves in your teacup means that you will receive a package in as many days as there are tea-leaves.....................Blue Grass

576. Put the tea leaves from your cup of tea on the back of your hand and slap it with the other hand. If they fall from the hand with one blow, you will marry within the year. If not, the number of blows it takes to remove the leaves indicates the number of years which will elapse before your marriage...
...............................Blue Grass

577. If your thread knots while you are sewing, name it for your sweetheart. If he loves you, it will come untied.

578. If your thread tangles, your sweetheart is thinking of you.

579. If your thread knots while you are making a garment, you will marry before it wears out.

580. If you can blow all the seeds from a thistle-ball at one blow, you will succeed in your undertakings.

581. If you can blow all the seeds off a thistle-ball, your sweetheart loves you.

582. If a toad hops across the road in front of you, you will see your lover.

583. Follow this receipt to make love powders:

Catch a toad, put it under a rock, and let it starve to death. After it has dried thoroughly, beat it into a powder, and sprinkle this powder on the person whom you wish to fall in love with you.

584. If your great toe itches, you have a dear lover......
.... Mountains

585. If you stump your toe and kiss your thumb at the same time, you will see your lover.

"Stump your toe,
Kiss your thumb,
And see your beau."

586. A man whose second toe is longer than his great toe will be henpecked. (Compare 1004.)

587. When two persons tie their toes together and the string breaks, the one with the shorter string will marry first.

588. If two persons tie their great toes together, they will marry the first persons of the opposite sex with whom they shake hands.

589. If you peel a stick toothbrush, you will offend your lover.....................Southern Kentucky

590. If when two people are walking together they pass on opposite sides of a tree, post, or other obstacle on the way, they will never marry each other.

591. When you see a turkey-buzzard sailing, say:

"Sail, sail, lonesome turkey-buzzard.
Sail to the east, sail to the west;
Sail to the one that I love best.
Flap your wings before you fly out of sight,
That I may see my sweetheart before Saturday
night"..........................Blue Grass

592. Count the number of turkey-buzzards that you see
flying. The number will be the number of years
that you will live.

593. If you find twin peaches, apples, cucumbers, or the
like, you will be married soon. . Southern Kentucky

594. If you find a twin berry or fruit, sleep with it under
your pillow. The one that you dream of will be
your husband or wife.........Western Kentucky

595. If you can tie the tying-vine into a lover's knot, you
can get any one that you desire as married partner ....Mountains

596. If you raise an umbrella in the house, you will not
be married.

597. If a girl wears a wasp nest in her clothing, her lover
will love her more deeply............Blue Grass

598. Go to a deserted house, drop a ball of yarn, and
wind it as you walk around the house, saying, "I
wind, who holds?" Before you have completed the
circuit, something or someone will catch the yarn
and in some way disclose your future mate......
.... Mountains

599. If you spill water while you are drinking, your sweetheart is thinking of you. . North-eastern Kentucky

600. Dip a stick into water. It it drops fewer than five
drops of water, your sweetheart loves you........
.... Mountains

601. If you put your finger into a saucer of clean water, you will marry a young man; into an empty saucer, you will be an old maid; into a saucer of soapy water, you will marry a widower......Mountains

602. Sleep on wedding cake; the person dreamed of is your destined mate.

603. If you sleep on a piece of wedding cake three nights and dream of the same person, you will marry him.

604. Sleep on a piece of wedding cake. Have six names and the word "stranger" on seven slips of paper. Take one out each morning. The one left shows your fortune.

605. If you wear a wedding veil in a play, you will never be married.

606. If a bride wears something of yours, you will have a proposal within a year.

607. If a sister of the bride wears the bride's garter, she will be the next one to be married in that family.

608. If you look into a well at midnight, you will see your future husband.

609. 'Put your handkerchief on the growing wheat at night. In the morning arise and get the handkerchief before sunrise. On it you will find the initials of the man or woman that you will marry...
.........................Southern Kentucky

610. If you are caught in a whirlwind, you will receive an invitation to a wedding.

611. When two people break a wish-bone between them, the one that gets the shorter piece will marry first, and the one that gets the longer one will obtain whatever wish he may have made.

612. When two people pull a breastbone of a chicken, the

one getting the shorter piece will marry first, but the other will be rich.

613. When two people break a wish-bone of a chicken, the one that gets the shorter piece will marry first, and the one that gets the longer piece will have the better dinner......................Blue Grass

614. A sprig of yarrow is a good love charm.

615. If you marry young, you will have trouble in the future.

MARRIAGE

616. "Marry when the year is new,
You will always be loving, kind, and true."

617. Marriage and the months:
"January, always poor.
February, wed once more.
March, splendid catch.
April, happy match.
May, turn to hate.
June, enviable fate.
July, poorly mated.
August, better have waited.
September, very wealthy.
October, extremely healthy.
November, quick undoing.
December, Cupid's wooing."

618. Do not marry in March, unless on the twenty-seventh.

619. The months of April, June, and October are fortunate months for a wedding.........Blue Grass

620. May is a bad month for a marriage, especially the fourteenth of May.

621. If you marry in June, your husband will be good to you ....Mountains

622. June is the month of love and marriage.

623. "Marry when June roses blow,
Over land and sea you'll go"..........Mountains

624. It brings bad luck to marry on the last day of the year.

625. "Married on Monday, married for health,
Married on Tuesday, married for wealth.
Married on Wednesday, the best day of all.
Married on Thursday, married for losses.
Married on Friday, married for crosses.
Married on Saturday, no luck at all."

626. Thursday is a fortunate day on which to be married
.... Mountains

627. Saturday is now a favorite day on which to be married.

628. To postpone a wedding causes bad luck.

629. "Married in gray, you'll go far away.
Married in black, you'll wish yourself back.
Married in brown, you'll live out of town.
Married in red, you'll wish yourself dead.
Married in pearl, you'll live in a whirl.
Married in green, ashamed to be seen.
Married in yellow, jealous of your fellow.
Married in blue, he'll always be true.
Married in pink, your spirits will sink.
Married in white, you have chosen right."

630. "If you marry in blue, your love will be true."

631. "If you marry in green,
     You'll always be seen."
632. "If you marry in yellow,
     You'll get another fellow."
633. It is considered unlucky for the bride to wear red, yellow, or green.
634. Blue and white are considered lucky colors for a bride.
635. If a bride wears a pearl, she will shed tears.
636. If you marry in red, your husband will die.
637. A bad dream on the eve of her wedding is unlucky for a bride.................Central Kentucky
638. A bride must not ride a horse to a wedding nor a bride-groom a mare...........Central Kentucky
639. A bride should not ride a gray steed—by no means a gray horse and not even a gray mare..........
     ....Central Kentucky
640. A bride should ride a black mare to the wedding rather than any other steed.....Central Kentucky
641. To go through a spider web brings good luck to a bride.
642. The bride who finds a spider on her wedding dress may consider herself blessed.
643. The bride who marries on a rainy day will have a stormy married life.
644. Rain on the wedding day means just as many tears for the bride.
645. If it rains on your wedding day, you will have to scratch for your living.......Southern Kentucky
646. "Happy is the bride the sun shines on,
     Tears for the bride the rain falls on."

647. If rain falls on the wedding day, the bride will be a bad housekeeper .... Mountains

648. An especially bad thunderstorm during a wedding means an unhappy married life.

649. If it rains on your wedding night, you will shed as many tears as there are drops of rain............
.... Louisville Negroes

650. If it rains the day before your wedding day, the bridegroom will weep as many tears as there are raindrops.

651. Rain on the day after marriage means many sorrows for the bride........................ Negroes

652. Snow falling on the wedding day is a prophecy of great happiness.

653. Snow on the wedding day brings money.

654. The marriage will be unhappy if the bride is seen by her fiance an hour before the wedding.

655. It brings good luck for a bride to weep on her wedding day.

656. It is lucky to be married in the full of the moon...
.... Western Kentucky

657. A bride must not see the groom on her wedding day until the wedding.

658. If a bride-to-be gets to the altar before the groom, the love is mostly on the bride's side.

659. It brings bad luck to have peacock feathers in a room when a wedding takes place.

660. If a bat flies into a church during a wedding ceremony, very bad luck will follow.

661. A bride should wear "something old, something new, something borrowed, something blue, and a four-leaved clover in the heel of her shoe."

662. Money in the heel of the bride's left shoe insures wealth.

663. If a bride goes to the altar with salt in her pocket, she will always be happy.............Blue Grass

664. It brings good luck for a bride to carry another bride's handkerchief.

665. If the bridegroom carries a miniature horseshoe in his pocket, he will always have good luck.

666. Orange blossoms in wedding decoration or worn by the bride bring good luck.

667. It brings bad luck for a bride to make her own clothes ....Western Kentucky

668. It causes bad luck for the bride's dress to be seen on her until the night of the wedding.

669. A bride should not show her veil to anyone outside of her family, and she should especially not try it on before anyone.

670. To get the wedding veil torn accidentally is the best of luck to the bride.

671. A touch of blood on the bride's dress indicates bad luck.

672. If you prick your finger when sewing on a wedding dress, so that a drop of blood falls on it, the bride will never be married.

673. If while the trousseau is being made a needle is broken, this accident is ominous for the bride.

674. It causes bad luck for a bride to look into a mirror as the last act before marriage.

675. If a bride breaks a mirror, seven years of bad luck are in store for her.

676. Do not have a mirror in a room in which a wedding

takes place, for the first unmarried woman who
sees her image in it will die soon...............
.....................North-eastern Kentucky

677. The position before a mirror is unlucky for the married pair.........................Blue Grass

678. It is lucky for a wedding pair to stand on a white
fur rug.....................Western Kentucky

679. It is unlucky for a wedding pair to stand so as to face
across the boards of the floor.........Blue Grass

680. If a padlock is locked as a couple are pronounced
man and wife, they will separate.

681. If you marry as the hand of the clock goes up, you
will rise in the world.

682. If you marry as the hand of the clock goes down,
you will not succeed in the world.

683. Marry young, you marry trouble.

684. To drop the wedding ring in the service is unlucky.

685. If a physician witnesses a wedding, someone present
will die within a year.

686. It causes good luck for the family cat to be present
at a wedding......................Mountains

687. The throwing of an old shoe after the wedded pair
averts bad luck and malevolent influences.

688. The throwing of rice after a couple increases the
probability of their having children.

689. "A change of name but not of letter
Is a change for the worse and not for the better."

690. A bride should remove her wedding ring to put it
back on before leaving the church and then never
take it off again.

691. Do not give a bride gold........Central Kentucky

692. The bride's bunch of roses is caught by the one who will be the next to marry.
693. The wedding cake contains certain articles which are symbolic. These articles are a ring, a needle or thimble, bachelor's buttons, a coin, a pen, a wishbone, a four-leaved clover. These articles are cut from the cake.
694. If you lend something to a bride or a groom, you will yourself be married the next year.
695. To find anything belonging to a bride means good luck.
696. Kiss the bride for good luck.
697. If you kiss a bride after the ceremony has taken place and before the newly-made husband has a chance to kiss her, you will have good luck throughout the year.
698. If a newly-married couple both think of the same person on their wedding day, that person will be the first one to visit them......Western Kentucky
699. At an older sister's wedding the younger sister should dance without shoes. Otherwise there will be bad luck.
700. If a bridesmaid goes to bed backward with her hand over her heart, she will be married before the year is out, provided the first man she sees in the morning is an old one.
701. It brings bad luck for the bride and a bridegroom to part the day they are married.
702. The loss of a wedding ring is thought a prediction of a calamity.
"As the wedding ring wears,
So wear away life's cares."

To lose a wedding ring within the first month of marriage augurs great misfortune.

703. It indicates bad luck for a bride to stumble at her husband's door.

704. A bride who steps on the threshold of her new home when entering it for the first time will never have a happy married life.

705. If a newly wedded pair take a little meat and a little meal into the house, they will never want......
.... Mountains

706. Of a couple newly married, the first one in bed will be the first one to die...............Mountains

707. There will be no good luck for the bride until the wedding clothes are worn out.

DEATH AND BURIAL

708. If you play at having funerals, one of you will die
.... Mountains

709. If you wear anyone's mourning gown or wrap, there will be a death in your family.

710. It is bad luck to put on or try on a mourning veil, for you will have disaster.

711. Do not put the clothes of a living person on a corpse. It means death.....................Blue Grass

712. If you give a pin to go on a corpse, you will be the next to die.................Western Kentucky

713. After a death in the family, you should not sing or play any kind of music..............Mountains

714. If you see a star fall, expect a death in the family..
....................................Blue Grass

715. If you count the stars, you will die. If lying on

your back, you count the stars, you will die.......

............................Southern Kentucky

716. To see a shooting star is a death sign....Mountains

717. If you shiver without apparent cause, death has touched you............North-eastern Kentucky

718. When you shudder involuntarily, it is a sign that someone is walking over your grave (the ground where your grave will be)......Central Kentucky

719. A noise as of someone throwing down wood is a sign of death...........................Blue Grass

720. If large drops of rain fall, there is a death somewhere.

721. A storm precedes or follows the death of a very old person......................Central Kentucky

722. He who kills a man will die with his boots on, that is, die a violent death..................Blue Grass

723. If a man kills another and dies a natural death, the killing was justified.................Blue Grass

724. If a sick person picks and catches at the bed covering, he will die.

725. It is a sign that a death will occur in the family, if you grieve over the death of a pet.............

...........................Southern Kentucky

726. The last person whose name a dying man calls will be the next one to die...............Mountains

727. If a person just before death calls the name of someone in the family, that person will be the next in the family to die.

728. Death leaves the door open, that is, one death in the family will be followed by another soon.

729. If a person dies, his picture will fade.............

.....................North-eastern Kentucky

730. If a person is killed or dies a hard death, his spirit is seen ....Central Kentucky
731. If a man dies hard, he will go to hell....Mountains
732. It brings bad luck to take money off a dead person's eye ....Mountains
733. If you are ever cut with a razor that has shaved the dead, you will die...................Mountains
734. It brings good luck to wear a bullet which has gone through a dead body.................Mountains
735. If you touch a corpse, you will not be afraid of dead people ....Mountains
736. If you touch a dead person, you will never dream of him ....Blue Grass
737. If you touch the body of a dead person, you will never worry about him.
738. No person who touches a dead body will be haunted by its spirit.
739. If you touch a corpse, you will be rid of the fear of death.
740. Sailors will not touch a dead body.
741. Put a lock of hair of a corpse into a hole in a tree to localize the spirit. If you remove the hair, the spirit will haunt you.
742. All portraits in a room where there is a corpse should be turned to the wall, for otherwise a near relative of the deceased will die shortly.
743. You will be unlucky if you see a corpse in a mirror. Cover the mirror at the time of a death.
744. Stop the clock in the room where a death occurs, to avert bad luck.
745. If a corpse's nose bleeds, it is a sign that the murderer is in the room.

746. If the body of a corpse does not become stiff, expect another death in the family..............Negroes
747. If a corpse gets stiff and then limber, there will be another death in the family..............Negroes
748. If a corpse has a limber neck, this circumstance is the sign of another death in the family soon.
749. The will o' the wisp indicates the proximity of a corpse.
750. Never allow the coffin containing a corpse to pass through any other room than the one in which it has been lying. It may, however, pass through a hall.
751. If a corpse is carried from one house to another, death will occur in the second house within a year.
752. In taking a casket from a house, be sure to take the foot of it out first............Western Kentucky
753. It is unlucky to pass in front of a casket.
754. It brings bad luck to lock the door after a funeral procession has passed out.
755. If a vehicle that is to carry away a corpse stops in front of your house, someone in the family will die.
756. If you see your reflection in the glass of the hearse, you will be the next one to be carried in it.
757. It causes bad luck to point your finger at a funeral procession.
758. It brings bad luck to cross a funeral procession unless you turn your back on it.
759. It brings bad luck to count the vehicles in a funeral procession.
760. If a horse becomes frightened or unruly in a funeral procession, one of the family will die before the year is out.

761. It causes bad luck for a horse to balk in a funeral procession.

762. If a black cat crosses in front of a funeral procession, there will be a death in the family of the corpse within three days.

763. It brings bad luck, if on your way to a funeral you meet a lizard.

764. A thunderstorm during a funeral means that the soul will go down.

765. Very bad luck will follow if a street-car runs into or even grazes a hearse. This occurrence is a sure sign that someone will be injured before the end of the trip.

766. If you point toward a grave-yard, your finger will drop off.

767. It causes bad luck to visit a grave-yard after dark.

768. It brings bad luck for one to go through a cemetery at midnight.

769. If you walk over a grave, your grandmother will die.

770. You will have bad luck if you walk in a funeral vault ....Blue Grass

771. To meet a red-headed negro in a grave-yard brings good luck.

772. It brings bad luck to leave the grave-yard before the body is buried......................Mountains

773. It causes bad luck to take anything away from a cemetery ....Mountains

774. If you step over a grave, you will be the next one buried in that cemetery..............Mountains

775. If one of a family dies and his grave is started but not finished, the number of times it is started but

not completed will mark the number of those who will die within that family in one year..Mountains

776. If you dig a grave and leave it open, or if rain falls into it, there will come bad luck to a member of your family.

777. Dig a grave only on the burial day, because a grave left open over night will cause another death......
.........................Blue Grass Negroes

778. To bury a corpse with the feet toward the sunset is a sign that the soul will be lost at the Resurrection ....Mountains

779. Bury the body so that it will face the east.

780. If a turtle-dove flies upward after a death, the soul of the deceased will go to heaven......Mountains

781. If you are buried on a rainy day, you will go to heaven.

782. Thunder after a funeral shows that the spirit of the deceased has gone to heaven..........Mountains

THE HUMAN BODY

783. If you touch the beauty spot on your face, you will go abroad. Compare the Divination sign that if you can touch the beauty spot with your finger your sweetheart loves you.

784. You will have bad luck if you lie on your face at night......................Western Kentucky

785. If your face burns, some one is thinking of you....
.... Mountains

786. The number of wrinkles in the forehead shows the number of children you will have......Mountains

787. If you join your hands behind your head, someone in your family will be ill or will die......Blue Grass

788. When your nose itches, someone is coming. Rub it on wood, to make the arrival certain.

789. If the nose itches, someone is coming to be waited on.

790. If the right side of the nose itches, a man is coming; if the left, a woman; if the end of the nose itches, someone will come riding.

791. If your nose itches on the end, expect a negro.

792. If the right side of your nose itches, your sweetheart is coming.

793. "If your nose itches,
Somebody is coming with a hole in his breeches"
........................Western Kentucky

794. If your nose itches, you will quarrel with someone.

795. "If your nose itches,
Kiss a fool, meet a stranger,
Fall in love or be in danger."

796. If your nose itches when you are away from home, you may know you are wanted at home.........
........................Western Kentucky

797. An itching nose is the sign of money.....Mountains

798. People with pointed noses interfere with the affairs of others.

799. If your right ear burns or is red, someone is talking well about you.

800. If your left ear burns or is red, someone is speaking ill of you.

801. If the right ear burns, pull it nine times up, saying, "Talk up."
If the left ear burns, pull it nine times down, saying, "Talk down."

802. If either ear burns, moisten the fingers, touch the
ear, and repeat these words:
"Talk good, talk bad. If it's good, may good be-
tide you. If it's bad, may the devil ride you."

803. If your right ear burns, a man is talking about you
.... Mountains

804. If your left ear burns, a woman is talking about you
.... Mountains

805. If your ear burns, someone is talking about you.
Put saliva on it and it will stop burning if the re-
marks are kind; it will not stop burning if the re-
marks are unkind.....................Blue Grass

806. "Itching ear, a secret you'll hear."

807. As to the ear's burning—
"If left or right,
Good at night."

808. A burning ear is the sign of someone's talking about
you. Spit on it, and you will outwit the talker..
.... Mountains

809. If your right ear itches, a boy is going to tell you a
secret......................Central Kentucky

810. If your left ear itches, a girl will tell you a secret...
...........................Central Kentucky

811. A ringing in the ear foretells a death in the family.
It is called the death bell.

812. Small ears are marks of stinginess.

813. Large ears signify generosity.

814. Small ears set tight to the head indicate a mean,
roguish disposition.

815. If the ear is thin and angular, the owner is bad-
tempered and cruel.

816. If the ear is long and hangs down, the possesser will have long life.
817. If you can see the sunshine through a man's ears, he is a rascal.
818. If your right eye itches, you will get a letter.
819. If the right eye itches, you will see something pleasant.
820. If your right eye itches, you will get money.
821. It indicates bad luck for the right eye to itch.......
.... Mountains
822. "Itching left eye,
    Sign you'll cry."
823. It indicates good luck for the left eye to itch.......
.... Mountains
824. If your eye jerks, you may expect to see someone unexpectedly.........................Blue Grass
825. If your right eye twitches, you will cry.
826. If your eye bats, you will get a whipping. Blue Grass
827. Clear eyes are the sign of a clear conscience.
828. Put jimson-weed juice in your eye, to make light eyes turn dark.
829. When a large part of the white of a negro's eye shows, you may know that you have to do with a mean negro.
830. It brings bad luck to you, to see a cross-eyed person.
831. Avert the bad luck produced by the sight of a cross-eyed person by crossing your fingers.
832. To avert the bad luck that comes at the sight of a cross-eyed person, cross your fingers and spit over the cross.
833. You will have bad luck if you see a cross-eyed negro.
834. If the first woman you meet in the morning is either

cross-eyed or has red hair, you will have bad luck
that day.....................Western Kentucky

835. Heavy eye-brows that meet signify a deep mind on
the part of the possessor.

836. If your eye-brows meet, you will be rich.

837. A person whose eye-brows meet cannot be trusted.

838. If your eye-brows grow together across your nose,
you will become a murderer.

839. Anyone whose eye-brows grow in a straight line
across the forehead possesses a fiendish disposition.

840. If the eye-brows meet, the person has a jealous nature.

841. If you cut your eye-lashes, you will be able to see
the wind....................Louisville Negroes

842. The "evil eye" is supposed to have malevolent power.

843. A coral or jet hand with fingers clenched will keep
off the disaster threatened by an "evil eye".......
...............................Blue Grass

844. A dimple in your chin is a sign that Cupid has
touched you.
"A dimple in your chin,
Many lovers you shall win."

845. Beware of the girl with a dimple in her chin.

846. Place the hand over the mouth when you are yawn-
ing, to keep the evil spirits from entering.

847. A large-mouthed girl has a large womb..Mountains

848. A fever blister is a sign that you have been kissed.

849. If your lip itches, you will kiss an older person.

850. When the upper lip itches, it will be kissed by a tall
person.................North-eastern Kentucky

851. When the lower lip itches, it will be kissed by a short
person.................North-eastern Kentucky

852. If your lip itches, some one is coming with a mustache.

853. If you bite the apple off to use as bait in a dead fall, you will catch a rabbit.

854. A blister or sore place on your tongue is a sign that you have told a lie.

855. If you bite your tongue in speaking, the next statement probably would have been a lie............
..........................Southern Kentucky

856. It causes bad luck to count your teeth.

857. If you throw away a tooth and an animal finds it, your new tooth will be like a tooth of that animal.

858. If a dog steps on your pulled tooth, you will have a dog tooth.

859. If you do not put your tongue into the place of a vacant tooth, a gold tooth will grow there.

860. If you lose a tooth and put your tongue into the cavity, you will not have a tooth to come in.

861. After a tooth is pulled, if you will swallow a bubble from milk, a gold tooth will come.

862. When the juice stays in one's teeth after he chews tobacco, good luck will follow.........Mountains

863. If you put a tooth that has been pulled under your pillow on the same night, you will have good luck.

864. It brings good luck to carry a back jaw-tooth from the upper right side of the mouth......Mountains

865. If your teeth grow wide apart, you will be a traveler.

866. Teeth far apart in front are a sign of the owner's being separated from home and friends.

867. You will have good luck, if you carry your wisdom tooth with you....................Blue Grass

868. If you cut your wisdom teeth before you are twenty years old, you will not live long........Mountains
869. Some people cut three sets of teeth.
870. If you comb your hair after night-fall, you will get a whipping.
871. To comb hair after dark brings sorrow to the heart.
872. If you comb your hair at night, you will dream of the devil ....Mountains
873. To comb your hair after sunset will make you forgetful ....Southern Kentucky
874. If two people comb each other's hair, the mother of the younger will die.
875. If two people comb anyone's hair at the same time, the younger of the two will die.
876. If you let two persons comb your hair at the same time, you will die.
877. If someone begins to comb your hair and you finish the process yourself, bad luck will ensue........ ....Central Kentucky
878. If you comb your hair with a comb in which someone else has left some hairs, you will die before she does........................Central Kentucky
879. It causes bad luck to comb your hair in front of a looking-glass at night.
880. If you bury the combings of your hair under running water, your hair will grow as rapidly as the stream runs ....Mountains
881. If a bright flame is produced from the combings of your hair thrown into the fire, you will have good health.
882. If the fire smoulders after you throw your hair into it, your death is approaching.

883. Wrap the palate lock on the crown of the head, to keep the palate from falling.

884. Tangles in your hair show that witches have been riding you.

885. Tangles in your hair show that the rats have slept in it ....Mountains

886. If your hair is ruffied, mice have been playing in it.. ....Blue Grass

887. To find a hair in the mouth is a sign that you will kiss a fool.

888. If you hold a lock of your lover's hair, he will always be true to you.

889. If you plant some of your hair in the ground and it grows, you will die....Central Kentucky Negroes

890. You will have good luck, if you rub your hands through the hair of a negro.

891. If a straight-haired negro's head is touched by a kinky-haired one, the hair of one of them will come out ....Louisville Negroes

892. If you cut a lock of your hair out and put it under a rock, it will bring you good luck.....Mountains

893. Your hair will grow well if when it is cut you place some of it under a rock.

894. If a grandmother takes a lock of a little girl's hair and fastens it in the bark of a tree in her orchard, the child's hair will grow to be as long as the height at which the hair is fastened....Central Kentucky

895. Place a lock of your enemy's hair in running water, to make him lose his mind....Blue Grass Negroes

896. If you place a lock of your enemy's hair under your doorstep, he will be unable to keep away from your home....................Blue Grass Negroes

897. To find a feather in your head is a sign that you will get a whipping......................Mountains

898. If a feather is in your hair, there is a letter in the Post Office for you.

899. If you pull out a white hair, two or three or ten will grow in its place (according to various versions of this superstition).

900. If your head itches, you already have company..... .... Mountains

901. To test a girl's disposition, stretch a strand of her hair. If it curls up, she is high-tempered. The tighter the curl, the worse is her temper.......... ....Central Kentucky

902. A negro with fine, straight hair is sure to be vicious ....Central Kentucky

903. Men with fine, light hair are intelligent and conceited. If they do not marry until late in life, they are likely to be selfish.

904. Men with fine brown hair, light or dark, make the best husbands. They are quick, thoughtful, and less likely to be selfish than extremely light-haired or extremely dark-haired men.

905. Men whose hair turns gray prematurely are nearly always good fellows. They are nervous, but are brainy, sympathetic, and honorable.

906. Women with pale blond hair, or the ashy kind, are impulsive, loving, fickle. They can not be depended on, but they make good companions.

907. Women with dark brown hair are very loyal. They are full of sentiment and easily affected. They enjoy keenly and suffer in proportion.

908. Women with fine black hair are highly strung.

Those with coarse black hair are nearly always ill-tempered.

909. All women with dark hair are more tempestuous than those with light hair. The dark eyes and complexions that go with dark hair denote strong feeling. Dark-haired women are more faithful than light-haired women.

910. If a woman's hair grows in a widow's peak on the forehead, she is a woman of charm.............
...........................Central Kentucky

911. Red hair is a sign of a fiery temper.

912. A person's hair may turn white from fright.

913. If you have two crowns, you will live under two governments.

914. If you have a double crown, you will not live long...
...............................Blue Grass

915. To make yourself think clearly, put something on your head; for example, a ring or a bracelet.

916. A hair on your shoulder is the sign of a letter......
..........................Western Kentucky

917. A wart on the neck shows that you will be hanged..
.... Mountains

918. If the left palm itches, you will receive money.

919. When the palm itches,
"Scratch it on wood,
It's sure to come good."

920. Cold hands mean a warm heart.

921. Put the hand of a sleeper into water. He will then tell his secrets or the name of his sweetheart.

922. If you put the hands of a sleeping person into muddy water, he will answer any question that you ask him.

923. Hold your hands down awhile; if you have had

measles, you can see the marks in your hands.....
.... Mountains

924. If four people accidentally cross their hands in shaking hands, they will have good luck.

925. If the hair on the back of your hands grows long, you will be rich.

926. Back-handed writing shows a sly nature.

927. It brings bad luck to put a worm on a hook with the left hand.........................Mountains

928. If you wear a thimble on the left hand, you will be an old maid............North-eastern Kentucky

929. It causes bad luck to shake hands with your left hand.

930. A left-handed person owes three days' work to the Devil.

931. A left-handed person owes the Devil a thousand rails
.... Mountains

932. If your right hand itches, you will shake hands with a stranger.

933. An itching of the right hand indicates that you will shake hands with an old friend.

934. If your right hand itches, you will get a letter.

935. If the palm of your hand itches, a caller is coming.

936. If you stick your finger with a pin, you will be disappointed.

937. When you join your two hands, if you place your right thumb over the left, you will rule your married partner.

938. If the left thumb is placed over the right, when you join your two hands, you will be ruled by your married partner.

939. He who clenches his thumb within his fist is a coward.

940. Long thumbs indicate a stubborn disposition.

941. If your thumbs turn back at the end, you will not be able to save money.

942. "Wide thumbs will spin gold," that is, make or earn gold.

943. If you can see between your fingers, you are a spend-thrift.

944. If your finger-prints make impressions of circular or approximately circular lines, you will be a money-saver.

945. If your finger-prints make impressions that sweep out and do not make circles, you will be a money-waster.

946. A woman with short fingers will be a good manager.

947. Crooked fingers show that one's ancestors were la-borers.

948. A person with long fingers will not have to scratch for a living.

949. A man with long fingers is grasping.

950. A person with short fingers will have a good living.

951. If you can make your first and fourth fingers meet back of your hand without holding them you will rule your married partner.

952. If you can make your first and fourth fingers meet in front, you will rule your home.

953. The spreading out of hands and fingers in a gesture indicates a broad and generous mind.

954. If your little finger is crooked, you are a crook.

955. Hands clenched and not open are indicative of a mean and grasping disposition.

956. If a person wears a ring on the middle finger of each hand, he will have bad luck.

957. If you bite your finger-nails, you will not grow tall.

958. If you cut the nails of a sick person, he will die.

959. If your finger-nails have half-moons at the bottom end, you are of good stock.
A half-moon on each finger-nail shows that you are of good blood.

960. If your finger-nails are ridged, you will have a short life.

961. If your finger-nails are deep down in your fingers, you will be rich.

962. Long finger-nails are a sign of a long life. Blue Grass

963. People with short finger-nails are tale-bearers.

964. If your finger-nails do not taper at the end, you will have to work for your living.

965. If there is a white spot on your finger-nail, you are to receive a present.

966. White spots on the nails counting from thumb to little finger, indicate, "Friends, foes, presents, beaux, journeys to go."

967. White spots on your finger-nails show that you tell lies.

968. If a sick person in bed cuts his nails, he will not get well until his nails grow out.[5]

969. Leather worn on the wrist will make you strong.

970. If you kiss your elbow, you will change your sex.

971. A pointed elbow is the sign of a sour disposition....
.........................Central Kentucky

972. If you strike your "crazy bone," you may know that two ladies are coming.

973. If you measure yourself, a member of the family will die before a year is over.

[5] For significance of the days that you pare your nails, see *Days and Seasons.*

87

974. If your back aches, you are going (or deserve) to get a whipping.

975. If a woman who is menstruating touches a barrel of sour-krout, it will spoil..............Mountains

976. If you attend to a call of nature in the road, you will have a boil on your posterior part.....Mountains

977. To avert the penalty involved in the last superstition, spit on the refuse...................Mountains

978. To lie on the right side brings good luck.

979. Every time you sigh, a drop of blood falls from the heart.

980. If a chain of shingles meets in a continuous sore, you will die.   (Shingles really follow a nerve.)

981. If your left foot itches, you will soon walk on the ground that you later will be buried in..Mountains

982. If your left foot iches, you will walk where you are not welcome.

983. If your right foot itches, you will walk on strange ground.

984. If the bottom of the foot itches, you will step on strange ground.

985. It brings bad luck to stump the toe of the left foot.

986. To avert the bad luck incident to stumping the left foot, you must go back and start over.

987. The bad luck incident to stumping the left foot may be averted by turning around.

988. It is lucky to stump the right foot.

989. It causes bad luck to stump your toe.

990. You can avert this bad luck incident to stumping your toe if you kiss your thumb.

991. If you stump your toe, it brings bad luck unless you

go back over the same place without stumping your toe.

992. If you go anywhere and stumble, you are not welcome there.

993. If you stump your toe while on the way to make a visit, you are not welcome there.

994. If you stumble on your way to make a visit, you will gain an admirer.

995. If you stumble on your way home from a call, you lose an admirer.

996. It is bad luck to have anyone step over your feet.

997. Avert the bad luck which will come if anyone steps over your feet by making the person step backwards over them.

998. If someone should step over you while you are lying on the floor, you will die before he does unless he steps back.

999. It brings bad luck to step first on the left foot in the morning.

1000. Dress and undress with the right foot first for good luck.

1001. It is well to step into a court room on your right foot when you have business there.

1002. If a girl steps on another girl's toe, she will take her sweetheart from her..............Mountains

1003. If you cross your feet while you are dancing, the devil will get you.

1004. If your second toe is longer than the great toe, you will rule your mate. (Compare 586.)

1005. It brings good luck to carry a negro's toe........
..........................Western Kentucky

1006. Big feet are a sign of intelligence.

1007. If you bury an amputated limb, the patient will have pains until it rots. It should be burned.

1008. A red mole is a sign of intelligence.

1009. "A mole on the face, gentleman's taste."

1010. "A mole on the face, you'll suffer disgrace."

1011. A mole on your cheek is the sign that your mother's washing tub will leak.

1012. "Mole on the lip,
You're a little too flip". Central Kentucky Negroes

1013. "Mole on the ear,
Money by the year."

1014. A mole under the ear is a sign that you will be hanged.

1015. "Mole on neck, money by the peck."

1016. A mole on the neck is a sign that the person will be hanged.

1017. "Mole on your back,
Money by the pack."

1018. "Mole on your arm, you are a gentleman's charm."

1019. "Mole on your arm,
You'll live on a farm."

1020. "Mole on your breast, baby in the nest...........
....................Central Kentucky Negroes

1021. A mole on the right side means good luck.

1022. A mole on the left side brings bad luck.

1023. A mole in the life line on the hand is the sign of a terrible disaster.

1024. "Moly, moly, on the leg,
Money, money, by the keg."

1025. A mole on your left leg is the sign that you have a very bad temper...................Mountains

SALIVA[6]

1026. If you spit on yourself, the nearest one to you will tell a lie on you......................Mountains

1027. If you spit on yourself, the one nearest your right side will tell a lie on you.............Mountains

1028. If you spit on yourself, you will hear of a death before the end of the week.............Mountains

1029. It causes bad luck to spit on any one else.

1030. If you spit over your left shoulder, you can break a bad charm.

1031. If you spit into any one's tracks, you will have a headache...................Western Kentucky

1032. If you make a cross and spit in it, you will have good luck all your life.

1033. Spit on a rock, to make it strike the object that you throw at......................Mountains

1034. When you plant a bush or plant, spit into the hole .... Mountains

SNEEZES

1035. Sneeze on Monday for health.
Sneeze on Tuesday for wealth.
Sneeze on Wednesday for a letter.
Sneeze on Thursday for something better.
Sneeze on Friday for sorrow.
Sneeze on Saturday, see your sweetheart tomorrow.
Sneeze on Sunday, safety seek,
For the Devil will be with you the rest of the week.

[6] Spitting is often the means of averting some kind of disaster. Therefore the use of saliva appears in many of the classes of superstitions in this volume. To find them the reader may consult the index.

1036. Sneezes as in 1035, except—
"Sneeze on Sunday, from the Devil you will bor-
row."

1037. "Sneeze on Sunday, safety seek;
Old Nick will chase you all the week.
Sneeze on Monday, sneeze for danger,
Sneeze on Tuesday, kiss a stranger,"
And the rest as in 1035.

1038. Sneezes as in number 1035, except—
"Sneeze on Sunday, get a sweetheart's kiss that
day."

1039. "Sneeze on Monday, sneeze for danger.
Sneeze on Tuesday, kiss a stranger.
Sneeze on Wednesday, get a letter.
Sneeze on Thursday, something better."
And the rest as in 1035.

1040. If you sneeze three times before breakfast on Sunday morning, there will be three deaths before the
week is out.

1041. It brings bad luck to sneeze before arising in the
morning.

1042. If you sneeze before seven, you will have company
before eleven.

1043. If you sneeze before breakfast, you will cry before
dinner and weep before supper.

1044. If you sneeze twice before breakfast, you will have
a beau that day.

1045. To sneeze three times before breakfast is a good
luck sign.

1046. If you sneeze before you eat,
You will have visitors before you sleep.

1047. To sneeze at the breakfast table is a sign of death.

1048. If the youngest in the family sneezes at the breakfast table on Sunday morning, a death will follow.
1049. A sneeze at the table is a sign of death.
1050. If you sneeze at the table when your mouth is full of food, there will be a death.
1051. To sneeze at table is the sign that there will be one more or one fewer at the next meal.
1052. If you sneeze once, someone will come into or leave the house within an hour.
1053. If you sneeze twice, you may expect two callers within two hours.
1054. Sneeze three times for a letter.
1055. If you sneeze three times in succession, you will be an old maid.
1056. If one sneezes in a group of people, what is being said will come true.
1057. A sneeze in a crowd means that the crowd will be increased or decreased by one.
1058. Look at the sun if you feel inclined to sneeze.

CURES AND PREVENTIVES

1059. When a finger, a toe, or an arm is amputated, it should be buried in a straight position; otherwise the patient will suffer pains from cramp. Secrecy should be observed in the burial of the amputated member.
1060. If after the amputation of any member of the body the absent member itches, scratch the other arm or foot, to make the itching cease.
1061. Asthma in a child may be cured if a lock of its hair is placed in a hole in a post or tree above its head.

When the child grows to that height the disease will be cured.

1062. You may cure asthma by wearing a string of amber beads about the neck.

1063. For back-ache use pine-resin plasters.

1064. In setting tobacco, you often have a pain in your back. Have someone kneel on your back. The pain will cease.

1065. To cure your back-ache, let a seventh child walk seven times up and down your back.............
.........................Central Kentucky

1066. Rub a plantain leaf on a honey-bee sting.........
.........................Central Kentucky

1067. You may remove birth-marks by rubbing them with the hand of a corpse.

1068. To prevent blindness, wear ear-rings.

1069. A dusty spider web is good for a cut.

1070. Some people can stop the flow of blood in other people or in animals. The power runs in families, and a man must teach it to a woman, and a woman to a man.

1071. Hemorrhages can be stopped by the use of pills made of cobwebs.

1072. To stop the flow of blood from a cut, use soot from the chimney..................Southern Kentucky

1073. Hemorrhages can be stopped by the swallowing of tea brewed from the soot of a wood fire.

1074. If you stick the knife or other instrument with which you have cut yourself into the ground, the blood will cease to flow..............Mountains

1075. If a knife which has caused a cut or wound is destroyed, the wound will be healed......Mountains

1076. When you cut your hand on a piece of tin, bury the tin in the ground, to cure the wound...........
...................North-eastern Kentucky

1077. A cut may be cured by the victim's drawing a charcoal ring around the cut............Mountains

1078. To stop hemorrhages, have a second person repeat with the patient: "And when I passed by thee and saw thee polluted in thine own blood, I said unto thee, 'Live'." [Ezekiel 16: 6.]

1079. Hemorrhages are checked by laying an axe under the bed of the patient...............Mountains

1080. To stop the nose from bleeding, drop a key down the back of the sufferer.

1081. To stop bleeding of the nose, pour water on the back of the head.............Western Kentucky

1082. Keep your nose from bleeding by wearing lead which has not been on the ground.....Mountains

1083. You can stop your nose from bleeding by wearing lead around your neck, and putting it on your shoulder when the nose begins to bleed.

1084. To stop nose-bleeding wear around the neck a bullet that has killed something..........Mountains

1085. Hold a piece of silver under the upper lip, to cure nose-bleeding ....Mountains

1086. You can stop your nose from bleeding by tying a red yarn string around your thumb............
..........................Central Kentucky

1087. You can keep the nose from bleeding by wearing a string of red corn around the neck.....Mountains

1088. Wear a string of corn around your neck to cure nose-bleeding ....Western Kentucky

1089. To prevent bleeding of the nose, a yarn string is worn around the left little finger..............Western Kentucky

1090. As a cure for nose-bleeding, wear a certain gristle taken from a hog's ear.

1091. To stop the nose from bleeding, put a piece of silk paper under the upper lip.

1092. To prevent your nose from bleeding, place a piece of stiff card board between your front teeth.

1093. If your nose bleeds, let it bleed a little bit on the point of a knife; then stick the knife into the ground before the blood gets cold. This process will stop nose-bleeding......................Blue Grass

1094. Nose-bleeding is stopped by allowing the blood to fall on a sharp axe.................Mountains

1095. You can stop your nose from bleeding by putting a knife dipped in the blood under a doorstep....... Mountains

1096. For nose-bleeding, hold a Bible over the sufferer's head and read Ezekiel 16: 6, three times........ Mountains

1097. Eat nutmeg for boils.........Western Kentucky

1098. For blood-poisoning, place a piece of bacon on the eruption ....Mountains

1099. Put a piece of copper on an eruption from blood-poisoning ....Mountains

1100. To cure a boil, turn up a kettle, get some soot, and make a cross on the boil.............Mountains

1101. You can cure your boils by swallowing shot.

1102. Boils are treated with a poultice of a mud-dauber's nest......................Western Kentucky

1103. To cure a boil, boil a bar of lead (about one third of a pound) in one pint of milk. Boil it down until about two teaspoonfuls are left. Drink it, and you will never have any more boils........Mountains

1104. Clover boiled in a kettle with a crystalline rock makes a salve for boils and other skin eruptions..
.... Mountains

1105. To cure a bone-felon, have a person who, before he was seven years old, had held a mole until it died, hold the finger for half an hour.................
........................Western Kentucky

1106. It causes bad luck to burn a rag that has been around a bone-felon.................Mountains

1107. To cure bots in horses, rub the animal nine times from the tip of its nose to the end of its tail, repeating some lingo; then slap its side............
........................Western Kentucky

1108. Burns can be cured by persons who have the miraculous power of "blowing the fire out" of the wound.

1109. Do not burn a bandage that has been wrapped about a burn. If you do, the burn will not heal.

1110. To throw the dressing from a burnt wound into the fire will cause the wound to burn as if it were in the fire ....Mountains

1111. To cure a burn, one must blow on the burn, repeating these words:
"Three angels from the north;
Go out fire, come in frost"...........Mountains

1112. To blow the fire out of a burn, the curer says: "You look east; you look west; you look south; you look north. I saw three angels coming. One had fire; one had frost. Blow out, Fire. Blow in, Frost.

Father, Son and Holy Ghost." Without the taking in or the letting out of breath, these words must be said in the mind three times, with the patient's wound against the curer's mouth......Mountains

1113. To take the fire out of a burn, the curer wets his forefinger with saliva and rubs it over the burnt place, repeating a charm of some kind..........
..........................Western Kentucky

1114. You may cure cancer by going at daybreak to an apple tree on three successive mornings and pronouncing a certain incantation........Mountains

1115. A cure for cancer. Get a double handful of red-oak bark from the north side of the tree, a double handful of persimmon-tree bark, the north side, a double handful of the bark of the roots of dogwood, the north side, a double handful of the bark of sassafras roots, the north side, and a handful of dewberry briar roots. Put these together, boil them slowly for about twelve hours, then drink the mixture ....Blue Grass

1116. A tobacco leaf is a sure cure for a carbuncle......
..........................Central Kentucky

1117. If you let a dog lick a cat, the latter will recover from its illness.

1118. If you wash your hands in the first snow, they will not chap that winter................Mountains

1119. If your chickens are sick, take the best one that is well and cut off its head, to cure the sick ones.

1120. Chicken-pox is treated with the water in which the feathers of a black chicken are boiled...........
..........................Western Kentucky

1121. As a cure for chicken-pox, the victim may sit in the henhouse for an hour......Western Kentucky

1122. Bathe a child in greasy dish-water, to avert illness.

1123. Gunpowder is given to a woman, to facilitate childbirth ....Mountains

1124. Carry an Irish potato in your pocket, to prevent chills ....Western Kentucky

1125. Frizzly chickens keep off cholera.......Mountains

1126. Mullein tea is a cure for colds, bronchitis, or croup .... Mountains

1127. To cure colds, rub the chest, the palms, and the soles of the feet with goose-grease.

1128. Tallow rubbed on a baby's foot will cure a cold.... .... Mountains

1129. To keep off cold (or other disease) cut an onion in two, hang it by a string, and knock it when you pass.

1130. If you accidentally fall into a creek, your cold will be cured.........................Mountains

1131. To keep off cold, wear a "sow bug" around your neck.

1132. Put a hair or a piece of toe-nail of the patient into a hole of a tree or stump, to cure a cold.

1133. If you drink water out of a stranger's shoe, your sore throat will be cured.............Mountains

1134. To cure sore throat, mouth or eyes, use yellow root.

1135. For a sore throat, tie your right sock, when you remove it at night and while it is warm, around your neck. Let it remain all night.

1136. As a cure for a sore throat, let a man who has smoked for several years blow his breath down the throat ....Central Kentucky

1137. Salt pork will prevent sore throat.

1138. If you wish to prevent a baby's having colic, blow tobacco smoke on its stomach.

1139. Eggs laid on Friday will cure colic.

1140. Red pepper and salt in your shoe will keep off conjures.

1141. Butterfly root is good for consumption.

1142. To eat the hind leg of a fat dog is a sure cure for tuberculosis of the lungs......Louisville Negroes

1143. Tuberculosis in a child may be cured if a lock of the child's hair is placed in a hole in a post or tree higher than the child's head. When he grows up to that height, he will be cured.

1144. For tuberculosis, stick a table fork into the head of the bed of the sufferer........Southern Kentucky

1145. To eat a snail each morning for nine mornings will cure consumption...........Southern Kentucky

1146. For consumption, eat three snails in the morning and three at night; then three or four days later drink a gill of cow's water and four gills of new milk mixed.......................Blue Grass

1147. A cure for tuberculosis is to burn dried cow dung to ashes, make a weak lye, and drink it now and then
................................Blue Grass

1148. As a cure for tuberculosis, cut off a rattlesnake's head, put the snake into rum, and then drink of the concoction two or three times a day.Blue Grass

1149. Tie a hemp string around the great toe of your left foot, to cure a cold...........Western Kentucky

1150. A string around the neck will keep off cold.

1151. If you have small-pox, you will never have tuberculosis.

1152. You can cure a corn by cutting it with a blade that has shaved the dead.

1153. To cure corns, use soft lye soap ("tub soap").

1154. To cure a corn, rub a snail (without a shell) on the corn nine times; then stick the snail on a thorn bush ....Mountains

1155. When a cow's bag is hard and will not break, rub the bag three mornings with a flat rock; then put the rock back where you got it. The fever will then leave the bag...........Central Kentucky

1156. If you feed a cow a soiled dish rag, she will recover her cud.

1157. If you place a bowl of water under the bed at night, your feet will not cramp.

1158. Croup is treated with skunk oil, taken internally and applied externally.

1159. Carry sulphur in the pocket, to keep off cramps in the arms and legs..................Mountains

1160. Tie a string of yarn around the ankle, to cure a cramp.

1161. A leather band worn around the wrist prevents cramp......................Western Kentucky

1162. Wear a brass ring, to keep off cramp...Mountains

1163. To prevent the feet from cramping, place the shoes with the toes pointed under the bed.

1164. You can cure a crick in the neck by rubbing the neck against a tree where a hog has rubbed itself..
................................Blue Grass

1165. Wear amber beads, to keep away croup.

1166. Croup may be prevented by placing the baby's bare foot in the first snow which falls after its birth..
...........................Western Kentucky

1167. To avert cramp in the legs, place a pair of scissors or some other piece of steel in your bed.........
.........................Central Kentucky
1168. Wear a pot hook around the neck, to cure a crick in the neck.
1169. Tea made from elder bark peeled upward will cure diarrhoea ....Mountains
1170. To cure diphtheria, put a part of a freshly killed chicken against the throat.....Western Kentucky
1171. The hair of a dog is good for its bite.
1172. If a dog that bites a person goes mad later, so will the person. Therefore kill the dog straightway.
1173. A madstone, a stone-like substance sometimes found in the body of a deer or other animal, will prevent the bite of a mad dog from producing hydrophobia.
1174. The herb angelica boiled in the urine of a healthy man-child is good for dropsy.........Blue Grass
1175. If you take a bess-bug and cut off its head, one drop of blood will flow. It will cure earache......
.........................Western Kentucky
1176. Three drops of blood from three different kinds of insects dropped into the ear will cure earache.....
....................Central Kentucky Negroes
1177. Cure earache by putting a lock of a negro's hair into the ear..................Central Kentucky
1178. Roast an onion in the ashes and then put the juice of it into your ear, to prevent earache again......
.........................Northern Kentucky
1179. Blow smoke into the ear, to prevent earache.
1180. Rub the hand of a corpse over the face of one who has eczema.

1181. Epilepsy is kept off by the victim's wearing a hemp string around the throat.......Central Kentucky

1182. Epilepsy can be kept off by the sufferer's wearing bones of a rattlesnake around the neck..Mountains

1183. A black cat's blood and a black chicken's will cure erysipelas ....Mountains

1184. Erysipelas is cured by "striking fire" over the patient's head.................Western Kentucky

1185. If you have your ears pierced, you will not have sore eyes.

1186. If you wear ear-rings, you will not have sore eyes.

1187. March snow is good for sore eyes.

1188. Bottled snow water is good for sore eyes.

1189. To wake up your foot when it is asleep, make a cross on your leg with a wet finger.

1190. To wash your feet in dish water will cure sore feet.

1191. Fill your shoes with corn and put a little water on it. Your shoes will thereafter never hurt the feet.

1192. If you will wear a bag of rhubarb around your neck, your children will not have club feet....... ....Western Kentucky

1193. A remedy for frozen feet is to wrap the feet in the skins of rabbits killed in the dark of the moon.... .... Mountains

1194. As a remedy for frozen feet, bury a crooked penny at the northeast corner of the cabin outside, where water drops from the eaves..........Mountains

1195. Frozen feet can be cured by wrapping them in the skin of a newly-killed rabbit, the fur on the outside.

1196. Your feet will not be frost-bitten if you wrap them with rabbit hide....................Mountains

1197. For frost bite, bathe the feet in the running water from a stream that runs west.

1198. A pine knot placed in drinking water will prevent typhoid ....Mountains

1199. Place steel under the bed for fever; it draws out the electricity from the body.

1200. As a cure for a "fever" or cold blister, take wax from your ear and rub it on the blister..........
..........................Southern Kentucky

1201. If you have cold blisters, kiss a dog's forehead, and they will get well...........Louisville Negroes

1202. One of the rattles of a rattlesnake will keep a person from having fits.................Mountains

1203. To cure freckles, go to a still branch in the mountains and bathe your face each day for nine days..
.... Mountains

1204. To remove freckles, wash your face in buttermilk.

1205. You may cure freckles by rubbing grass over your face before the dew is off.

1206. The first shower in May is said to cure freckles.

1207. To remove freckles, wash your face in dew off grass the first nine mornings in May.

1208. If on the first day of May you walk backward from your bed outdoors and then wash your face in dew, the freckles will leave.

1209. To remove freckles, wash your face with melon rind.

1210. To wash in water standing in an oak stump, will remove freckles.....................Mountains

1211. To cure freckles, go to a stone and step over it three times backward and then three times forward.

1212. To cure freckles, get up before the sun rises, go out to a wheat field, and wash in the dew.

Some say that this should be done for seven days.

1213. Glandular swellings are treated with two-year-old marrow taken from the inferior maxillary of a hog .... Western Kentucky

1214. You can stop a goitre from growing by burying a live toad under the drip of the house...Mountains

1215. If you rub a goitre with a toad, it will go away.... .... Mountains

1216. A gold bead necklace prevents a goitre or cures it .... Mountains

1217. "Job's tears," (a kind of smooth, gray bean) tied around the neck, will cure a goitre............. .... North-eastern Kentucky

1218. If you have a goitre on your neck, rub a dead person's hand over it three times. As the body decays the goitre will disappear.......Louisville Negroes

1219. To cure grip, hang your hat on the bed post and drink whiskey until you see two hats.

1220. Rub the sap from a grape vine on your hair to make it grow...........................Mountains

1221. Put burnt leather on a galled place on a horse to prevent the hair from coming out white.Mountains

1222. When a servant finds that her hair is falling out, she should seek a new situation, somewhat removed from her present one, in order to stop the trouble.

1223. For headache, apply brown paper and vinegar.

1224. One subject to headache may prevent it by carrying a buckeye in his pocket.

1225. For headache, use a poultice of cornmeal.Mountains

1226. You can cure headache by pressing the hand on the forehead so as to press each pulse-beating place.

1227. Plait the front hair into four plaits, to avert headache ....Central Kentucky

1228. To cure a headache, place the hair that comes from
the head in combing under a hidden rock somewhere ....Mountains

1229. Carry one of your teeth around your neck, to keep
off headache......................Mountains

1230. For headache, bruise a horse-radish leaf, wet it,
and tie it to the head..........Central Kentucky

1231. Wear a snake-rattle in the hair day and night, to
prevent headaches.

1232. You can cure a headache by swallowing a spider
web ....Western Kentucky

1233. Wear a match in your hair, to keep from having a
headache.

1234. Cure hiccough by holding the breath and counting
nine.

1235. To cure hiccough, take nine sips of water, count
nine backwards, and then turn around nine times.

1236. If somebody tells somebody else to get you a drink,
it will stop hiccough.....North-eastern Kentucky

1237. You can cure hiccough if you put the ends of both
thumbs behind the ears and push inward........
..................................Blue Grass

1238. You can cure hiccough if you frighten the victim
badly ....Blue Grass

1239. If you have a hiccough, think of your lover. If he
loves you, you will not have it anymore.

1240. You can cure a child of hives by "scarifying," that
is, by making three cuts in the child's back, mixing
the blood with breast milk, and giving the mixture
to the child to drink................Mountains

1241. To cure a baby of hives; place a hot, moist cloth just under the shoulder blade, remove it, cut the skin two or three times with a razor; draw about fifteen or twenty drops of blood, and feed it to the baby.

1242. When you break out with hives, mix Irish potato peelings, peanut-butter, and lard; cook them to a syrup and rub with it.........Louisville Negroes

1243. To cure hollow horn, cut a gash in a cow's tail, put in salt, and sew up the wound...Central Kentucky

1244. If a horse hurts his feet, take a nail from the shoe and put it into a lard-can............Mountains

1245. May butter will make an ointment that will cure any ill; it never grows rancid..Western Kentucky

1246. Carry a castor-bean for indigestion.

1247. For indigestion, boil chicken-gizzards and drink the broth.

1248. A sure cure for stomach trouble is a tea made from dog-fennel.

1249. A sure remedy for all kinds of stomach troubles is ginseng.

1250. A nutmeg carried in the pocket or in the clothes is a preventive for stomach troubles.

1251. Keep a goat with a herd of cattle, to keep off infectious diseases...................Blue Grass

1252. A mole's foot will keep off infectious diseases.....
...............................Blue Grass

1253. Kiss an injured spot to make it well.

1254. Iron gives strength. It may be given in the form of simple filings, rust of iron, or salt of steel......
...............................Blue Grass

1255. To cure itch in the toe, tie a yarn string around the toe which is affected.................Mountains

1256. Roll the baby in sulphur and lard for itch........ .... Mountain

1257. To cure itch, rub the body with sulphur, wear your clothes three weeks without change or bath, and bury the clothes. Later dig them up in the dark of the moon and launder them........Mountains

1258. For jaundice, catch about a half-dozen "old sows" (gray hearth bugs) and boil them in water. Then stir into the mixture enough meal to make a cake. Place it on the chimney piece. When the cake is done, the person will be well. (It is not necessary to eat it.)....................Central Kentucky

1259. Wet the index-finger in the mouth, rub it on the bottom of a "pot-vessel" of some sort, and make a cross-mark on a kernel under the jaw, to make it disappear ....Mountains

1260. To cure kernels which result from a bruise or sore, cross them with soot from the chimney.

1261. For an affection of the kidneys, pills made of pine-pitch are taken.

1262. For gravel or other kidney disorders, drink tea made from nine buds picked from as many different stalks of mullein.

1263. You can cure a liver complaint in a child by having him touch his left foot with his right hand........ .... Mountains

1264. For difficult and painful menstruation, take the largest grown pullet you can get, that never laid an egg, pick her without scalding, beat her to pieces and boil her well. Let the patient drink the soup about the time of the change..........Blue Grass

1265. For measles, use "sheep-nanny" tea, that is, a drink made by pouring hot water over the dried manure of sheep.

1266. Flesh moles may be removed by the juice of milkweed.

1267. Some people have the power of removing flesh moles simply by rubbing grass over them.

1268. To ward off mumps, wear a silk cord around the waist.

1269. If from stumping your toe you break your nail, place it with two stones in a rag; then throw the rag over the house..................Mountains

1270. When a nail is stuck into the foot, drive the nail into the ground, to make the swelling go down.

1271. If a nail is stuck into the foot, do not drive the nail high into a door or wall because the swelling in the foot will then rise.

1272. If you stick a rusty nail into your foot, hide the nail where no one can find it, to prevent your foot from getting sore.

1273. If you stick a nail into your foot, grease the nail and carry it in your pocket. The wound will heal quickly.

1274. If you pull a nail out of a horse's foot and put it into your pocket, the horse's foot will not get sore.

1275. Neuralgia can be cured if the sufferer will for three consecutive days take nine swallows of water after rising in the morning and before speaking.......
.... Mountains

1276. Use a red silk handkerchief for neuralgia........
...........................Central Kentucky

1277. If you are suffering from neuralgia in the left side of the head, take a piece of red wrapping string, ignite it, and sniff the smoke into the right nostril, and vice versa......................Blue Grass

1278. Tie a certain bone from a hog's head around the neck, to keep off neuralgia......................
....................Central Kentucky Negroes

1279. Neuralgia is cured by the wearing of a nutmeg around the neck..............Central Kentucky

1280. If you go to sleep on the flat of the back, you will not have a nightmare................Mountains

1281. A cure for nightmare is found by turning the shoes upside down with the toes toward the head of the bed.

1282. A pan of water under the bed prevents night sweats.

1283. In slicing onions, place a pin between the teeth, to prevent crying.

1284. For a fallen palate, the hair on top of a patient's head is pulled "till it pops"; the patient at the same time must swallow twice......Western Kentucky

1285. To cure phthisic, you must measure yourself with a broom-stick and then put the broom-stick upstairs where you will never see it again......Mountains

1286. To cure phthisic, stand the one affected against a tree, fasten a lock of his hair in the tree, and then cut that lock off. When the place grows over, the sick one will be cured.

1287. Cockle-burr tea is good for phthisic.............
..........................Central Kentucky

1288. Carry a horse chestnut in the pocket, to avert piles.

1289. Carry alum, to keep off piles.........Mountains
1290. To cure pheumonia, place a part of a freshly killed chicken on the chest..........Western Kentucky
1291. A dime under your tongue will enable you to eat without danger of poison......Central Kentucky
1292. A nutmeg tied around the neck with a silk cord prevents quinsy.
1293. Carry an acorn in the pocket, to prevent rheumatism.
1294. A piece of alum carried by a person who is suffering from rheumatism will cure the disease.
1295. Wear amber beads about the neck for rheumatism.
1296. To cure rheumatism, fill a can with angleworms, let it stand in the sun all day, and rub the oil on the stiff joints.
1297. A brass ring worn on the left thumb prevents rheumatism.
1298. If you wear a brass ring on the middle finger of the left hand, you will prevent rheumatism..........
.....................North-eastern Kentucky
1299. To avert rheumatism, carry a horse-chestnut in the pocket.
1300. Put a bumble-bee sting between the fingers, to keep off rheumatism.
1301. Use carbon from an arc-light that has not touched the ground, to prevent rheumatism.
1302. For rheumatism, wear a copper wire around the affected parts...............Northern Kentucky
1303. Rheumatism may be prevented by the sufferer's sleeping with a dog.................Mountains
1304. For rheumatism, wear an eel skin around the neck.

1305. You can cure your rheumatism by carrying elder leaves in your pocket................Mountains

1306. Wear red flannel on the wrist, to cure rheumatism
................................Blue Grass

1307. Carry a round ham bone, to avert rheumatism.

1308. Bend a horse-shoe nail into the form of a ring, to avert rheumatism.

1309. If you break the ice in winter time and jump into the water, the bath will cure rheumatism.

1310. Wear a lead ring, to keep off rheumatism.

1311. For rheumatism, wear a nutmeg around the neck.

1312. Pokeberries are thought to be a cure for rheumatism. The berry mixed with whiskey is drunk as a tea. The dried berry gathered in the fall is also made into tea. The raw berry is also eaten......
.... Mountains

1313. Rheumatism is treated with skunk grease or red-worm oil...................Western Kentucky

1314. An Irish potato in the pocket may avert or cure rheumatism. If the potato hardens, it will cure the ailment. If, however, it rots, it will do no good.

1315. Carry a round ham-bone in your pocket, to avert rheumatism.

1316. Carry a potato filled with tacks in your pocket, to keep off rheumatism.........Northern Kentucky

1317. You can cure your rheumatism by crossing your shoes at night...............Northern Kentucky

1318. If you wish to keep from having rheumatism, place your shoes side by side under the bed at night....
.....................North-eastern Kentucky

1319. Wear a silver ring, to keep off rheumatism.

1320. As a cure for rheumatism, tie a red string around the toe.

1321. A white silk ribbon worn about the body will prevent rheumatism....................Blue Grass

1322. A belt made of a rattlesnake skin will cure rheumatism ....Mountains

1323. To cure rheumatism, kill a rattlesnake which has had no chance to strike, skin it, dry the remains, place them in a jug of corn whiskey, and drink the whiskey ....Mountains

1324. Carry sulphur in the pocket for rheumatism......
.... Mountains

1325. To cure rheumatism, bind a live toad to the back. The pain will pass from the back of the sufferer into the toad......................Blue Grass

1326. Put a string of yarn around the neck, to keep off rheumatism.

1327. You can cure rheumatism if you will tie a wool string around your ankle.

1328. To cure ringworms, wet the index finger in the mouth, continue to move it in a circle on the bottom of a used pot, chanting this incantation the while:
"Ringworm round,
Ringworm red,
Ringworm die,
To make ―― ―― glad."
The person afflicted with ring-worm goes through with the ceremony using his given name in the blank space ....Mountains

1329. To cure a ringworm, let some one rub the ringworm

with each of his fingers wet with saliva. Do not let him see the ringworm.............Mountains

1330. To cure a ringworm, rub around it nine times with a thimble.........................Mountains

1331. Scratch a cross with a pin on the finger, to make a "run-around" go off...............Mountains

1332. For shingles, rub the sores with blood obtained from cutting off a black cat's tail. They will then never meet.......................Central Kentucky

1333. For shingles, cut off a black cat's tail and nail the tail against a door.................Mountains

1334. Kill a black chicken, and put the blood on shingles, to cure them.

1335. To cure a pain in the side, spit on the bottom of a stone, put it back in its place, and repeat rapidly an indefinite number of times, until the pain leaves your side: "Pain, get off my side; pain, get off my side"..........................Mountains

1336. For a pain in the side, stoop over until the nose touches the ground.

1337. For a pain in the side, stoop and take a drink of water from a spring.

1338. Hops in the pillow are soothing and induce sleep.

1339. You will never have small-pox so long as you carry an onion in your pocket.............Blue Grass

1340. For a snake-bite, bury the wounded part in the earth.

1341. For a snake-bite, put grease on the wound and let a dog lick it..........Central Kentucky Negroes

1342. For a snake-bite, tie the half of a freshly killed chicken to the bitten place......Central Kentucky

1343. If a snake bites you, kill the snake, split it open,

and wrap it around the wounded member........
.... Mountains

1344. Bind the liver and the intestines of the snake to its bite, as a cure for snake-bite.........Blue Grass

1345. A rattlesnake-bite is cured by salt and fresh pork.. .... Mountains

1346. A piece of red yarn around your little toe will take sores off your feet..................Mountains

1347. Take jimson-weed and fat meat on a penny and apply the mixture to a sore; it will stop pain...... ....Louisville Negroes

1348. A sore may be cured by a dog's licking it......... ....Louisville Negroes

1349. After you have extracted a splinter from your flesh, there will be no pain if you put the splinter in your hair..................Louisville Negroes

1350. Sprains are treated with goose grease........... ....Western Kentucky

1351. For insect stings, take three kinds of weeds and rub the place that is irritated..Southern Kentucky

1352. To cure a stone bruise, bind a live toad on the bruise. When the toad dies, the bruise will disappear.

1353. Rub a black cat's tail over your eye nine times, to remove a sty.

1354. To remove a sty, steal a dish-cloth, rub the sty with it, and bury the dish-cloth secretly.

1355. Rub an incipient sty with a plain gold ring warmed by friction with a woolen garment. Pronounce the following couplet:
"Sty, sty, leave my eye;
Go to the next passer-by."

1356. A sty may be cured by one's rubbing it with a wedding ring that has been blessed..Central Kentucky

1357. Take gravel from a running stream, rub it on a sty or other place of pain, and then replace it........
.... Mountains

1358. If any one has a sty on his eye, tell him he has told a lie. This statement will relieve him..Mountains

1359. If some one on seeing that you have a sty says that it is a sty and you say it is a lie, the sty will go off..
.... Mountains

1360. If you wear a nutmeg around your neck, you will cure the sty on your eye.

1361. At a cross-roads say: "Sty, sty, leave eye; Go to the next passer-by."

1362. Remove a sty by turning three times on the heel at a cross-roads.

1363. If you have a sty, walk backwards to a cross-roads and spit on the ground three times over the right shoulder. The sty will leave you and infect the next passer-by.

1364. Remove a sty by picking up a rock, spitting on it, and returning it to its place.

1365. To keep off sun-stroke, put a wet cabbage leaf on the head.

1366. If you have a sun pain in your head, clip a small bunch of hair from the top of your head and place it in a branch running from west to east.Mountains

1367. If you have a tape-worm, get a handful of the bark of the root on the north side of a mulberry tree and boil it in a gallon of new milk; take this mixture for three days before the full, and three days before the change, for three moons......Blue Grass

1368. To cure tetter, wear a brass ring on your thumb...
..........................Southern Kentucky

1369. Thrush in a child can be cured if a person who has never seen his father will blow his breath three times into the child's face for three days.........
.............................Blue Grass

1370. You may cure thrush by putting the blood of a chicken into the child's mouth........Mountains

1371. To cure thrush, place a lock of the child's hair into a hole in a tree..............Central Kentucky

1372. Rainwater from a stump will cure thrush.

1373. Thrush in a child can be cured by washing the child's mouth with nine sage buds......Mountains

1374. For thrush, take three bunches of green sage of three buds each; rake each bunch through the mouth; hang the three bunches before the fire; when they dry, the child will be cured..Mountains

1375. The seventh son or daughter by blowing into the mouth of a child will cure thrush...............
..........................Western Kentucky

1376. To avert thrush, drink water from a man's right shoe ....Mountains

1377. You can cure thrush in a child by giving him to drink water that has been tossed in a stranger's right shoe from heel to toe three times..Mountains

1378. Cure thrush by having the child drink water out of an old shoe.....................Mountains

1379. As a cure for thrush, place nine sow-bugs (little white insects found under stones near dwellings) in a small sack and wear it around the neck for nine days.

1380. To cure a child of thrush, let a stallion snort into the child's face.....................Mountains

1381. The wearing of amber beads around the neck will help teething.................Central Kentucky

1382. Black wooden beads worn about the neck will avert the pains of teething.................Blue Grass

1383. Black hen's brains make babies' teething easy.....
...........................Central Kentucky

1384. For a baby's teething, let it have nine pieces of burdock root on a string around its neck........
...........................Central Kentucky

1385. Rub an unbroken egg shell on a baby's gums, to ease the pains of teething............Mountains

1386. Suspend a borrowed egg in a paper sack from the ceiling, to cause the baby to cut its teeth easily....
...........................Western Kentucky

1387. Sore gums in a baby may be cured by the application of a groundhog's brains..........Mountains

1388. Put the eye-tooth of a hog about the neck of a child. to keep it from having a hard second summer. (This tooth is found with a hole through the center)
...........................Central Kentucky

1389. For sore gums, let the child wear a necklace of "Job's Tears" (a kind of smooth, gray bean) about its neck.

1390. To aid a baby in cutting its teeth, rub a minnow or other small fish on the baby's gums....Mountains

1391. To make all teething pains in a child cease, fasten about its neck in a small cloth "poke" or bag the right front paw of a ground mole.

1392. Make a baby's teething easy by putting a quarter of a dollar around its neck.

1393. For teething, cut off a rabbit's head, roast the head with the hair on, take the brains out, and rub them on the gums.................Blue Grass Negroes

1394. Rub warm and raw rabbits' brains on the baby's gums ....Mountains

1395. A snail or slug is placed on the gum for tooth-ache ....Western Kentucky

1396. If you put a string of warm seed roots about a baby's neck, its teething will not be painful...... .... Mountains

1397. For teething, use a necklace of whole spice soaked in whiskey ....Blue Grass

1398. For toothache, make the gums bleed, put the blood on a long cotton string, and tie the string around a dogwood tree at a place where an incision has been made in the bark............Western Kentucky

1399. To cure a toothache, steal a dishrag and bury it... ....North-eastern Kentucky

1400. For toothache a faith doctor writes, "Gaffa, gaffa, gaffa," on the wall. With a nail he points at each letter, at the same time asking the sufferer if the tooth feels better. When he reaches a letter where the tooth is said to be better, he drives in the nail, and the toothache ceases......Western Kentucky

1401. If you keep a hog's jaw tooth, you will not have a toothache ....Mountains

1402. To cure toothache, cut a wart off a horse's leg and rub it on the gums...........Western Kentucky

1403. For toothache, carry the skull of a horse as far as you can, holding its teeth with your teeth........ .... Mountains

1404. To cure toothache, choke a mole with your hands

behind your head and hang one of its feet around your neck ....Mountains

1405. For toothache, secure a tooth from a live mole and rub this on the aching member. Western Kentucky

1406. Avert or cure toothache by cutting your nails on Friday.

1407. You can cure toothache by promising not to cut your nails or do similar things on Sunday........ .... Mountains

1408. If you stand a person against a tree and drive a nail into the tree just above his head, this process will cure toothache............Western Kentucky

1409. To cure toothache, pick your tooth with a poplar peg until it bleeds, then wrap a yarn string around the peg, and get someone to bury it. Relief will come soon....................Central Kentucky

1410. To cure toothache, pick up a rock, spit on the under side, and put it back into the same place. Mountains

1411. If after your tooth is pulled you throw it over the left shoulder (or put it under a rock), you will have no toothache...................Mountains

1412. Pick your aching tooth with a splinter from a tree that has been struck by lightning.............. ....Western Kentucky

1413. To prevent toothache, make a wish by the full moon .... Mountains

1414. To cure toothache, go to a wood, find a small hickory tree, take your knife, stand by the tree and mark the place even with your mouth; then move back, turn up the bark, spit into the place, and turn the bark down again. If it grows back, your tooth will not hurt any more........Mountains

1415. If you have swollen tonsils, place a live toad against them. The swelling will disappear............
................:.............Southern Kentucky

1416. To cure abrasion in the toe, tie a yarn string around the toe............................Mountains

1417. Place hops in a bag or in your clothes as a cure for train-sickness or sea-sickness.

1418. Put Irish potatoes in a traveling bag, to keep off train-sickness.

1419. A newspaper inside the shirt next to the skin will keep off train-sickness.

1420. To prevent train-sickness, wear a piece of writing paper on the chest.

1421. To prevent train-sickness, wear a pair of soles made of butchers' brown paper. North-eastern Kentucky

1422. You must not take turpentine externally unless you take it internally.

1423. For typhoid, cut a chicken in half and put one part against the sole of each foot.

1424. Sprinkle lime around the house, to protect the family from typhoid.................Mountains

1425. A piece of onion will keep off typhoid. .Mountains

1426. Tea made from the lining of a chicken's gizzard will cure vomiting.

1427. Tea made from elder bark peeled downward will cure vomiting......................Mountains

1428. Peach-tree bark taken internally will cure vomiting

1429. To cause vomiting, put a wet tobacco leaf beneath the foot, under the arm, or on the stomach.

1430. You can make a wart go away by burying an apple secretly and saying this charm:

"As this apple decays, so let my wart go away"...
..............................Blue Grass

1431. Make an incision in the bark of an apple tree. When the place grows over, your wart will be gone.

1432. Rub the wart with bacon rind. Bury it secretly. As it decays, the wart will disappear.

1433. Rub the warts with a piece of bacon. Tie a string around the bacon and bury it secretly. The warts will leave within nine days.

1434. Rub the wart with fresh beefsteak, tie a string around the steak, and bury it secretly. The wart will leave within nine days.

1435. Buy five cents worth of candy, eat it all, and your warts will disappear.

1436. For a wart cure, bury one bean or three beans secretly. When the beans sprout, the wart will be cured.

1437. Put wart blood on a bean leaf and bury it secretly. The wart will leave within nine days.

1438. As a cure for a wart, put blood from the wart on a bean leaf, pour water on the rock, and leave it. The wart will disappear.

1439. Take a bean leaf and squeeze its juice onto a wart. The wart will be gone in three days.

1440. Get nine bean leaves and rub them nine times over your wart; then bury them where they will rot.

1441. Rub the wart with the underside of a round or ring bone. Bury the bone secretly. Within three weeks the wart will disappear.

1442. Kill a black cat, take it to a graveyard at midnight, and rub the cat on the wart.

1443. To make a wart go away, wash it in the blood of a black cat which was killed in the light of the moon.

1444. Pick 'the wart with a brass pin. Let one drop of blood fall on a stone. Cover the drop with another stone and then bury them secretly.

1445. Put castor oil on a wart.

1446. Rub a chicken gizzard or chicken intestine on a wart, to make it disappear.

1447. Rub coffee grounds on a wart; then put the coffee grounds into a bag and bury them.

1448. If you have warts, put as many cords under a rock as you have warts. When the cords rot, the warts will disappear.

1449. To cure warts, rub seven grains of corn on the warts; then feed the corn to your neighbor's chickens.

1450. To cure a wart, cut it, take ten grains of corn, and put them on the wart; then put them into a crawfish hole. The wart will go off.

1451. Pick a wart with a red grain of corn until it bleeds; then give the grain of corn to a red rooster.

1452. Pick the wart, put the blood from it on a grain of corn, and give it to a gander.

1453. Rub a wart with a grain of corn, and drop the grain into a well; when it rots the wart will disappear.

1454. Pick the largest or "seed" wart with a needle until it bleeds; then take as many grains of corn as you have warts and put a drop of blood on each. Feed these to a rooster.

1455. To remove warts, pick the part until it bleeds, put the blood on seven grains of corn, and feed them to one chicken.

1456. Some people can count warts off.

1457. Some people can rub a wart and conjure it off.

1458. If you cut a cross mark on a tree and then pick the wart until it bleeds and rub the blood on the cross mark, the wart will leave when the mark goes off the tree.

1459. To cure a wart, go to a cross-roads, make a cross, and spit into the middle of it.

1460. Rub a wart with the juice of a dandelion, to make it leave.

1461. If you have warts, wait until some one dies; then just at midnight go to the graveyard and call to the devil. He will take away the warts.

1462. Rub the wart with an old dishrag (some say, a stolen dishrag). Bury the rag. When it rots, the wart will be gone. The process must be done secretly.

1463. In the use of a stolen dishrag for the cure of a wart, throw it over your left shoulder into a pond.

1464. Tie a dog's hair around a wart very tightly; the wart will disappear.

1465. Steal an egg, rub it over the wart, and then bury it. Do not tell any one of your act. The wart will disappear.

1466. Cut your finger-nail to the quick. When it grows out, the wart will be gone.

1467. Catch a fish and rub the wart with it.

1468. Rub the wart seven times with a gold ring.

1469. Rub a wart with the end of a goose quill.

1470. In order to cure a wart, place a fresh piece of grape vine over the wart; then bury the vine in a secret place.

1471. If you drop some dirt from a new grave on a wart, it will go away.

1472. Get three pieces of gravel where the rain-water falls on them off the house; apply them to the wart; then tie them in a white rag and bury them. . Mountains

1473. To remove a wart, rub it with nine pieces of gravel, and then place the pieces in the fork of the roads. . . . . Mountains

1474. Select an herb of each of three different kinds. Spit on each herb and touch the wart with it. Bury the herbs. Tell no one. The wart will disappear.

1475. Cut the wart off with a horse hair.

1476. Cut the wart off with a silk thread.

1477. If you kiss your wart and then kiss some one, your wart will come off. . . . . Mountains

1478. Warts may be removed by lemon juice.

1479. As a cure for warts, steal a piece of meat, grease the warts, bury the meat under a rail fence or the eave of the house. When the meat rots, the warts will be gone.

1480. Rub the juice of milk-weed on the wart. It will be cured by the next morning. This remedy is possibly medicinal.

1481. When you see the new moon, pick up any object on which your foot rests and rub this article on the wart; then walk backwards ten steps and throw the object over your right shoulder. Very soon the wart will disappear.

1482. If you look at the new moon and rub your hand over the wart three times, saying each time, "You grow and you go," the wart will disappear. . . . . Mountains

1483. When you see a new moon, rub your finger-tip around the wart. It will leave.

1484. Rub the wart with a stalk of green mustard.

1485. To remove a wart, one must pick it until it bleeds, then put the blood on a rusty nail, and drive the nail into the root of an oak tree.

1486. Give the warts on your hand names that you have never heard of and make some good wish about them; the warts will go off.

1487. To cure warts on cattle, name the animal that has the warts "Finny," and call it always by that name ....Southern Kentucky

1488. Smoke a nettle and stick it in the wart; then throw the nettle away.

1489. Count the warts each night for nine nights. They will leave.

1490. Let a friend of yours cut the wart on your hand and then put a drop of the blood on a piece of paper and hide it. The wart will leave.

1491. Cut the wart. Put a drop of blood on a piece of the wart on paper. Throw the paper away at a cross-roads or over the left shoulder. If any one picks up the paper, your wart will pass to him. Secrecy must be observed.

1492. Rub the warts with peach-tree leaves and bury the leaves. When they rot, the warts will leave.

1493. Go unseen to a young peach-tree and cut with a butcher knife as many notches in the tree as you have warts. Put the knife back into its place. In seven days the warts will go away.

1494. Cut three notches in a peach-tree limb. When the notches are filled up, the wart will be gone.

1495. To remove a wart, rub a penny over the wart for nine mornings.

1496. Pick the wart until it bleeds. Split the bark of a persimmon tree and put the blood within. When the split grows up, the wart will leave.........
............................Western Kentucky

1497. If someone gives you a pin and if you then close your eyes and turn around three times, your wart will disappear ....Central Kentucky

1498. Pick your wart with a pin; blindfold yourself and stick the pin into the ground; the wart will disappear ....Southern Kentucky

1499. Thrust a pin entirely through a wart; heat the point of the pin; pull the heated point back through the wart ....Western Kentucky

1500. Pick a wart with a pin that has never been used and throw it where it can never be found. Your wart will disappear......................Mountains

1501. To remove a wart, rub it with a pin that belongs to someone other than a relation of yours. Then hide the pin....................Western Kentucky

1502. The warts will go away if you give a girl who is not related to you a pin or anything like a pin.......
.... Mountains

1503. Put poke-root on the warts, to remove them.

1504. If you rub a wart with a fresh piece of potato once or twice each day, it will fall out within two weeks.

1505. Throw a piece of potato over your left shoulder. When the potato sprouts, your wart will be cured.

1506. If you boil potatoes and wash your hands in the juice, your warts will leave.

1507. Rub a person's wart three times; on the third time say, "Father, Son and Holy Ghost"...Mountains

1508. Pick a wart until it bleeds; rub salt over it; wrap the salt up in a piece of paper; throw the paper into the road. The wart will disappear.

1509. Cut as many notches in a sassafras root as you have warts; plant the root; if it grows, the warts will leave ....Mountains

1510. Call each wart by the name of a preacher, cut a notch for each one in a sassafras stick, and stick it into the ground up to the first notch. The warts will then disappear.................Mountains

1511. Cure a wart by selling it to someone and keeping the money.

1512. Warts may be cured by the touch of the seventh son of a seventh son, who must utter the words, "Go away, wart." No pay must be offered to the healer.

1513. Tie a black silk thread around the wart. When the thread wears out, the wart will disappear.

1514. Rub the warts with a snail obtained from the woods; place the snail on a stick; when the snail crawls away from the stick, the warts will be gone.

1515. Spit on a wart and rub it seven times upward with the finger while someone chants a hocus-pocus rhyme.....................Western Kentucky

1516. Rub a steel ring on a rug, and then touch the wart It will be gone at the end of three weeks.

1517. Cut as many notches in a stick as you have warts, and place it under the drip of the house. When it rains, the warts will go off..........Mountains

1518. Measure each wart with a stick, and break off the

piece. Bury the pieces of stick. When they rot, the warts will be gone.

1519. Get a stone at midnight, spit on it, and put it on a rafter in the attic. In eight weeks turn it over. Secrecy must be observed.

1520. Touch each wart with a stone, and speak certain secret words of charm. The warts will leave.

1521. Go out secretly in the morning, rub a stone on the wart, and put the stone back exactly as you found it. Repeat this action daily until the wart disappears.

1522. A good cure for warts is to prick them with a broom straw, and then break the straw into as many pieces as there are warts.

1523. Get a piece of straw for every wart; touch each wart with a separate straw. Bury the straws in a wet place. When they rot, the warts will be gone.

1524. Pick three straws from a broom. Rub the wart three times. Bury the straws where water drops. When the straws rot, the cure is effected. This process must be done secretly.

1525. Rub a bundle of straws over a wart, and place it in a path where it will be picked up. If some one picks the bundle up, the wart will go away within a month.

1526. A witch-doctor takes a flat stick and cuts a notch for each of your warts. Then he chants: "Come, witches, take these warts away." He then hides the stick. When it is moved, the warts will leave.....
. . . . Mountains

1527. Take a string out of a dish rag, tie as many knots in it as you have warts on your hand, and bury it under a rock. When it rots, the warts will disappear.

1528. Let someone tie a string into a knot on the wart, and then hide it in a place unknown to the afflicted person. When the string rots, the wart disappears.

1529. To cure a wart, walk backwards in the moonlight to an old stump full of water and stick your hand into the water.

1530. In order to remove a wart, you must get up some morning without speaking to anyone or allowing anyone to speak to you and walk down the steps backward and out of the house to a thorn bush. Take a thorn from the bush, and stick it into your coat; then address the thorn bush: "Mr. Thorn, I wish to trade you my warts for a thorn."

1531. Tie a black thread around the wart, and then put the thread where the water drips off the house. . . . . Mountains

1532. Put a thread on the wart; then take the thread, and let some one bury it in a place you do not know. When the thread rots, the warts will come off.

1533. Any old woman who is possessed of supernatural power will remove your warts for so many pins. . . . . Mountains

1534. Point the fingers at a wart and say "Tige" three times. It will go away.

1535. In order to cure your warts, put tobacco juice on them.

1536. To remove your warts, rub a broken toothpick on them.

1537. If someone rubs your wart twenty-five times, it

will leave your hand and go to his..............

..........................Central Kentucky

1538. Stick a toothpick dipped in vinegar into your wart. It will leave.

1539. Rub the wart with half of a green walnut and then bury the pieces of walnut.....Western Kentucky

1540. If you tie three knots in a red yarn string and throw it into the fire, the warts will leave your hands.

1541. To cure a wart, hold your hand so deep in water that you cannot see the wart.........Mountains

1542. To awaken a sleeping part of the body, wet your finger, and make a cross on that part of the body.

1543. No matter how much contaminated water may be, it will be purified when it has passed over nine pebbles ....Mountains

1544. To remove a wen, wish it away with a formula, and strike it with a book.

1545. If you have a wen on your hand, rub it against a dead-man's neck, to make it go wway..........

..........................Louisville Negroes

1546. To cure a wen on your neck, place a string around the neck of a deceased friend of yours and afterward wear it around your own neck..........

..........................Louisville Negroes

1547. To keep off whooping-cough, wear a black velvet band around the neck........Blue Grass Negroes

1548. A tea made from white ants will cure whooping-cough....................,.....Louisville Negroes

1549. You will cure a pain in your leg if you tie a string around your leg just above the knee............

..........................Western Kentucky

FIRE

1550. To play with fire will bring bad luck.

1551. A child that plays with fire will wet its bed.

1552. You will have bad luck if you burn bones.

1553. If you burn the skin of onions, you will receive money......................Lousiville Negroes

1554. If you burn an egg-shell, you will get money......
..........................Louisville Negroes

1555. If the fire roars, there will be a quarrel in the family.

1556. Some negroes can foretell the arrival of strangers by the presence of figures in the fire.

1557. If a piece of burning wood or coal rolls from the fire-place, a stranger is coming.

1558. To avert the coming of a stranger when a piece of burning wood or coal rolls from the fire-place, spit on the burning pieces.

1559. Name a piece of burning wood or coal when it falls from the fireplace the person you wish to see, and then spit on it.

1560. If a log falls out of the fireplace, put it back in the same position as it was before falling. If you do not, you will have bad luck....Louisville Negroes

1561. You must not turn a log of wood over in the fire, for you will have bad luck; and if a piece falls down, you must not turn it around when you replace it.

1562. When fire pops, there will be a quarrel in the family. The one that punches the fire will start the quarrel.

1563. To avoid a quarrel in the family, stir the fire when it pops.

1564. If a spark pops out of the fire, company is coming.

1565. In making a garment, if the fire pops upon it, you will die before it is finished.

1566. To avert the disaster that follows the popping of fire upon your dress, throw salt into the fire.

1567. If a spark from a fire falls behind you, you will have trouble that comes from behind you.

1568. It causes bad luck to move into a house before the fire left by the last tenants has died out.........
...........................Western Kentucky

1569. If the soot hangs from the bars of a grate, some one is coming ....Mountains

1570. If soot on the back of a fire-place catches fire and if sparks creep and crawl along it, you will have fresh meat.

1571. If a fire goes out before the fuel is consumed, there will be bad luck.

1572. If a tree is struck by lightning, the fire may be put out by milk but not by water.

1573. If you burn the wood of a tree that has been struck by lightning, there will be a death in your family..
.... Mountains

HOUSEHOLD AND DOMESTIC LIFE[1]

1574. If the stone step of a newly built house cracks, there will be an early death in the family

1575. If a board warps in a porch, you may expect a death in the family.

1576. To build a new house where an old one stood will cause a death in the family.

1577. It brings bad luck to cut a door or a window in a

[1] For dates of moving see *Days and Seasons*. For the connection of witches and butter, see *Witches*.

house after it is built. If you cut a new door in an old house, there will be a death in your family.

1578. When dirt is lifted, if it is thrown away from the house, there will be good luck for the household.

1579. It causes bad luck when dirt is lifted, if it is thrown toward the house.

1580. If a chimney is blown from your house during a storm, you will have good luck if it falls on the right of the house...................Blue Grass

1581. If you build a new house and move at once into it, one of the family will die.

1582. If you give an entertainment upon moving into a new house, you will have good luck.

1583. If when you move into a new house you take into it first a basket of food, you will have good luck and a sufficiency of food.................Blue Grass

1584. If you take a cat with you when you move, you will have three years of bad luck..........Mountains

1585. It brings good luck, when you move into a newly built house, to hang a bag of salt in the kitchen behind the stove......................Mountains

1586. When she moves, the woman should not enter the new home without salt...............Mountains

1587. When you move, do not take salt into the house first.

1588. To carry an old broom to a new house brings bad luck.

1589. In moving into a new house, do not take the broom in first.

1590. It brings good luck, when you move into a new home, to take the handle of the broom in first.

1591. You must never take your broom with you when you move.

1592. In taking up residence at a new place, throw a broom before you through the front door.

1593. Never move from a house without throwing a broom over it.

1594. To sweep a house after the moving is done will bring bad luck.

1595. If you are hit by a broom, you will be arrested.

1596. If you hit a person with a broom, he will spend the greater part of his life in prison.

1597. If the person struck with a broom spits on the broom, he averts the prison omen.

1598. If you hit a person with a broom, you will make him lazy.

1599. To step over a broom is a sign of slovenliness.

1600. If you step over a broom when it is on the floor, you will have bad luck.

1601. To step backward over a broom brings bad luck.

1602. It brings good luck to fall over a broom handle.

1603. It causes bad luck to hand a person a broom from a window.

1604. It is unwise to carry a broom from the front door through the house to the back.

1605. If a broom falls in front of a door, there will be disaster to the one who goes through that door.

1606. You will have bad luck if you place a broom with the handle above.

1607. It causes bad luck to lean a broom against a bed.

1608. If you drop a great many broom-straws out of a broom, you will have good luck.

1609. If a bunch of straws comes out of the broom when

you are sweeping, name it and place it over the
door. The person named will call.

1610. If you drop a broom while you are sweeping, you
will get a new carpet.

1611. Do not sweep under one's feet, for he will never be
rich.

1612. If you sweep under a sick person's bed, he will die.

1613. If you let any one sweep under your feet with a
broom, you will have bad luck.

1614. If you let some one sweep under your feet, you will
never be married.

1615. If you sweep your feet with a broom, you will never
be married.

1616. It brings bad luck to sweep dirt from a room out
of the door.

1617. If you sweep dirt out of your door during the first
part of the week, you will have bad luck all the
week.

1618. It causes bad luck to stir the fire with a broom.

1619. If the broom falls across the doorway, someone will
call.

1620. If two people sweep a floor together, they may expect bad luck.

1621. If you sweep after dark, you will bring sorrow to
your heart.

1622. If you sweep dirt out of the house at night, before
a month is over a member of the family will be
carried out the door a corpse.

1623. It brings bad luck to sweep a porch after night.

1624. If you take up ashes or sweep them out after four
o'clock in the afternoon, you will have bad luck.

1625. If you sweep the house after the sun goes down, you may expect a man caller.

1626. If you move the furniture in your sitting room every month, you will have good luck.

1627. Never put your foot on a bed, for you will have bad luck.

1628. If spinning rolls are not laid in the same direction in which they come off the cards, they will not spin . . . . Mountains

1629. It brings bad luck to sit on a trunk.

1630. If you turn a chair around, whoever sits down in it will have bad luck all of his life.

1631. You will shorten your days if you turn a chair around on one leg.

1632. To turn a chair around on one leg is a sign that you will soon get a whipping.

1633. To avert the disaster incident to turning a chair around, turn it in the reverse direction.

1634. It causes bad luck for anyone to put a foot on your chair.

1635. If one unconsciously turns a chair, a calf will die. . . . . Mountains

1636. Two chairs with their backs together promise good luck.

1637. Two chairs set back to back accidentally promise company.

1638. It brings bad luck for a chair or a table to creak.

1639. The rocking of an empty rocking-chair indicates the coming of bad luck.

1640. To rock a chair when no one is in it, is a sign that you are rocking someone out of the family.

1641. To avert the bad luck incident to rocking an unoc-
cupied chair, one may place a pillow in the chair.

1642. If you sit on the front edge of your chair, you are
of a grasping disposition............Blue Grass

1643. It is a sign of death if an old clock strikes that has
not been running.

1644. If an old clock that has not been running strikes,
one of the family will die in the number of years
indicated by the number of the strokes.

1645. If a weight in the family clock falls, there will be a
death in the family.

1646. If the clock ticks loudly at midnight, there will be
a death in the family.

1647. If the family clock stops, there will be a death in
the family.

1648. It causes bad luck to have two clocks running in one
house. ....Mountains

1649. A watch-tick sound in the wall is the sign of a death
in the family. A "death-ticking" in some article
of furniture is a sign of death.

1650. If you hear the furniture creaking, bad luck will
follow.

1651. If you hear the furniture crack in the night, there
will be a death.

1652. A creaking wall indicates death.

1653. To go in at one door and out at another indicates
that you will have company.

1654. A person will have bad luck who goes in at one door
and out at another.

1655. To stumble when going upstairs is a sign that you
will receive a letter.

1656. To hang out clothes after dark brings bad luck.

1657. To shake out a table-cloth after dark brings ill luck.

1658. If you take a hoe or a spade into the house, someone will dig your grave.

1659. If a hoe is carried through one door and out at another, the youngest member of the family will die.

1660. If you carry a hoe through the house, your calf will die .... Mountains

1661. It causes bad luck to throw a hoe over the fence.

1662. It brings bad luck to carry an axe into the house.

1663. Avert the bad luck of carrying a spade or an axe into the house by carrying the implement out the same way that it was brought in.

1664. It causes bad luck to step on an axe.... Mountains

1665. It brings bad luck to draw a rake or a hoe across a porch.

1666. If you carry a plant into the house through one door, you must take it out through the same door, or a person in your family will soon die. Blue Grass

1667. If you pour some of the first of each milking into the creek, the cow will not go dry.

1668. In milking if you throw milk on the ground, the cow will go dry. Throw it into the running water.

1669. Lightning and thunder will sour milk.

1670. If you lend a churn, your cow will go blind or suffer some other disaster.................. Mountains

1671. You cannot make butter when elders are in bloom.
.... Mountains

1672. Hold a buttercup under your chin. If it casts a reflection upon your chin, you like butter........
.... Mountains

1673. If while currying a horse you drop a curry-comb

or brush, you will miss your aim that day in hunting.

1674. It causes bad luck to knock a vase off a mantel....
....................................Blue Grass

1675. If you iron the hem of your husband's shirt, you iron his money away..............Central Kentucky

1676. It brings good luck to bury your fish bones.......
.... Mountains

1677. If a working woman leaves the place of her employ·· ment after five o'clock in the afternoon without at least a morsel of food in her pocket, she will be without food the next day............Blue Grass

1678. If a working woman in leaving the place of her employment after five o'clock in the afternoon turns back for a forgotten morsel of bread, she will have bad luck. The bread must be brought to her.....
....................................Blue Grass.

1679. It brings bad luck for the kettle to move on the hearth without apparent cause.

1680. It brings bad luck for the door to push in and out without wind.

1681. If your thread knots, you will die before the article that is being made is worn out.

1682. If while hemming a napkin you prick your finger and the blood gets on the napkin, you will die before it wears out...................Blue Grass

1683. If two people sew on the same piece at the same time, the older will outlive the younger.

1684. If you accidentally drop a needle and it sticks into the floor, some one is coming.

1685. To hang up the calendar before the old year is out will bring you bad luck.

1686. If you walk over a rug and turn up the edge, you will have bad luck.

1687. If you walk back over a rug which you have turned up at the edge, you will avert the bad luck.

1688. To pass any one on the stairs causes bad luck.

1689. If you stand in a friend's open door, you will bring bad luck to that friend.

1690. You will have bad luck if you walk through a door backward...................Western Kentucky

1691. It brings bad luck to go through a doorway when some one is sitting in it.

1692. You will have bad luck if you bump against any one while you pass through a door.

1693. Do not knock on your own door. Western Kentucky

1694. Never hang any thing on a door knob.

1695. If you break a glass door or a window, you are certain to have bad luck.

1696. It brings bad luck to shake hands across a door-sill.

1697. It causes bad luck to jump out of a window unless you jump in again backward.

1698. Shaking hands over a fence or a gate is unlucky.

1699. It brings bad luck to close an open gate.

1700. It is unlucky to touch an open gate.

1701. A bed should head toward the north.

1702. Never sleep with your head toward the east.

1703. You must not place your bed with the head to the west, as that position is the one in which the dead are buried.

1704. If you lie with your head out the door, you will die before the year is out...............Blue Grass

1705. If you lie with your head toward the fire, you will be ill.

1706. "Early to bed and early to rise,
You'll be healthy, wealthy, witty and wise."

1707. It brings bad luck to get into bed over the foot-board.

1708. It causes bad luck to climb over any one in bed.

1709. If you get into bed on the side opposite to the one you are used to getting in, you will have bad luck.

1710. If you go to bed backwards, you will have pleasant dreams.

1711. If you say your prayers after going to bed, you say them to the Devil............Central Kentucky

1712. If you go to bed thirsty, your spirit will wander off and drink from foul mud-puddles.......Negroes

1713. If you go to bed very happy, you will awake ill the next morning.

1714. If you laugh in bed, you will cry before morning.

1715. If you whistle in bed, you will cry before you retire again.

1716. To sing in bed brings bad luck.

1717. If a solid crown of feathers is found in a pillow, misfortune will fall on the household.

1718. If a cross of feathers is found in a pillow, misfortune will fall on the household.

1719. If you get up in the morning with a feather in your hair, you have slept one hour late.....Mountains

1720. If a person walking in his sleep is awakened, the awakening will kill him.

1721. It brings bad luck for three people to make up one bed.

1722. Never put a broom on the bed; it brings bad luck.

1723. To lay an umbrella on the bed causes bad luck.

1724. It brings bad luck to raise an umbrella over any

one's head in the house. He will not grow any more.

1725. If you raise an umbrella in the house, you will have bad luck.

1726. If a man gives a woman an umbrella, bad luck will follow.....................Louisville Negroes

1727. New sheets must not be slept in unlaundered, as the occupant will have bad luck.

1728. It brings bad luck to keep a quilt of hexagonal pattern. This pattern is sometimes called "Job's Trouble"....................Central Kentucky

1729. In quilting, if you leave out a line, one in the family will die.........................Mountains

1730. You will have good luck if you use tablecloths, towels, and the like before they are laundered.

1731. If two people use a towel at the same time, they will fight.

1732. "Wash and wipe together,
You'll be good friends forever."
or
"Wash and wipe together,
Live and love forever."

1733. Do not empty the water that someone else has washed in, as a quarrel will follow.

1734. If you wash in the same water that some one else has used, the two of you will quarrel.

1735. When a candle is allowed to burn entirely out, a death will follow.

1736. If a short flame rises from the candle, expect a small stranger.....................Central Kentucky

1737. If a long, straight flame rises from the candle, expect a tall stranger............Central Kentucky

1738. If a candle flame, instead of being straight, spreads around the tallow, it forms a winding sheet and is prophetic of death.

1739. A spark on the wick of a candle flame is the sign that you are to receive a letter..Central Kentucky

1740. If a guest blows out a candle, he will come again.

1741. If there are three candlesticks in a row, you must move them to different parts of the room before lighting them.

1742. It causes bad luck to let a lamp go out. You should blow it out.

1743. If a lamp goes out in the room, there will be a death in the family.

1744. It causes bad luck to bring a lighted lamp into a room where there is one already lighted.

1745. You will have bad luck if you put two lamps on a table at one time.

1746. It causes bad luck to have three lighted lamps in a room.

1747. If you light a lamp after you sit down at the table, some one will die............Southern Kentucky

1748. You will have bad luck if a lamp chimney breaks in your hand.

1749. As many times as it takes you to blow out the lamp, just so many lies have you told.......Blue Grass

1750. If your lamp chimney breaks after you have gone to bed, there will be a death in the family........
...............................Blue Grass

1751. It brings good luck to drop a knife if the blade sticks into the ground. The direction towards which the knife points is the one from which the good fortune will come.

1752. If you drop a table-knife, you will have a disappointment.
1753. If you drop a knife at the table, the one who picks it up will have good luck............Blue Grass
1754. Do not give a sharp instrument to a friend of yours; if you do, trouble will follow.
1755. Avert the ill luck that comes from giving a sharp instrument to a friend by sticking the friend with the sharp point.
1756. Avert the ill luck that arises from giving a sharp instrument to a friend by receiving a penny.
1757. If a person lends you a knife open, return it open.
1758. If a person hands you a knife shut, return it shut.
1759. It brings good luck to find a knife open. Mountains
1760. "A dull knife, a dull wife"............Mountains
1761. It causes bad luck to sit on a pair of scissors......
.... Mountains
1762. To sing at the table causes bad luck.
1763. If two forks are accidentally put at your plate, instead of one knife and one fork, you will go to New York..................Western Kentucky
1764. If by some mistake someone puts two forks by your plate at the dinner table, you will go to a funeral or a wedding.[1]
1765. An accidental dropping of a knife brings a woman caller.
1766. An accidental dropping of a fork brings a man caller.
1767. If you drop a fork, your best friend is coming....
.... Mountains

[1] Other superstitions concerning the accidental placement of two forks, two knives, or two spoons at one's plate at table are given under *Divinations*.

1768. If you drop your fork, some one is coming from the direction in which the fork points.

1769. An accidental dropping of a spoon brings a child.

1770. If you drop a spoon, a baby will be born in the family.

1771. If a spoon is dropped, a negro woman is coming... .... Mountains

1772. If a large spoon is dropped, a large family is coming.

1773. If you drop a tablespoon, you may look for a woman and a baby............Northern Kentucky

1774. The presence of two forks at one place at table means that two fools are coming............... ....Western Kentucky

1775. If you drop a knife during a meal, you are exactly one half through the meal......Central Kentucky

1776. If when you drop a knife and fork they cross, you may expect bad luck.....North-eastern Kentucky

1777. To drop a spoon brings disappointment.

1778. It causes bad luck for a woman to break a plate and step on the pieces.

1779. It brings bad luck to break any kind of dish.

1780. To avert ill luck, throw the pieces of a broken dish into a gully.

1781. If you burn sassafras for stove wood, you will break all the dishes......................Mountains

1782. The dropping of a dish-rag indicates the coming of a caller. If it opens out when it falls, the guest will arrive for the next meal.

1783. If you wish to prevent a visitor's arrival that has been forecast by the dropping of a dish-rag, step backward over the rag.

1784. If a dish-rag that drops is spread out, a woman is coming.

1785. If a dish-rag that falls is not spread out, a man is coming.

1786. If when you drop a dish-rag on the floor you shake it under the table and name it the person that you wish to come, he will come. . . . Southern Kentucky

1787. If you drop a dish-cloth, pick it up, and think about some one. The first one you think about will arrive within an hour. . . . . Mountains

1788. If after dropping a dish-rag you kiss it, your sweetheart will come. . . . . Mountains

1789. If you drop a dish-rag, a slouch is coming.
If you drop a dish-rag, a worse slouch than you is coming.

1790. If you drop a dish-rag and it spreads out, you will have bad luck.

1791. If you drop a dish-rag and it does not unfold, no bad luck will befall you.

1792. The boiling of a dish-rag in soiled water breaks bad luck.

1793. If you drop a tea towel, someone is coming.

1794. If you leave your dish water in a pan over night, you will dream of the Devil. . . . . Blue Grass

1795. If a woman forgets to wash a skillet, she may expect a guest for the next meal.

1796. It brings bad luck to pour water out of a pail over the end of the handle.

1797. If two women run together in preparing a meal, they will work together next year.

1798. "A watched pot never boils."

1799. Lightning and thunder will addle eggs.

1800. Make jelly on sunny days...........Mountains
1801. If you drop a spoon into pickles while you are making them you will be a sour old woman......
...............................Blue Grass
1802. If you cook frog-legs and set them by, they will become raw again...............Central Kentucky
1803. If when you are cooking onions you place a pan of water over them, there will be no odor........
.........................Western Kentucky
1804. If you boil a biscuit with cabbage, there will be no odor......................Western Kentucky
1805. If anything that may be eaten is burned, you will have to pick it out of hell-fire with your hands in the after-life.
1806. If you burn salt on the stove or in the grate, you will have to pick each grain out of fire in hell.
1807. Be sure to throw a pinch of borrowed salt into the fire.
1808. Do not return the salt that you have borrowed.
1809. It causes bad luck to spill salt.
1810. If you spill salt on the table, you will get a scolding before Friday.
1811. If you spill salt between yourself and the person next you at table, you two will quarrel.
1812. You can avert a quarrel from spilling salt by throwing a pinch over your left shoulder.
1813. If salt is spilt at table, there will be a guest at the next meal.
1814. If salt is passed you at table, it passes you trouble.
1815. If salt is thrown away, bad luck will follow.
1816. If you throw salt into a whirlwind, you will see the Devil ....Mountains

1817. If you throw salt behind someone who has done you a bad deed, he will never return. Louisville Negroes

1818. If someone comes to your house whom you do not like, throw salt into his tracks. He will then not bring you bad luck. . . . . Louisville Negroes

1819. When a stand of pepper is overturned, there will be bad luck, unless the person who turns it over burns an old dish-rag.

1820. If the pepper falls toward you from a pepper stand, you will have bad luck.

1821. Do not eat too much meat, for, if you do, your face will become roughened.

1822. If you eat too much meat at supper, you will have bad dreams.

1823. If you eat meat for supper, you will dream of negroes. . . . . Southern Kentucky

1824. If you drop a piece of meat from your mouth at the table, there will be a death in the family. . . . . .
. . . . Louisville Negroes

1825. If you drop anything while you are eating, the act indicates that someone else desires it.

1826. Eat a dozen onions before you go to bed, to become beautiful.

1827. Eat a pickle, to settle your love.

1828. If you eat the crust of bread, your hair will become curly.

1829. If you eat burnt bread, your hair will become curly.

1830. If you take the last biscuit on the plate, you will have to kiss the cook.[1]

1831. To take the last portion from a dish brings bad luck.

[1] For other signs connected with taking the last biscuit, or the last but one, on a plate, see *Divinations*, numbers 227-231.

1832. If you drop a biscuit while taking the bread from the stove, a hungry person will call.

1833. If you drop a biscuit, you will marry a poor man.. . . . . .Western Kentucky

1834. It causes bad luck to break bread in anybody else's hand.

1835. If you break bread in your friend's hand, the act is said to bring bad luck.

1836. If you count the biscuits as you put them into the pan, they will not be good.....Central Kentucky

1837. If someone gives you a cake of yeast, do not thank him. If you do, the bread will not come.

1838. If you burn bread, you and Satan will have to pick that amount out of hell-fire.

1839. When the cook's bread burns, her husband is angry.

1840. The burning of bread shows that the cook is angry.

1841. If you burn the biscuits, your sweetheart is angry with you.

1842. If you burn the bread, your sweetheart is thinking of you.

1843. If you burn your bread, you may expect the arrival of a black-headed person...........Blue Grass

1844. It brings bad luck to stir bread toward you.

1845. It causes good luck to stir the bread away from you.

1846. If bread or cake rises and then suddenly falls, the maker's digestion is bad.

1847. Bread should be set to rise before the sun rises.

1848. If you bake bread after the sun goes down, your bread will also go down.

1849. If the bread cracks open while you are baking it, there will be an increase in the family..Mountains

1850. If you put too much soda into the bread, someone is coming......................Blue Grass

1851. A loaf of bread on its back means that a ship is in distress at sea.

1852. If you serve yourself to butter or bread when you already have butter and bread, someone is coming hungry.

1853. When you bake a cake, do not burn the egg shells until the cake has risen, but burn them then.

1854. Place egg shells on the top of the oven, to make the cake rise......................Mountains

1855. In cake-baking if you burn the egg shells before the cake has risen, the cake will burn......Mountains

1856. If you bake a cake in the afternoon, it will sink as the sun sinks.

1857. If you bake a cake in the morning, it will rise as the sun ascends.

1858. Do not make a cake on a rainy day, for it will not rise well.

1859. It is a good sign to have a piece of pie point toward you.

1860. If a piece of pie is pointed toward you, you may expect a letter that day.

1861. If a piece of pie points half-way around, you may expect a letter the next day.

1862. If a piece of pie points more than half-way around, you may expect a letter later on.

1863. If you cut the point off a piece of pie and eat it last, you will get a letter.

1864. If the point of another person's piece of pie is directed toward you and the person begins eating his piece at this point, you will get a letter.

1865. It causes bad luck to begin eating pie at the point.

1866. If the crust end of a piece of pie is placed next to you, you will get a postcard.

1867. If in drinking you look above the rim of the glass, you are a flirt.

1868. If at the table you do not drink all your milk or water, you will be disappointed soon...........
.........................Southern Kentucky

1869. If you have water in your glass and pour more into it, there will be trouble.

1870. If you pour water into a glass that already contains water, you will quarrel with your mother-in-law.

1871. It brings bad luck to burn coffee.......Mountains

1872. It causes bad luck to stir the coffee pot with a knife or fork.

1873. "Stir with a knife,
Stir up strife."

1874. If you drink all the coffee from your cup, so that upon the turning of it over no drop comes out, you will cry later................Louisville Negroes

1875. If you can get a bubble off the coffee and drink it, you will receive money.

1876. If you fail to get a bubble off the coffee, you will lose money.

1877. Never drink a cup of coffee at five o'clock, or you will die..........................Mountains

1878. After a meal if the coffee cup is left outside the saucer, there will be bad luck.........Mountains

1879. To leave coffee in a cup causes disappointment...
.................................Blue Grass

1880. The presence of tea grounds on tea is a sign of people coming.

1881. It causes bad luck to change places at the table.
1882. Do not cross hands with another at the table.
1883. It brings bad luck for two people at table to reach for the same thing at the same time.
1884. If two reach for bread at the same time, someone is coming hungry.
1885. If you sing at the table, you will miss your next visitor.
1886. "Sing before breakfast, cry before night."
1887. If you sing before breakfast, you will get a whipping before the week is gone.
1888. If you sneeze at the table, you will hear of a death before night.

DREAMS

1889. "Dreams go by contraries."
1890. "A dream out of season,
Trouble out of reason."
1891. Morning dreams come true.
1892. If you tell a dream before breakfast, it will come true.
1893. A dream told before breakfast on Friday morning will come true.
1894. "Friday night's dream on Saturday told
Is sure to come true—be it ever so old."
1895. "Saturday dreamed and Sunday told
Is sure to come true before a month old."
1896. If you sleep with the dream bone, taken from the ham of a hog, under your pillow, your dreams will come true...........................Mountains
1897. If some one goes to a strange place and sleeps under strange covers, his dreams will come true.

1898. What you dream on the first night that you sleep under a new roof will come true.

1899. If you sleep under a new quilt, your dream will come true.

1900. If you tell your dreams to an old hollow stump, they will come true................Mountains

1901. If you dream of the same thing three times, it will come true.

1902. When one has the same dream more than once, the dream will come true.

1903. If you do not wish to dream, put both shoes under the foot of your bed at night.

1904. To dream of an angel is a sign of death. Mountains

1905. If you dream of a baby, you will hear of a death.

1906. To dream of a bakery means that you will awake with cream puffs in your hand.

1907. To dream of bees at work means good luck........ .... Mountains

1908. It brings bad luck to dream about catching a bird.

1909. If you dream of blasting, one of your close friends will be shot soon...................Mountains

1910. It brings bad luck to dream of being blind....... ....Western Kentucky

1911. To dream of blood is the sign of coming disgrace.

1912. To dream of your brother or sister is a sign of sudden death in your family...Louisville Negroes

1913. If you dream of cats, you will have bad luck...... ....Blue Grass

1914. If you dream of cats, you will find money........ .... Mountains

1915. To dream of a black cat is a sign that some of your relatives are treacherous......Western Kentucky

154

1916. A dream of good children is followed by good luck.
1917. To dream of black clouds is a harbinger of bad luck.
1918. To dream of a coffin is the sign of a death in the family ....Mountains
1919. It is a good sign to dream of a filled coffin........
.... Mountains
1920. It is a bad sign to dream of an empty coffin......
.... Mountains
1921. It is a sign of death to dream of a fine-tooth comb
.... Mountains
1922. To dream that you cry is a sign that you will take a journey.
1923. If you dream of the dead, you will live a long time
...................Central Kentucky Negroes
1924. To dream of the dead is to hear from the living.
1925. A dream of one dead is a sign that the one dreamed of wishes you to pray for him.
1926. It is a sign of rain to dream of a dead person....
.... Mountains
1927. In dreaming of falling through the air, one ordinarily wakes before striking the ground. If he dreams that he strikes, or if in any way he dreams that he is killed, he will die.
1928. A dream of death is a sign of birth.
A dream of birth is a sign of marriage.
A dream of marriage is a sign of death.
1929. A dream of diamonds is a good-luck sign.
1930. It causes bad luck to dream of freshly dug earth..
.... Mountains
1931. It causes bad luck to dream of eating.
1932. If you dream of many eggs, you will receive much money......................Western Kentucky

155

1933. If you dream of eggs, you will be angry.

1934. A dream of eggs is a sign of enemies.

1935. To dream of unbroken eggs is a sign of trouble to come.

1936. If you dream of broken eggs, your troubles are past.

1937. It is a good luck sign to dream of eggs if they are not broken.

1938. It brings bad luck to dream of broken eggs.

1939. To dream of seeing one's eyes other than bright and healthy is a sign of bad luck..........Mountains

1940. If you dream of falling, bad luck will follow.

1941. To dream of fire is a sign of enjoyment. Blue Grass

1942. To dream of fire is a sign of the return of some relative.....................Western Kentucky

1943. If you dream of fire, you are too warm.

1944. If you dream of fire, you will be angry..........
..........................Central Kentucky

1945. A dream of catching large fish is a harbinger of prosperity.

1946. It means bad luck to dream of flowers, especially white roses.

1947. A dream of flying is a sign that you are climbing upward.......................... Mountains

1948. If you dream of flying, pleasant things await you next day...................Western Kentucky

1949. If you dream of a friend in distress and hear him cry out, you will receive news of an accident to him.

1950. A dream of perfect fruit is a forerunner of prosperity.

1951. A dream of imperfect fruit is a sign of bad luck.

1952. "Dream of fruit out of season,
You'll have trouble out of reason."

1953. To dream of a funeral procession is a sign of death
.................................Blue Grass

1954. To dream about the firing of a gun is unlucky.

1955. It brings good luck to dream of heaven. Blue Grass

1956. A dream of helping somebody to dress is a sign of
a sudden death...............Central Kentucky

1957. If you dream of finding a hen's nest, you will have
good luck...........................Mountains

1958. It is a sign of good luck to dream of being on a
very high place.....................Blue Grass

1959. To dream of a hog is a sign of bad luck. . Mountains

1960. It brings good luck to dream of a bay horse.

1961. It causes bad luck to dream of a black horse......
.... Mountains

1962. It brings good luck to dream of a gray horse......
.... Mountains

1963. To dream of sorrel horses is an indication of good
luck........................Central Kentucky

1964. If you dream of a white horse, you will hear of a
death before the week is out. To dream of white
horses is a sign of bad luck.... Southern Kentucky

1965. If you dream of a gray horse, you will get a letter
.........................Southern Kentucky

1966. It brings bad luck to dream of the death of a horse
.................................Blue Grass

1967. To dream of the Judgment Day is a sign of death
inside of a month..................Mountains

1968. If you dream of a letter, you will see a stranger...
.... Mountains

1969. A dream of lice in your head is a sign of approaching illness.

1970. To dream about new lumber is a sign of bad luck
.... Mountains

1971. A dream of marriage means that a death is near.

1972. If you dream of milk, there will be an increase in
the family ....Mountains

1973. It brings bad luck to dream of money...........
...........................Southern Kentucky

1974. To dream of money is a sign of illness..Mountains

1975. To dream of large pieces of money is a good-luck
sign.

1976. To dream of small coins means that bad luck is in
store for you.

1977. It is lucky to dream of silver money.

1978. It augurs good luck to dream of paper money....
.... Mountains

1979. To dream of seeing the moon is a sign of good luck.

1980. It brings bad luck to see the moon in a dream.

1981. It is a sign of death to dream of more than one
moon.

1982. It brings bad luck to dream about mules.Mountains

1983. To dream of a necklace is a sign of jealousy......
.... Mountains

1984. It causes very bad luck to dream of negroes......
.... Mountains

1985. You will quarrel with some one if you dream of a
negro.

1986. A dream of a negro man is a sign of the coming of
a friend...........................Mountains

1987. A dream of a negro woman is the sign of the coming of an enemy...................Mountains

1988. To dream of riding is a sign of fleeting pleasure...
...........................Western Kentucky

1989. It indicates bad luck to dream that you strike the bottom of a river in diving....................
....................Central Kentucky Negroes

1990. To dream of a house with many rooms is a sign of bad luck.

1991. A dream of teeth is a sign of death.

1992. If you dream that your teeth fall out, there will be a death.

1993. If you dream that you lose a tooth, you will lose a friend.

1994. If you dream that your jaw teeth fall out, an elderly person will die.

1995. If you dream that your side teeth fall out, a middle-aged person will die.

1996. If you dream that your front teeth fall out, a child will die.

1997. If you dream that your front teeth fall out, a member of your family will die.

1998. If you dream that your back teeth fall out, a distant relative will die.

1999. If you dream of a turkey, you will shortly see a fool.

2000. A dream of vermin augurs serious illness among your friends........................Blue Grass

2001. To dream of sheep is a sign of bad luck..Mountains

2002. If you dream about old shoes, you will hear of a death.............................Blue Grass

2003. It causes bad luck to dream that you lose a shoe...
........................Southern Kentucky

2004. It brings bad luck to dream about being shot......
.... Mountains

2005. If you dream of smoke, there will be a death.

2006. A dream of a snake is a sign that you have enemies.

2007. If you dream that you have killed a snake, the dream is a sign that you have killed an enemy.

2008. You will have bad luck if you dream of being bitten by a snake.........................Mountains

2009. A dream about snow is a sign of disappointment or loss.........................Central Kentucky

2010. It brings good luck to dream of a squirrel........
.... Mountains

2011. To dream of a strange place is a sign of good luck.

2012. If you dream of eating a dish of strawberries, you will be in a large, new crowd.

2013. If you dream of a white swan, you may expect a death in the family.

2014. If you dream of sweeping, you will receive a letter
.... Mountains

2015. It is a sign of bad luck or death to dream of a wagon.

2016. To dream of a wagon moving away from you is a sign of death...................... Mountains

2017. If you dream of water, you are too cold.

2018. You will have good luck if you dream of clear water.

2019. If you dream of muddy water, your best friend is angry with you.

2020. A dream of walking through muddy water is a death sign.

2021. If you sleep on wedding-cake, your dream will come true.[1]

2022. To dream of anything solid white is a sign of death.

---

[1] Divination in connection with sleeping on wedding cake is treated under *Divinations*, numbers 602, 603, 604, 693.

DRESS

2023. "If a pin points toward you and you let it lay.
You'll have bad luck all that day.
If you see a pin and pick it up,
All that day you'll have good luck."

2024. "See a pin and let it lie
Sorrow will come by and by."

"Find a pin, and let it lie,
You'll want a pin before you die."

2025. If you find a pin with the point toward you and place it on the shoulder of your coat with the point toward the back, and leave it there for three days, good luck will come to you.

2026. If you see a pin with the point toward you and pick it up and stick it into wood, you will have good luck. If the point is away from you, pick it up and give it to someone else for good luck...Blue Grass

2027. If you find a pin with the head towards you, there is mail for you at the Post Office......Mountains

2028. If you pick up a pin lying with its side toward you, you will get a letter.

2029. If you find a pin lying with its side toward you, you will go buggy-riding the next day.

2030. If you pick up a pin lying with its side toward you, you will receive a kiss, or you will see your sweetheart that day.

2031. If you find a pin with the side towards you, you will get a new dress................Mountains

2032. If anyone takes a pin from your dress, bad luck will follow....................Louisville Negroes

2033. If a pin stands on the point in your dress, someone is "on his head" to see you.
2034. If when you are trying on a dress, the dressmaker sticks a pin in your other clothes, you will not be married that year...................Blue Grass
2035. To prick your finger as you pin your waist is unlucky.
2036. Avert the disaster of the last mentioned superstition by burning the pin.
2037. It brings good luck to find a brass pin, if you stick it on your shoulder.........Western Kentucky
2038. You will lose a friend if you give a person a pin. She must pick it up after you lay it down.
2039. If you drop a pin and it sticks into the floor, someone is coming.
2040. You will have good luck if you find a safety pin.
2041. It is unlucky to find a safety pin in water, for a sad visit awaits you................Blue Grass
2042. If a needle falls and sticks into the floor, you will have bad luck.
2043. If you break a needle in a garment while making it, the person for whom it is made will not live to wear it out.
2044. If you find a hairpin and hang it up on the first thing you see, you will get a letter.
2045. If you find a hairpin and hang it on the first nail you see, you will get a friend.
2046. If you find a hairpin, hang it on a nail or anything iron. It will bring good luck.
2047. If your hairpin drops out of your hair, someone whom you like is thinking of you..............
................................Louisville Negroes

2048. If a woman drops a hairpin and fails to pick it up, she will lose a friend.

2049. If you pick up a hairpin, you will fall...Mountains

2050. If a hairpin is about to come out of a girl's hair, someone is "on his head" about her..............
..........................Western Kentucky

2051. If you accidentally leave your gloves and have to go back for them, the next person you call on will be out.

2052. It is unlucky to pick up an old glove in the street.

2053. If you find a wet handkerchief, you may know that all your tears have been shed and that you will live happily ....Blue Grass

2054. The moonstone is a lucky stone.

2055. If you wear an opal ring and it is not your birth-stone, you will have bad luck.

2056. If you wear an opal ring and it is not your birth-stone, you must give it away to avoid bad luck.

2057. If you wear pearls, you will shed tears.

2058. If you count pearls in a ring or a brooch, you will lose them.

2059. When danger is imminent to a person who has pearls, they lose their lustre.

2060. It brings good luck to carry a piece of pearl jewelry
.... Mountains

2061. Do not let anyone take a ring off your finger.

2062. If you take a ring off your friend's hand, you will have bad luck.

2063. Turn one hundred seal rings for good luck.

2064. If you find a button and put it into your shoe, you will have good luck.

2065. If you find a button, you will receive a letter soon.

2066. It causes bad luck to find a button smaller than a
penny ....Mountains

2067. The finding of a pearl button means that there is
a letter for you in the Post Office...............
...........................Central Kentucky

2068. If you find a button with so many holes in it, you
will receive a letter with the same number of pages
.... Mountains

2069. When you find a button, count the holes in it. You
will find that number of pieces of money before
you come to your stopping place. Central Kentucky

2070. To carry in your pocket a button that you have
found brings good luck.

2071. To sew a button on a garment that you are wearing
brings bad luck.

2072. If you drop a comb, somebody is coming.

2073. If you drop a comb, you will be disappointed.

2074. If the comb with which you are combing your hair
falls behind you, you will have trouble...........
...........................Western Kentucky

2075. Avert the bad luck of dropping a comb by putting
your foot on it................Central Kentucky

2076. If you are combing your hair and let the comb fall,
you will get money...........Louisville Negroes

2077. It brings bad luck to count the teeth of a comb....
.... Mountains

2078. If you count comb teeth, the youngest one in the
family will die.

2079. Do not count the teeth of a comb, for if you do they
will come out...............Southern Kentucky

2080. When your skirt turns up, spit on it and turn it
down, to obtain good luck.

2081. If your dress is turned up, spit on it, and turn it down, to get a new one.

2082. If the hem of a dress is turned up, and someone calls the wearer's attention to it, the wearer will get a new dress.........................Blue Grass

2083. If the hem of a girl's dress is turned up, the person calling her attention to this fact will get a new dress ....Blue Grass

2084. If a girl's dress turns up and she spits on it, she will become wealthy.

2085. If a part of the hem of your skirt is turned up, and you spit on it, you will have a joyful day.

2086. If your skirt turns up, you will catch a sweetheart.

2087. If you tear a hole in a new dress before it is washed, you will have good luck.......Western Kentucky

2088. It is a sign of bad luck to tear your dress behind...
...........................Western Kentucky

2089. If you drop ink on a new white dress, you may look for company.

2090. If your underskirt hangs, you will have to shovel coal ....Mountains

2091. If your petticoat hangs lower than your skirt, your father loves you better than your mother does.

2092. If a woman kicks up her dress behind, she is a thief.

2093. After a number of boys have been in swimming, the boy who after dressing puts on his cap or hat first will have good luck.

2094. If a boy or a man comes into the house with his hat on, he will have bad luck.

2095. It causes bad luck to place your hat higher than your head.

2096. It brings bad luck to lay a hat on a bed.

2097. If you put two hats on your head, you will get a whipping...................Louisville Negroes

2098. If you put on two hats, you will get a double-whipping......................Louisville Negroes

2099. If a wife loses her apron, she will lose her husband.

2100. If you lose your apron, you will lose your best friend.

2101. If a woman drops her apron, she will lose one of her friends ....Mountains

2102. "A stitch in time saves nine" (felt by many as a superstition.)

2103. To sew a garment that you are wearing is a sign of bad luck or death.

2104. If you mend a garment on you, there will be a slander about you with as many words as you put stitches into the garment.............Mountains

2105. You can avert the hard luck that follows the mending of a garment while you are wearing it by holding a straw in your mouth.

2106. If you talk while sewing something that is on you, a lie will be told about you for every stitch taken while you were talking.

2107. It causes bad luck to sew new pieces on an old garment.....................Blue Grass Negroes

2108. If you leave the bastings in a dress, the dress is not paid for.

2109. It brings bad luck to sew polka-dotted goods.....
......................North-eastern Kentucky

2110. You will have bad luck if you make clothes for people who are ill......................Blue Grass

2111. If any kind of garment is made or bought for a sick person, that person will never get well..Mountains

2112. If you tear a garment, you may break the spell of a bad luck sign that is connected with it.

2113. It brings good luck to put on clothes accidentally wrong side out.

2114. Clothes put on in the morning wrong side out, if changed at twenty minutes past one, will bring good luck.

2115. If you put a garment on wrong side out and discover the mistake yourself, you may change it without bad luck.

2116. A person wearing a garment inside out will have good luck if he turns the garment right side out at midnight.

2117. After you have on your clothes wrong side out, it is bad luck to change.

2118. If you put your clothes on wrong side out and someone else than you takes them off, good luck remains ....North-eastern Kentucky

2119. If you burn a hole in a new garment and wear it, there will be a death.

2120. If two women help a third to dress, the youngest of the three will die.

2121. If you put your night gown on inside out by mistake, there will be a fire in town soon...Mountains

2122. It brings bad luck to the passengers if a woman dressed in black gets on a passenger train at night.

2123. It causes bad luck to meet a woman dressed in black, after midnight.

2124. It brings bad luck to put a black pin into a white dress..................North-eastern Kentucky

2125. It brings bad luck to put a white pin into a black dress....................North-eastern Kentucky

2126. It brings bad luck to put on the left stocking first.

2127. A hole in your stocking indicates that you will get a letter. The size of the letter depends on the size of the hole........................Blue Grass

2128. It is well for an aviator to wear a lady's stocking about his neck.

2129. If you dress one foot entirely before beginning the other, you will have bad luck.

2130. Put on the left garter and the right shoe first for luck.........................Central Kentucky

2131. Remove the left shoe and the right garter first for luck ....Central Kentucky

2132. If you put your left shoe on before your right, you will have a headache.................Mountains

2133. To put the left shoe on the right foot is to produce misfortune for yourself.

2134. If you pull off your right shoe first, you will never have toothache....................Blue Grass

2135. It causes bad luck to walk with one shoe off and one shoe on.

2136. It brings bad luck to walk around in one shoe because you will measure your mother's grave......
..........................Louisville Negroes

2137. If a child walks about with one shoe off and the other on, he will receive as many whippings as he takes steps........................Mountains

2138. As many steps as you take in one shoe, so many steps do you take into trouble.........Mountains

2139. For every step that you take with one shoe on and one off, you will have one year of misfortune.....
.... Mountains

2140. Never lace one shoe until you have put the other one on .... Mountains

2141. It causes bad luck to button the top button of your shoe first .... North-eastern Kentucky

2142. If the soles of your shoes are of black leather, your teeth will become loose .... Blue Grass

2143. If your shoe-string comes untied, somebody is talking about you.

2144. Your left shoe-string untied shows that someone is speaking evil of you.

2145. Your right shoe-string untied shows that someone is speaking well of you.

2146. "If you wear your shoes out on the side, you will be a rich man's bride."

2147. "If you wear your shoes out on the toe, You will spend money as you go."

2148. If you wear your shoes out in the middle of the sole first, you will be rich some day. . Central Kentucky

2149. Put your shoes with the points away from the bed, so that bad dreams may walk away from you.

2150. If you set your shoes under the bed always turn the toes out. To turn them in is a sign of bad luck during the night.

2151. If you put your shoes above your head, on the table or on the bed, you will have very bad luck.

2152. If you put your shoes higher than your head in the closet, you will never be married.

2153. It brings bad luck to place your stockings in your shoes when you are going to bed.

2154. Be sure to place your shoes at night with the inner sides against each other.

2155. If you spit on your shoe accidentally, you will get a new pair of shoes.................Mountains

2156. If you wear a hairpin in your shoe, you will meet a good friend.

2157. Put sugar into your shoe, to coax your trousers down ....Central Kentucky

2158. If your shoes squeak, they are not paid for.

2159. An old shoe is a sign of good luck.

2160. If you burn an old shoe, you will have rheumatism.

2161. If you lose one of your rubbers, it is a sign that you are going to lose one of your friends.

SHADOWS, PORTRAITS, AND REFLECTIONS

2162. If you sit with your shadow thrown on the water, you will not catch fish..............Mountains

2163. If a portrait hangs on the wall crooked, there will be bad luck.................Louisville Negroes

2164. If you turn a picture of a friend of yours upside down, he will have a headache..Louisville Negroes

2165. If you hang your sweetheart's photograph upside down, he will die soon.......Blue Grass Negroes

2166. If a portrait falls, there will be bad luck.

2167. It a portrait falls from the wall, someone in the family will die..............Louisville Negroes

2168. The falling of anyone's picture means death in the household. When the death occurs, the clock stops until after the funeral.

2169. If a large family portrait falls, there will be a death
...................................Blue Grass

2170. If a portrait falls, you will have a quarrel with the original.

2171. If a portrait falls in a room where someone is dead, the original will die.

2172. If a portrait falls in a room where someone is dead, the original will die within three years.

2173. To have a picture drop out of a frame is a bad omen......................Southern Kentucky

2174. It is a bad luck sign to hear knocking behind a picture ....Blue Grass

2175. If the glass on a picture breaks of its own accord, a death will occur in your family.....Mountains

2176. If your photograph is buried by an enemy, your life will fade as the photograph fades.

2177. If you draw a picture of your enemy and shoot it with a silver bullet, he will suffer pain where the bullet strikes.

2178. Bury the picture of your enemy face down in the direction that Jesus Christ was buried, that is, with head toward the west. As the picture fades, your enemy's life will fade................Mountains

2179. If you break your mirror, you will have seven years of trouble.

2180. Avert the penalty attached to breaking a mirror by throwing all the pieces into running water.

2181. If you break a mirror, the number of pieces will indicate the number of years of bad luck that you will have....................Louisville Negroes

2182. It brings bad luck for two people to look into a mirror at the same time..............Blue Grass

2183. If two people look into a mirror at the same time, they will both be disappointed before the day is gone......................Southern Kentucky

2184. If two persons look into a mirror at the same time, one will soon die......................Negroes
2185. It brings bad luck to look into a mirror while you are putting on your night gown.
2186. To look into a mirror at night brings bad luck....
.... Mountains
2187. If you look into a mirror after dark, you will see the Devil..........................Mountains
2188. If you see your image double in the mirror, your death will follow..............Central Kentucky
2189. To see one's shadow while one is looking into a mirror is a sign of death.................Mountains
2190. It brings bad luck to look into a mirror when one is ill...............................Blue Grass
2191. If while lying in bed you see yourself in a mirror, you may expect bad luck or death.
2192. To look into a mirror over anyone else's shoulder leads to disappointment.............Blue Grass
2193. If you see a dead man's face in a mirror, you will be the next one to die.
2194. If a mirror hangs in a room where a death occurs, turn it to the wall or cover it, as the first person that sees himself in it will be the next one to die.
2195. If you look into a mirror while you are drinking, you will never be married...........Blue Grass

MOON[1] AND SIGNS OF THE ZODIAC

2196. If a stray dog howls in the moonlight with his nose pointed at a person, that person will die........
........................Western Kentucky

[1] For weather signs connected with the moon, see *Weather*, numbers 2572-2594.

2197. If the moon stays away all night, there has been much robbery going on during the night.........
.... Mountains

2198. Moonlight will dull a razor....Southern Kentucky

2199. If you sleep in the moonlight, you will have rheumatism.

2200. If you sleep in the moonlight, you will become insane.

2201. It makes one homely to sleep with the moon shining on his face.............North-eastern Kentucky

2202. If you shoot toward the moon, you will fall dead..
.... Mountains

2203. If you see the reflection of the moon in a well, you will have good luck..........Southern Kentucky

2204. A red moon is a sign of war.

2205. If you can see a woman in the moon, you will obtain riches............................ Mountains

2206. If you can see a man in the moon, you will have bad luck ....Mountains

2207. It is lucky to look at a dollar while the moon is shining upon it over your left shoulder.

2208. It brings bad luck to see a woman combing her hair in the full of the moon...North-eastern Kentucky

2209. People who have moods of meanness are ruled by the moon.

2210. If you plant seeds in the moonlight, the crops will be good.

2211. If you plant your seed in the full moon, you will have bad luck.

2212. To see the new moon over the left shoulder is an omen of bad luck.

2213. To see the new moon over the right shoulder brings good luck.

2214. To see the new moon through brush or clouds portends more or less trouble until after the moon fulls.

2215. After you have seen the new moon through trees, you will have trouble that month if you are not good.

2216. If you look at the moon through the tops of trees, your sister or brother will die.........Mountains

2217. If you see the moon through brush that makes a cross, you will have bad luck. If the brush is straight, for example, canebrush, you will come to no harm.....................Central Kentucky

2218. If you see the new moon through brush, you will shed as many tears as any vessel will hold that you have in your hand..................Mountains

2219. It means good luck to you to see the new moon clear of clouds and brush, especially if you take hold of a piece of money and turn it over in your pocket.

2220. When you see the new moon clear, kiss the first person you meet, so that you may get a new dress....
................................Blue Grass

2221. It causes bad luck to you if you look at the new moon through a pane of glass.

2222. If you look through the window at a new moon, there will be illness in the family.

2223. It is unlucky for a bride and groom to see a new moon out of a car window. North-eastern Kentucky

2224. If you see the moon as you go up hill, you will have good luck........................Blue Grass

2225. If you see the moon as you go down hill, you will
have bad luck......................Blue Grass

2226. It is a sign of fire to see the new moon through telephone wires.

2227. Show the new moon a piece of money.

2228. If you have some money in your pockets when you
see a new moon, look over your shoulder, and you
will never be bankrupt...............Mountain

2229. If you show your pocket-book to the new moon, you
will have twice as much money in it....Mountains
If you shake an empty pocket-book at the new
moon, you will have it full of money before the next
new moon.........................Mountains

2230. If you see the new moon with something in your
hand, you will receive a present.

2231. The thing that you hold in your hand when you see
a new moon will trouble you all the month.......
................................Blue Grass

2232. When you see the new moon, stop, reach down, and
get some dirt out from under your left heel, tie it
in a rag, and put it under your pillow. What you
dream will come true................Mountains

2233. The first appearance of a new moon on Saturday is
lucky.

2234. If the new moon appears on Saturday, there will
be rain for the next forty days........Mountains

2235. Vegetables that mature under ground must be
planted in the dark of the moon.

2236. Vegetables that mature above ground must be
planted in the light of the moon.

2237. Plant root vegetables in the dark of the moon, vegetables for leaves (as cabbage and lettuce) in the

new moon, and vegetables for blossoms and fruit (as peas and beans) in the full moon.

2238. For little vine, plant in the dark of the moon. If potatoes are planted in the light of the moon, the crop will be near the ground.

2239. Only Irish potatoes, say some, should be planted in the dark of the moon.

2240. If you plant potatoes when the sign of the zodiac[1] is in the heart, the insects will not attack them.....
.... Mountains

2241. All tuber plants should be planted in the dark of the moon, say some. This opinion contradicts the superstition that only Irish potatoes should be planted in the dark of the moon. For example, corn should be planted in the dark of the moon, so that the ear will be low and large.

2242. Plant asters in the light of the moon...Blue Grass

2243. Plant flowers in the light of the moon, that they may be large and beautiful.

2244. Plant flowers (everything in which vine is desired) when the sign is in the fingers.

2245. Plant all vines in the light of the moon.

2246. Sow grass always in the light of the moon.

2247. Plant melons, cucumbers, and the like when the sign is in the twins.

2248. Crops will not be successful if planted in the new moon.

2249. If anyone becomes ill in a March that has two new moons, he will die.

---

[1] Many people, especially in rural communities in Kentucky, are guided in their daily actions by the sign of the zodiac, the position of which at any time is shown by almanacs.

2250. Early in the fall and late in spring, frost in the new moon does not bite much.

2251. If you gather apples in the light of the moon, the bruises will dry up.

2252. If you gather apples in the light of the moon, they will not rot.

2253. Beans should be planted when the sign is in the arm........................Central Kentucky

2254. Butterbeans should be planted when the sign of the zodiac is in the arm.

2255. Briars should be cut up in August when the sign is in the heart.

2256. Cabbages planted when the sign is in the head will be large.

2257. If you plant your cabbage on Friday when the moon is new, it will not be killed by the frost..Mountains

2258. Plant corn when the sign is in the arms.

2259. Corn grows more rapidly in the light than in the dark of the moon.

2260. If you plant your cucumbers or pumpkin seeds when the sign is in the heart, the insects will eat them up.

2261. Transplant a blooming flower in the light of the moon.

2262. Fruit is never killed during the light of the moon..
.........................Western Kentucky

2263. Do not plant onion sets when the sign is up, for they will jump out of the ground, and you will have to replant them after the sign changes.

2264. Plant trees before the moon is old. As many days as you wait, so many years you will wait for fruit
.................................Blue Grass

2265. The new of the moon is the time to kill timber.

2266. Never peel the bark to a tree during a dark moon.

2267. If you cut the weeds out of your yard in the dark of the moon in March, they will not come again.

2268. If you cut a few inches of bark from the trunk of a tree on the twenty-fifth of May in the light of the moon, the tree will die.............Blue Grass

2269. To kill a tree so that it will not sprout, cut it down or mutilate it in the dark of the May moon in June ....Blue Grass

2270. Deaden locust trees in the dark of the moon.

2271. Obviate the presence of locust sprouts by killing the tree in the dark of the moon in August.

2272. Trim trees when the sign is in the heart in August, the best time of the whole year for that purpose... ....Blue Grass

2273. If you prune a tree in the light of the moon, it will not die.

2274. If peach trees are in bloom during the light of the moon, they will not freeze, however cold it may be.

2275. If osage-orange bushes are cut down in the dark of the moon in August, they will not grow again.

2276. Peel tan bark in the light of the moon, so that it will slip with ease.

2277. Wean a calf, horse, or mule colt just after the new moon. Otherwise they will fret.

2278. Calves will cry for the mother cow, unless they are weaned when the sign of the zodiac is in the legs.

2279. If you wean a calf in the light of the moon, the cow will not "bawl."

2280. If you wean a colt when the sign is in the heart, it will cry itself to death.

2281. When calves, colts, pigs, and so forth are altered, let it be when the sign is in the leg, that is, between the knee and the ankle.

2282. Some say that it is in the altering only of colts that you need wait until the sign is in the leg.

2283. It is best to alter hogs when the sign is below the waist.

2284. Kill hogs in the light of the moon. Otherwise the meat will shrink (or go to grease, or taste bad).

2285. Kill hogs when "the sign has gone out of the body," that is, when the sign is in the legs or the head. Otherwise the meat will shrink, go to grease, or taste bad.

2286. If you kill hogs in the dark of the moon, they will make much lard.

2287. If you kill hogs in the light of the moon, the meat will draw up and be flabby..........Mountains
This superstition and the next one, strongly prevalent in one section of the mountains, are contradictory to the general belief.

2288. If a hog is killed in the old of the moon, it will have a great deal of lard in it.............Mountains

2289. If you butcher on Saturday when the moon is full, the meat will be tough...............Mountains

2290. The best time to fish is the period when the sign of the zodiac is in the feet.

2291. To fish when the sign is in the head causes bad luck.

2292. Fish bite best in the dark of the moon, because on moonlight nights they feed at night.

2293. If you shoot game when the sign is in the breast, it will be easily killed................Mountains

2294. Horse-breeders put faith in the moon as to the sex of a coming colt....................Blue Grass

2295. If you pick geese when the moon is shining, you will get more feathers than at other times........
................................Blue Grass

2296. If you wean a baby when the sign is in the heart, the baby will die....................Mountains

2297. Bathe only in the dark of the moon.....Mountains

2298. To trim your nails in the light of the moon brings good luck.

2299. If you trim your finger nails in the dark of the moon, you are sure to have bad luck.

2300. If you have your hair cut in the dark of the moon, you will become bald.

2301. If you have your hair cut in the light of the moon, it will grow.

2302. If you cut your hair when the moon is new, you will have twice as much hair during the first new moon of the next year....................Mountains

2303. Always cut your hair in the change of the moon.

2304. Cut your hair when the sign is in the feet.

2305. If you singe your hair at the ends when there is a new moon, it will grow.

2306. Any work begun in the full of the moon will be disastrous.

2307. Move when the moon is new, before it goes into the first quarter.

2308. If you clean beds in the dark of the moon in March, there will be no vermin.............Blue Grass

2309. If you clean house in the dark of the moon in March, there will be no moths........Blue Grass

2310. Dirt will not come out of clothes in the dark of the moon ....Mountains

2311. That part of the fence laid in the dark of moon will rot, or the bottom rail will go into the ground.

2312. Planks laid on the grass in the dark of the moon will kill the grass.

2313. Planks laid on the grass in the light of the moon will not injure the grass.

2314. If you put a post into the ground in the light of the moon, the hole cannot be filled.....Mountains

2315. If you make preserves in the light of the moon, the fruit will yield more than in the dark of the moon.

2316. Cut rail timbers when the moon is old.

2317. It brings bad luck to put on a board roof or lay a worm fence in the new moon.

2318. If you cover a house with shingles in the light of the moon, they will crimp. Therefore, shingle a house in the dark of the moon.

2319. In making shirts, cut them when the sign of the zodiac is in the legs or at least going down. Otherwise they will crawl up the back and "out of the breeches."

2320. Make soap in the light of the moon.

2321. Lye soap made in the dark of the moon will not thicken.

2322. To make soap, stir it with a sassafras stick in the dark of the moon............Western Kentucky

2323. Do not make sauer-kraut or put pickles in brine when the sign is in the "fish," or they will become shiny and soft.

2324. The man in the moon is carrying brush as fuel for hell-fire ....Mountains

2325. The man in the moon is carrying brush as a punishment for working on Sunday..........Mountains

2326. The man in the moon is carrying cane as a punishment for murdering his brother.......Mountains

WEATHER SIGNS[1]

2327. If animals have heavy fur, expect a hard winter.

2328. If you step on an ant, there will be rain.

2329. In spring and summer, during the season of thunderstorms, the barometer is unsteady preceding rain, a condition that is not observed during colder months ....Lexington

2330. Before spring and summer rains, the barometer usually falls to 29.90 or below, and before autumn and winter to 30.......................Lexington

2331. After a drought the cry of a rain crow near a settlement is a sure sign of rain.

2332. The singing of birds and hens during rain is an indication of approaching fair weather.

2333. If birds gather together in multitudes on the ground, there will shortly be snow.....Mountains

2334. If you see a bluebird today, you may expect a fair day tomorrow ....Mountains

2335. If a bob-white says "Bob" only once, that is, does not repeat the first note, there will be rain......
.........................Western Kentucky

[1] The weather signs in this list from Lexington and Louisville are taken from "Weather Folk-Lore and Local Weather Signs," by Edward B. Garriott, U. S. Department of Agriculture, Weather Bureau, page 101 for Lexington; page 103 for Louisville.

Many of the weather signs given below are based on logical causes. They are included with the weather superstitions because they are all folk signs and because no distinction is felt by the superstitions between the logical signs and the superstitions.

2336. If you take the last piece of bread on a plate by accident, you may look for rain........Blue Grass

2337. To burn brush will cause rain.

2338. When the rain makes large bubbles on the ground, there will be rain the next day.

2339. Yellow butterflies in the fall show that within ten days there will be enough frost to turn the leaves the color of the butterflies.

2340. If a calf plays, there will be falling weather.

2341. If the camphor bottle is not clear, you may expect rain...............................Blue Grass

2342. If the camphor bottle is clear, you may expect pretty weather.....................Blue Grass

2343. The rising of camphor in a bottle signifies rain... ....Western Kentucky

2344. If candy will not get hard, there will be rain. The condition is really caused by relative humidity.... ....Blue Grass

2345. There will be rain soon when the carpet on the floor becomes wet.

2346. If a cat sleeps before the fire with its nose turned up, there will be rain soon.........Central Kentucky

2347. If a cat turns on its back with its nose up, there will be rain..............................Mountains

2348. If a cat sits with its back toward the fire, cold weather may be expected.

2349. If cats play with their tails, bad weather is imminent.

2350. When a cat runs about the house and plays, you may expect high winds.

2351. Expect rain when a cat washes its face around its ear.

2352. Caterpillars in the fall that are brown in the middle and yellow at each end prophesy a severe middle winter with mild weather at each end.

2353. You may expect rain when you see a chicken lying on its side.

2354. When a chicken oils its feathers, one may expect rain.

2355. When chickens fly upon something and pick their feathers, the rain is over.

2356. If chickens seek shelter during a rain, the rain will be only a shower.

2357. If chickens do not seek shelter during a rain, it will rain all day, or at least for some hours.

2358. "If the cock goes crowing to bed,
It will rise with a watery head."

2359. You may expect a cold winter if the inside of a chicken gizzard sticks tight when you take it out.

2360. When the inside of a chicken gizzard comes out easily, you may expect a light winter.

2361. If cocks crow at about eight o'clock at night, there will be rain the next day.

2362. If a rooster crows after dark and before midnight, there will be rain before morning.

2363. The crowing of chickens at midnight indicates the approach of bad weather.

2364. The coming of the robin is the surest sign of spring.

2365. If a chicken crows more than ten times, there will be bad weather......................Mountains

2366. If when it is raining the cock crows before noon, the afternoon will be clear..............Blue Grass

2367. The crowing of a cock before twelve o'clock noon means a change of weather...........Blue Grass

2368. If a chimney that is blown from your house during a storm falls on the left of the house, you will have bad luck..........................Blue Grass

2369. If the wind comes down the chimney, the weather will be very cold........North-eastern Kentucky

2370. Cirrus, cirro-stratus, and alto-stratus clouds are almost invariably forerunners of rain in all seassons .... Lexington

2371. Cirrus and cirro-stratus clouds indicate rain, but are far from being a sure sign. They frequently appear for several hours, disappear, and re-appear the next day........................Louisville

2372. No special cloud formation is known on which it would be safe to predict rain more than twenty-four hours in advance. Some cloud formations are of decided assistance, however, if used in connection with a knowledge of the location of approaching storm areas.....................Louisville

2373. Pink clouds seen in the west in the evening prophesy rain ....Mountains

2374. There will be fair weather if the clouds have a golden appearance ....Mountains

2375. Buttermilk clouds are seen before rain.

2376. Three successive cloudy mornings mean that there will be rain on the third.

2377. Cobwebs on the grass are a sign of rain.

2378. When corn twists up, there will be rain.Mountains

2379. Red corn is a sign of a hard winter..............
...........................Central Kentucky

2380. If corn blades wither, there will be rain.

2381. When a large number of tumble-bugs are seen, it indicates a hard winter is coming.

2382. If your corns itch, expect rain.

2383. Cows coming home in the middle of the day are a sign of a bad storm.

2384. When the crawfishes do not throw up their usual little mounds, expect a wet summer...........
........................Central Kentucky

2385. A crow's cry indicates fair weather that day......
.....................Northeastern Kentucky

2386. If a crow drinks out of a stream running by a house before breakfast, it will rain before dark.

2387. The presence of a large flock of crows together is followed by a change of weather......Blue Grass

2388. The first three days of the year determine the general character of the weather during the year.

2389. The weather of the first four days of the year indicates that of the first four months of the year....
........................Western Kentucky

2390. The first twelve days of January foretell the weather of the twelve months respectively.

2391. The weather from new Christmas to old Christmas—twelve days—governs the weather of the following twelve months respectively....Mountains

2392. The weather of the first three days in December determines the weather for December, January, and February.

2393. The first three days of any season determine the weather for that season.

2394. The first thunder in spring means that winter is broken.

2395. The first thunder in the spring awakens the snakes
........................Western Kentucky

2396. If a spring bird calls late in the winter, while the

weather is still cold, there will be colder weather or more snow..................Central Kentucky

2397. A cold winter is followed by a hot summer.

2398. Frosts in summer indicate that the crops have been planted in some cold planet like the moon.

2399. Frost is likely to damage fruit or other crops from March twentieth to April thirtieth, and from September fifteenth to October fifteenth...Louisville

2400. A rain on the first day of the month is a sign of fifteen rains that month.............Blue Grass

2401. If it rains on the first day of any month, it will rain seventeen days that month...........Blue Grass

2402. The date of the month of the first snow indicates the number of snows that will fall during the winter.

2403. Count the number of days from the date of the first snow until Christmas, to find the number of snows that will fall that winter......Southern Kentucky

2404. When there is thunder in the winter time, very cold weather may be expected.......Central Kentucy

2405. If the wind blows from the south on the first day of January, it will blow from the south every day of that month......................Blue Grass

2406. Just as many foggy mornings as there are in January, there will be just so many frosty mornings in May and on the same days of the month.Mountains

2407. The number of times it thunders in January indicates the number of frosts there will be in April.

2408. The days that are cold in February will be warm in March, and the warm days in February will be the cold ones in March.

2409. If it thunders in February, there will be snow in May.

2410. If it thunders on a certain day in February, there will be frost on that day in May.

2411. The number of times it thunders in February, so often will it frost in May.

2412. If it thunders on the last day of February, there will be frost on the last day of May.

2413. If it thunders in February, goose eggs will not hatch......................Western Kentucky

2414. If the ground hog sees his shadow on February second, there will be six more weeks of cold weather.

2415. It is between eleven and one o'clock on February second that the ground hog's shadow is significant.

2416. If it freezes on February twenty-second, there will be forty more freezes..............Blue Grass

2417. There will be heavy rains on the first Monday in March ....Mountains

2418. If it snows the first day of March, there will be snow for thirty days..........Central Kentucky

2419. If March comes in like a lion, it goes out like a lamb.

2420. If March comes in like a lamb, it goes out like a lion.

2421. Fruit is never killed by frost in March..........
.........................Western Kentucky

2422. Mists in March mean frost in May.

2423. The sun never shines on Good Friday.

2424. In whatever direction the wind blows on Good Friday, it will blow for forty days.

2425. If there is enough rain on Easter Sunday to wet a pocket handkerchief, there will be a good crop year.

2426. If it rains on Easter Sunday, it will rain on seven Sundays in succession.

2427. If the wind blows a certain way on Easter Sunday, it will blow that way for six weeks.

2428. When there is an early Easter, there is an early spring.

2429. When there is a late Easter, there is a late spring.

2430. If it rains on the first day of April, there will be rain for fifteen successive days.....Western Kentucky

2431. If you remove your flannels on the first day of May, you will not take cold.

2432. Cool weather in May is called blackberry winter.

2433. If the weather is cool when the dogwood blooms, the term dogwood winter is used for the cool period.

2434. If it rains June first, there will be fifty-seven rains in June, July, and August.....Central Kentucky

2435. If it rains the first three days of June, there will be no wild grapes..................Blue Grass

2436. There will be no blackberries if it rains on June second.

2437. If it rains on the sixth of June, there will be no mast ....Mountains

2438. A dry June means a good corn crop.

2439. If it rains on the first of the dog days, it will rain thirty days.

2440. If it rains on July first, it will rain seventeen days in the month.

2441. If it rains on July first, there will be no grapes that year ....Mountains

2442. If it rains between the first and the fourth of July, it will rain for forty days...........Mountains

2443. If it rains on the fourth of July, there will be no grapes that year...................Mountains

2444. It never rains at night in July...Central Kentucky

2445. If it rains on St. Swithin's day, July fifteenth, it will rain for forty days.

2446. There will be as many snows in the following winter as there are rains in August.

2447. As many foggy mornings as there are in August, so many snows will there be in the winter.

2448. There will be as many snows in the winter as there are foggy mornings in October.

2449. If it thunders in December, there will be cold weather.

2450. A green (warm) Christmas makes a fat graveyard.

2451. A white (snowy) Christmas means a lean graveyard.

2452. If it sleets between the Christmases (old and new), there will be a good mast year........Mountains

2453. The number of fogs in summer indicates the number of snows in winter.

2454. If you stick an axe into a tree during "dogwood winter" (see 2433), the tree will die.

2455. If it rains on Sunday, there will be only one fair day in the week.

2456. If the sun sets behind a cloud on Wednesday evening, there will be rain before Sunday.

2457. If the sun shines on Monday, it will shine every day in the week.

2458. If the leaves on the trees turn up on Monday, it will rain before Wednesday.

2459. If the leaves on the trees turn up on Wednesday, it will rain before Sunday.

2460. If it rains on Monday, it will rain all the week.

2461. A rain on Monday means rain two more days of that week.

2462. If the weather is cloudy on Monday, there will be cloudy weather on three days of the week.

2463. If the sun goes down behind a bank of clouds on Wednesday, there will be rain before the week is gone.

2464. A cloudy sunset on Thursday means no rain before Sunday.

2465. Friday is either the fairest or the foulest day of the week.

2466. The sun always shines brightly sometime on Friday and Saturday.

2467. A rain on Friday means rain on Sunday.

2468. If the weather is clear on Friday, it will rain on Sunday.

2469. If the sunset is clear on Friday, there will be rain before Monday.

2470. The weather at Friday noon determines the weather for the following Sunday.

2471. If the sun sets behind a cloud Friday night, it will rain before Tuesday.

2472. When the moon sets clear on Friday, there will be rain before Tuesday.

2473. The sun shines every Saturday but three during the year.

2474. If the clouds open before seven and close again, there will be rain before eleven. "Open and shet is a sign of wet."

2475. "Rain before seven, stop before eleven."

2476. It always clears off at milking time.

2477. It never rains so hard at three o'clock in the afternoon as it does at other times in the day.

2478. When the wind is high, it will blow hardest about five o'clock—night or morning.

2479. "Night red, next morning gray,
Sure sign of a pretty day."

2480. "Red in the morning, sailors take warning.
Red at night, sailors delight."

2481. "Red sunrise at morning, sailors take warning.
Red sunset at evening, storms are leaving."

2482. "If at morn the sky be red, it bids the traveler stay in bed;
If at night the sky be gray, it bids the traveler on his way."

2483. "Evening red, morning gray, speed the traveler on his way;
Evening gray and morning red, brings down rain upon his head."

2484. "Evening red and morning gray, sets a traveler on his way.
Evening gray and morning red, put on your hat and wet your head."

2485. If the sun sets clear, there will be fair weather for the next three days; if cloudy, it will rain within three days.

2486. If the sun throws a reflection on the window when it is going down, the next day will be fair.

2487. If the weather clears off during the hours of darkness there will be rain again within thirty-six hours.

2488. Butterflies in the fall are a sign of cold weather immediately.

2489. If it thunders at midnight, the frogs will soon look through glass windows (that is, there will be ice-cold weather).

2490. "Blessed are the dead the rain falls on."

2491. If anyone dies, it will rain . . . . Mountains

2492. If there is dew on the grass at night, there will be good weather.

2493. If there is no dew at night, there will be bad weather.

2494. "If the dew is on the grass,
Rain will never come to pass."

2495. If there is not much dew on the ground in the morning, one may expect rain.

2496. When a dog chews grass, there will be rain.

2497. If a dog howls toward the moon, you may expect snow.

2498. When a turtle-dove calls in the spring, winter is broken.

2499. The cry of a turtle-dove foretells warm weather.

2500. When turtle-doves coo, there will be rain.

2501. To dream of the dead is a sign of rain or snow...
........................Western Kentucky

2502. If you dream of eating something, there will be bad weather.

2503. If ducks fly high, there will be clear weather.

2504. If ducks fly low, there will be falling weather.

2505. If your feet hurt, it will rain.

2506. Itching of frostbitten feet indicates the nearness of snow or rain.

2507. If firelight is seen reflected on the woodwork in the room, cold weather will follow.

2508. When fire spits, there will be snow.

2509. The crackling of the fire with a fluffy sound as if snow were falling into it indicates the coming of snow.

2510. If a fire sighs, there will be very cold weather.

2511. When fish jump above the surface of the water, you may expect rain................Blue Grass

2512. When flies sting you, expect rain.

2513. If a flower or a fruit tree which should bloom or bear but once a year, blooms or bears twice in a season, you may look for a hard winter.

2514. If the fog lifts early, it will rain.......Mountains

2515. If the fog lifts late, the day will be clear.

2516. If the fog goes up, there will be falling weather.

2517. If the fog comes down, there will be pretty weather.

2518. A dense fog line near water, indicates the height to which the water will rise by means of the rain which will follow the fog.............Mountains

2519. In winter, if the fowls seek a more elevated place to roost, there is colder weather coming.

2520. Frogs freeze up three times before spring comes to stay ....Mountains

2521. If frogs croak in the daytime, it will rain.

2522. A white frost is a sign of rain.

2523. After three white (heavy) frosts, expect rain.

2524. If frost hangs on the timber late in the morning, snow may be expected.

2525. The general conditions that precede heavy frosts are: rising barometer, falling temperature, low humidity, west to northwest winds diminishing in force, and clear or clearing weather....Lexington

2526. Fruits, vegetables, and other crops are likely to be damaged by spring frosts...........Lexington

2527. Autumn crops in Kentucky are generally not injured by frost.....................Lexington

2528. The continual slamming of a gate means that cold weather is approaching...North-eastern Kentucky

2529. When the gnats swarm, rain and warmer weather will follow..................Central Kentucky

2530. If the breastbone of a goose is white, expect clear, warm weather.

2531. If the breastbone of a goose is dark, you may expect cold weather.

2532. If the breastbone of the goose is mottled, expect varied weather.

2533. The weather goose must be hatched in June and killed on December first.

2534. You may expect rain when a number of geese flap their wings in the water..............Mountains

2535. If wild geese fly low when they go south, the winter will be mild.

2536. If wild geese fly high when they go south, the winter will be severe.

2537. A heavy wild-grape crop is followed by a hard winter.

2538. If a grasshopper is seen dancing, there will be rain within three days...........Southern Kentucky

2539. When guineas cry in the afternoon, there will be rain later.

2540. When your hair curls, you may expect rain.

2541. If a hog looks toward the north, cold weather may be expected.

2542. There will be cold weather when hogs begin to build their beds.

2543. If a hog's liver points towards its head with the little end, the first part of the winter will be warm and the second part cold...........Blue Grass

2544. If a hog's liver points towards its head with the large end, the first part of the winter will be cold and the second part warm..........Blue Grass

2545. When hogs are killed in the winter, if the large end

of the hog's spleen is behind, most of the winter
is over............................Blue Grass

2546. When hogs are killed in the winter, if the large
end of the hog's spleen is in front, the hardest part
of the winter is yet to come..........Blue Grass

2547. The squealing of pigs foretells cold weather.

2548. The loud sound of horses' hooves shows that rain is
near.

2549. "Horses' tails and fishes' scales
Make sailors spread their sails."

2550. If a hornet builds his nest low, there will be a cold
winter ....Western Kentucky

2551. If the hornet's nest is high, the winter will be mild
...........................Western Kentucky

2552. Rapidly increasing moisture after a period of low
humidity is a strong indication of approaching rain,
but by no means a sure one...........Louisville

2553. Except as a sign of more rain during an intermis-
sion in a rainstorm, high humidity is not usually a
forerunner of rain, unless the rain is about to begin
.... Lexington

2554. There is generally a decrease of relative humidity
before rain ....Lexington

2555. As a rule, humidity can not be depended upon as an
indicator of rain.....................Lexington

2556. If you see an insect carrying material for its bed,
there will be cold weather.....Western Kentucky

2557. Ninety days, or three months, after the first katydid
is heard, there will be frost.

2558. If a lamp flickers continually, there will be rain...
...............................Blue Grass

2559. Lightning in the north means rain within twenty-four hours.................Central Kentucky

2560. Lightning in the north is a sign of dry weather.

2561. If you see lightning in the northwest, it will rain within forty-eight hours.

2562. If there is lightning in the east, one may look for dry weather.

2563. Lightning in the south means dry weather.

2564. When you see a flash of lightning, count as fast as you can until it thunders. The number will show how many miles away the lightning has struck.

2565. If locusts are noisy, dry weather will follow.

2566. If locust blooms are heavy, expect a cool summer.

2567. If everything is eaten at a meal, the weather will be clear the next day.................Mountains

2568. There will be rain if mice cry loudly at night.

2569. When the thick part of milk rises to the top, there will be rain.

2570. If the rain gets thick and heavy, almost like mist, the weather will turn cold.

2571. The presence of a great quantity of mistletoe in the fall indicates that a severe winter will follow.

2572. An abundance of wild fruits in the fall is a sign of a cold winter.

2573. When the new moon stands on end, it is generally thought that the weather during the following month will be dry.

2574. When the new moon lies on its back, that is, when the horns extend upward, it is generally thought that the following month will be dry, for the moon will hold water. Some believe, however, that such a moon betokens wet weather.

2575. When a new moon lies sufficiently on its side to allow an Indian's powder horn to be hung on the point, the moon will be a dry one.

2576. A ring around the moon with a star in it brings clear weather.

2577. "Circle around the moon, rain soon;
Circle around the sun, rain none."

2578. When the moon has a ring around it, there will be as many rainy days that week as there are stars in the ring.

2579. A ring around the moon is a sign of rain or bad weather, which will begin in as many days as there are stars enclosed in the circle.

2580. The number of rings around the moon shows how many days there will be before the rain.

2581. A circle around the moon with two stars in it is a sign that it will rain in two days.

2582. If there are seven stars in a circle around the moon, there will be rain for seven hours.

2583. The presence of two rings around the full moon brings snow within twenty-four hours.

2584. If the moon changes in the morning, there will be rain...................North-eastern Kentucky

2585. If the moon changes in the afternoon or evening, there will not be rain....North-eastern Kentucky

2586. A ring around the moon is a sign of cold weather.

2587. No frost will fall when a full moon is shining.

2588. Any month when the moon is north of due west is a cold month.

2589. Any month when the moon is south of due west is a hot month.

2590. If there is a ring around the moon, rain may be expected. The nearer it is, the sooner will the rain come.

2591. When the moon hangs low in the south, there will be mild weather.

2592. The number of days old the moon is when it snows for the first time is the number of times it will snow that year.

2593. The bad weather of January 1915 was explained by the presence of two full moons that month.

2594. The growing of moss on the south side of trees means that a cold winter may be expected.

2595. If a mule looks toward the north, expect cold weather.

2596. If you drive a nail into the ground, there will be rain the next day............Western Kentucky

2597. If you see a negro, it will rain.

2598. If the nut crop fails, the winter will be mild......
.... Mountains

2599. If the nut crop is heavy, the winter will be severe..
.... Mountains

2600. An owl's hooting indicates the coming of heavy rain
.... Mountains

2601. The hooting of owls indicates a change of weather..
.... Mountains

2602. When an owl screams on the top of a mountain, dry weather may be expected............. Mountains

2603. When peacocks cry a great deal in winter, the cold weather is over.

2604. There will be rain when the peacocks run crying along the ground.

2605. The cry of a peacock is followed by rain.

2606. It brings bad luck to play a piano when a storm is going on.

2607. If you lick your plate at breakfast, there will be rain before supper...........Southern Kentucky

2608. Preparation for rain scares it away.

2609. The crying of rabbits is followed by heavy and continuous rain ....Mountains

2610. "Rainbow at night, shepherds' delight.
Rainbow in the morning, shepherds' warning."

2611. "Rainbow in morn, sailors warned.
Rainbow at night, sailors' delight.
Rainbow at noon, more rain soon."

2612. If a rainbow bends over a house, there will be a death in that house...........Western Kentucky

2613. A rainbow in the west is a sign of wet weather.

2614. A rainbow in the east is a sign of dry weather.

2615. If you see a rainbow, there will not be any more rain that day.

2616. If a raincrow calls late in the evening, there will be rain next day.

2617. The redbird's whistle is a sign of rain.

2618. When a redbird says, "Wet, wet," a heavy rain may be expected.

2619. If a redbird that you are looking at flies to the right, the weather will turn cold.

2620. When redbirds fly low, you may look for bad weather.

2621. An attack of rheumatism means the coming of rain soon.

2622. Every time your rheumatism hurts you, you may look for rain.

2623. Sweating rocks are a sign of rain.

2624. If you kick up the rug several times, you may look for rain.

2625. If you drop salt on the ground, you may look for rain .... Western Kentucky

2626. If the sun draws water in the evening, it is a sign of approaching rain (cf. 2656).

2627. If it has not been raining for a day and is cloudy, and if a patch of sky large enough to make a sailor a pair of trousers is seen before ten o'clock, it will not rain that day.

2628. "Mackerel sky, not twenty-four hours dry."

2629. "A mackerel sky never leaves the earth three days dry."

2630. A mare's tail in the sky is a sign of rain.

2631. A blue spot of sky as large as a Dutchman's trousers means that the weather will be clear.

2632. If smoke goes straight up, there will be clear weather.

2633. If smoke stays close to the ground, there will be high winds and bad weather.

2634. If the smoke from a train is white and cloudlike, there will be fair weather.

2635. If smoke goes down stream, expect rain.

2636. If smoke goes down the valley, rain may be expected.

2637. When coal smoke and gas puff out into the room with a singing noise, snow may be looked for.

2638. If a snake crosses your path, there will be rain.

2639. To kill a snake and turn it over will cause rain.

2640. If a black snake is killed and hung on a fence, rain will come.

2641. The hanging of a black snake up by the tail will bring rain before night.

2642. When snipes cry, winter is over...............................North-eastern Kentucky

2643. If the snow melts from the trees, the snow will leave the ground in a rain.

2644. If the snow is blown off the trees, there will be another snow soon before the current snow melts.

2645. Snow left unmelted in the fence corner brings another snow.

2646. When you see snowbirds flying along a rail fence, you may expect the weather to be much colder within the next twenty-four hours.

2647. If you kill a spider, there will be rain that day.....................................Mountains

2648. If you kill a spider on a rainy day, it will rain the next day ....Mountains

2649. You may expect bad weather when a squirrel gathers nuts.

2650. When the squirrel hoards are large, there will be a cold winter.

2651. If the stars are thick, there will be rain.

2652. If an old person stumbles, there will be rain the next day ....Central Kentucky

2653. If the sun shines while it is raining, there will be rain the next day.

2654. If it rains while the sun is shining, there will be rain at the same time the next day.

2655. "Ring around the sun, rain none;
Ring around the moon, rain soon".....Mountains

2656. If the sun draws water in the morning, there will be rain in the evening.

2657. If the sun shines while it is snowing, there will be snow the next day.

2658. It always rains for five days in succession after an eclipse of the sun.

2659. When the telephone wires sing, a change of weather may be expected.

2660. To kill a toad will cause rain.

2661. If rain drops cling to the twigs of trees, there will be more rain.

2662. If tree leaves wither, there will be rain.

2663. If you see the white on leaves when the wind is blowing, there will be rain.

2664. When maple leaves turn up, there will be rain.

2665. If you hear whistling among the trees in a mountain, you may expect rain before dawn. . Mountains

2666. When the trees have heavy foliage, there will be a hard winter.

2667. If bark grows on the north side of a tree, there will be a cold winter.

2668. If snow sticks to the sides of trees and houses, there will be snow again in forty-eight hours.

2669. If sycamore trees are white and smooth in the autumn, a mild winter may be expected.

2670. If a tree toad croaks, it will rain.

2671. Turkeys dance (that is, jump up and down) before rain.

2672. The carrying of an umbrella scares the rain away.

2673. Foam on the water is a sign of rain. . . . .
. . . . Southern Kentucky

2674. A sweating water pitcher is a sign of rain.

2675. A whirlwind going east is a sign of rain.

2676. If a whirlwind goes down stream, there will be rain soon.

2677. Whirlwinds of dust are a sign of dry weather.

2678. If it begins raining while the wind is blowing from the east, there will be rain every day for seven days.

2679. Precipitation is generally preceded for eighteen to twenty-four hours by southeast to northeast winds and falling barometer.................Lexington

2680. In all seasons rain is preceded for twelve to thirty-six hours by southeast to northeast winds and falling barometer, and the barometer generally falls to 29.90 or below in spring, summer, and winter and to 30 or below in autumn before the rain begins ....Louisville

2681. If the wind is in the south on the first day of the year, it will not be out of the south forty-eight hours within forty days.......Western Kentucky

2682. During periods of abnormally high temperature the wind is from the south in spring and winter and from the southwest in summer and autumn.......
.... Lexington

2683. Cold winds of all seasons are from the northwest...
.... Lexington

2684. During periods of very high temperature prevailing winds are from southeast to east in spring, southwest to northwest in summer, and south to southeast in autumn and winter........Louisville

2685. During very low temperature prevailing winds are from the west, northwest, or north......Louisville

2686. Severe winter storms are preceded by east to northeast winds ....Lexington

2687. Before summer rains the wind is usually from south to east ....Lexington

2688. Stretch a yarn string over beans and other young plants in the early spring, to protect them from frost. The frost will collect on the yarn and the plants will not be injured.

2689. Any noise during a thunderstorm is dangerous...
.... Central Kentucky

2690. Music during a thunderstorm is very dangerous...
.... Central Kentucky

2691. If you sit on a feather bed, the lightning will not strike you.

2692. If the lightning strikes twice in the same place, there is mineral in the ground there near the surface
.... Central Kentucky

2693. Many negroes will not burn the wood of a tree that has been struck by lightning for fear that their houses will burn or be struck by lightning.......
.... Western Kentucky

2694. When sunshine and rain come together, the Devil is beating his wife. If you put a black-headed pin into the clay and put your ear to the pin head, you may hear them.

2695. There is a pot of gold at the bottom of the rainbow.

2696. If an east wind blows for three days in the spring, there will be no acorns, beech nuts, and the like that year............ ...North-eastern Kentucky

2697. If it thunders heavily while a hen is sitting, it will kill the chickens.

2698. If it thunders while ducks are sitting, the eggs will not hatch.

2699. If the sun looks red like blood at the sunset of a rainy day, a sudden death will soon take place.

DAYS, SEASONS,[1] ETC.

2700. Monday's child is fair of face.
Tuesday's child is full of grace.
Wednesday's child is loving and giving.
Thursday's child must work for a living.
Friday's child is full of woe.
Saturday's child has far to go.
But the child that is born on the Sabbath day,
Is blythe and bonny and good and gay.

2701. Wednesday's child is merry and glad.
Thursday's child is sour and sad.

2702. Cutting Nails.
Monday for health;
Tuesday for wealth;
Wednesday for news;
Thursday for a new pair of shoes;
Friday for sorrow;
Saturday, see your beau tomorrow.
But you had better never been born than have your
nails on Sunday shorn.

2703. To cut the finger-nails on Monday means health,
on Tuesday wealth, Wednesday a letter, on Thursday something better, on Friday a wife, on Saturday long life, on Sunday means evil, for all of that
week you will be ruled by the Devil.

2704. To cut the nails on Monday will bring good luck.

2705. If you cut your finger nails on Monday morning
before breakfast, you will receive a present before
the week is over.

---

[1] For the significance of sneezes on certain days, see *Sneezes*, numbers 1035-
1038. For days and months of weddings, see *Weddings*, numbers 616-627.
For the connection of days or seasons with crops, see *Crops*.

2706. It brings bad luck to cut the nails on Thursday.

2707. If you cut your toe nails on Friday, you will never have toothache ....Western Kentucky

2708. If you cut your nails on Sunday, you will have a plague.

2709. It brings good luck to have the nails pared on Monday, Tuesday, Wednesday. It brings bad luck to have the nails pared on other days, especially Sunday.

2710. If you trim your nails on Sunday, someone will catch you with your clothes down before the end of the week........................Mountains

2711. If you burn brush on Sunday, you will be put in the moon.

2712. If you burn brush on Sunday, when you die your body will burn all the time.

2713. It brings good luck to move on Monday, Tuesday, or Wednesday.

2714. You will have good luck if you are born on Sunday.

2715. A person born on Sunday can talk to animals at midnight of old Christmas...........Mountains

2716. It brings good luck to wear a new dress on Sunday ....Western Kentucky

2717. If it thunders on Sunday, goose eggs will not hatch .... Mountains

2718. If you work on Sunday, you will be sick on Monday.

2719. It brings bad luck to fish on Sunday.

2720. If you turn a spinning wheel around on Sunday, you will get a whipping..............Mountains

2721. One will have to pick each stitch out with his nose that he sews on Sunday.

2722. If you sew on Sunday, on Judgment Day or in

hell you will have to take the stitches out with
your nose.

2723. It brings bad luck to use scissors or to sew on Sunday, unless you do not wear a thimble or unless
you carry your work to a friend's house. Mountains

2724. If you sew on Sunday, you will die on Monday.

2725. It brings bad luck to iron on Sunday.

2726. It is harmful to darn on Sunday, unless you cross
your feet........................Blue Grass

2727. It brings bad luck to comb your hair on Sunday..
.... Mountains

2728. Sunday is the best day to move.

2729. It causes bad luck to move on Sunday..Mountains

2730. It brings good luck to start on a journey on Sunday.

2731. If you start on your journey on Sunday, you will
be gone a long time.

2732. If you set tobacco on Sunday, the grub worms will
attack it.

2733. If you turn a cow dry on Sunday, her calf will be
born in the day time.

2734. It brings bad luck to count eggs on Sunday.

2735. It brings bad luck to turn a feather bed on Sunday.

2736. If you take up the hoe on Sunday, you will not be
able to turn it loose.

2737. To burn paper on Sunday brings bad luck.

2738. As goes Monday, so goes the week.

2739. If you have company on Monday, you will have
company every day in the week.

2740. If you go visiting on Monday, you will go every
day in the week.

2741. Your whole week will be unlucky if you eat in a
strange house on Monday.

2742. If you are in a bad humor on Monday, you will be in a bad humor all week.

2743. If you hurt your foot on Monday, it will not get well until Sunday...................Mountains

2744. If you take out ashes on Monday, you will have bad luck.

2745. It brings good luck to begin a job on Monday.

2746. A letter on Monday means that you will receive two more letters that week.

2747. It brings good luck to receive a nickel early Monday morning.................Louisville Negroes

2748. If you keep all you take in on Monday, the amount will increase during the week.

2749. If a man comes to your house the first thing on Monday morning, there will be good luck all that week.

2750. If on Monday morning a woman comes to your house before a man, you will have bad luck all that week.

2751. If the first person that you meet Monday morning is a negro woman, you will have bad luck.

2752. Avert the bad luck that will come to you from meeting a negro woman on Monday morning by turning and going back..........Southern Kentucky

2753. Monday and Friday are unlucky days for all women who are born in April...........Mountains

2754. Monday, Friday, and the thirteenth day of the month are unlucky days for a journey.

2755. Set the first hen on Monday for good luck........
..................................Blue Grass

2756. You will not have good luck that week if you start to work on Tuesday.................Mountains

2757. It is unlucky to meet a left-handed person on Tuesday ....Mountains

2758. Wednesday is a lucky day for collecting money.

2759. Wednesday is the luckiest day of the week for a wedding.

2760. Thursday is the best day for business transactions.

2761. Do not comb your hair on Thursday............ ....Western Kentucky

2762. One never sees a blue jay on Friday because these birds carry sand to the Devil on that day. Another version says that every blue jay carries a piece of wood to hell on Friday, to heat the lawyers.

2763. Eggs laid on Friday never decay........Negroes

2764. On Friday, the thirteenth, wear odd shoes for good luck ....Western Kentucky

2765. It brings good luck to begin anything on Friday.

2766. It brings bad luck to pay a debt on Friday........ .... Mountains

2767. It is unlucky to fish on Friday.

2768. It causes bad luck to kiss your girl on Friday..... ....Western Kentucky

2769. Do not wash your face on Friday.............. ....Western Kentucky

2770. It causes bad luck to sweep dirt out of the house on Friday, for the house will burn later...Blue Grass

2771. Never carry ashes out of the house after four o'clock in the afternoon on Friday. Wait until Monday morning, or you will lose a dollar that week.

2772. It brings bad luck to move on Friday or Saturday.

2773. It brings bad luck to be born on Saturday. You will have to work hard for a living.....Mountains

2774. If you cut a garment on Saturday, you will never live to wear it out. "Quick done or never done."

2775. It causes bad luck to begin building a house on Saturday.

2776. You must not bake a cake on Saturday.

2777. The sun always shines on Saturday, if only for a few minutes.

2778. If you cut your finger nails on Saturday, you will get joy tomorrow.

2779. If you feel that it is Saturday when it is not, you will soon hear of the death of a friend of yours.
. . . . Mountains

2780. What you do on the first day of the year indicates the character of your actions throughout the year.

2781. If a man enters your house before a woman on New Year's Day, you will have a good year.

2782. If a woman enters the house before a man does on New Year's Day, there will be bad luck.

2783. If a negro is your first visitor on New Year's Day, he brings bad luck.

2784. As the first caller on New Year's Day, a dark man brings the best luck.

2785. As the first caller on New Year's Day, a fair-haired man brings the next best luck.

2786. As the first caller on New Year's Day, a dark-haired woman brings the third best luck.

2787. As the first caller on New Year's Day, a red-haired person brings bad luck.

2788. If a woman comes on the first day of the year, some one will come every day in the year.

2789. If a woman visits you on New Year's Day, you cannot raise chickens successfully that year. Mountains

2790. To break something on the first day of the year causes bad luck for the remainder of the year.

2791. If you dip your head into the ocean on January first, you will not be ill during the year.

2792. If you wash anything on New Year's Day, you will wash a member of the family away....Blue Grass

2793. If you eat cabbage on New Year's Day, you will have money all the year.......Western Kentucky

2794. If you cook white beans the first day of the year, you will have money all the year..............
.......................Western Kentucky

2795. Poultry raisers are interested in the first person who comes into their houses on New Year's Day. The sex of the caller signifies whether the house will raise pullets or roosters that year, and the size of the chickens will compare with the size of the visitors ....Blue Grass

2796. You will have good luck if while walking up grade you hear the first turtle-dove of the new year.

2797. You will have bad luck if while walking down grade you hear the first turtle dove of the new year.

2798. The cutting of the hair in March causes a year of headache.

2799. If you cut your hair in March, you will be sick before the year is out.

2800. If you cut your hair in March, you will lose a horse.

2801. If you have your hair cut in March, you will never live to see another March.

2802. To move in March brings bad luck.....Mountains

2803. If a person lives through March, he will live the rest of the year.

2804. If it rains on Good Friday, rains will be without

value all summer, that is, they will be too hard,
will come at the wrong time or for some other reason will be valueless..........Southern Kentucky

2805. Rain on the Friday before Easter Sunday is a good-
luck sign.

2806. An early Easter means an early Spring..........
.....................North-eastern Kentucky

2807. Unless you wear something new on Easter Sunday,
you will be unlucky throughout the year.

2808. If you have a man for a guest on the morning of
May first, all the chickens that year will be roosters
...............................Blue Grass

2809. If you have a woman for a guest on the morning
of May first, all your chickens that year will be
hens.

2810. "A maid who on the first of May,
Goes to the fields at break of day,
And washes in dew from the hawthorn tree,
Will ever after handsome be."

2811. If you wash your hair in the first rain of May, it
will grow.........................Mountains

2812. It causes bad luck to look into a well on the first
day of May, for if you see your reflection, there
will be a death in your family before the next May.

2813. Do not pluck a four-leaved clover in May........
.....................North-eastern Kentucky

2814. If you go in swimming on the first morning of May
before the sun is up, you will not have any con-
tagious disease during that year.......Mountains

2815. If a colt is born in May, he will lie down in the
water with you.............Louisville Negroes

2816. It is dangerous to take off your winter clothing until the tenth of May.

2817. To become beautiful, wash your face in dew before sunrise on Mayday.[1]

2818. If you set hens in June with eggs laid in June, the chickens will die.

2819. If you go in swimming on the first of June, you will not be sick the whole summer.........Mountains

2820. If a turtle-dove sits on a tree the first day of June and calls, looking at you, you have enemies.

2821. The time to cut shrubbery so that it will not come up again, is Ember Day (the day in the Episcopal Church when special prayers are made for those going into holy orders).

2822. Trees are easily killed on Ember Day by removing the bark.

2823. If you hack the bark of a tree on Ember Day, it will die ....Mountains

2824. Dog days begin with the cry or song of the katydid .... **Mountains**

2825. If it rains on the first day of dog days, it will rain for forty days.....................Mountains

2826. There will be no chestnuts if it rains on the fourth of July.

2827. If it rains on the fourth of July, there will be no grapes ....Blue Grass

2828. Martens go south on the fifteenth of August.....
.........................Western Kentucky

2829. If you cut your foot while swimming in the water

[1] For other superstitions associated with May first, see *Divinations* and *Weddings*.

during the first ten days of August, you will have
blood poisoning....................Blue Grass

2830. You will have good luck if you are the first to say
"Merry Christmas" or "Happy New Year."

2831. A green Christmas makes a full graveyard.

2832. If the sun shines on Christmas, and if it snows on
Easter, there will be a fat graveyard.

2833. Never take up ashes from the fireplace during the
Christmas season..................Blue Grass

2834. It brings bad luck to kill the Christmas fly......
..........................Central Kentucky

2835. A white New Christmas and a white Old Christmas
are the signs of a good fruit year. (Old Christmas
is twelve days after New or regular Christmas)...
.... Mountains

2836. At Christmas Eve, trees bleed (because of the
Cross).

2837. At Christmas Eve, spirits walk.

2838. At midnight on Christmas Eve all cows kneel (because Christ was born in a manger).

2839. On Old Christmas Eve, all animals talk to spirits
and get on their knees and pray.......Mountains

2840. At midnight of Old Christmas, the elders bloom...
.... Mountains

2841. It brings bad luck to leave up the Christmas greens
after New Year's Day.........Central Kentucky

2842. If you stay up until midnight on December thirty-
first, you will see an old man go out your door and
a little child come in................Mountains

2843. If you talk to animals at midnight on New Year's
Eve, they will understand you and you them.

215

2844. Oysters are not good except in those months which contain the letter r.

2845. If you turn water into a cistern during any month that has not an *r* in the spelling, the water will sour and not be fit to drink.

2846. It is unlucky to marry a person born in the same month with you. You will not be happy together because you are ruled by the same stellar influence.

2847. The girl born in January will be a prudent house-wife, goodnatured, and inclined to be melancholy.

In February, humane, affectionate as a wife, tender as a mother.

In March, a chatterbox, fickle, stormy, quarrelsome.

In April, pretty, dainty, inconsistent, not studious.

In May, handsome, contented, happy.

In June, gay, impetuous, will marry early.

In July, fair, surly, jealous.

In August, amiable, practical, will marry rich.

In September, discreet, generally beloved.

In October, pretty, coquettish, moody.

In November, liberal, kind, amiable, thoughtful of others.

In December, fond of novelty, extravagant.

2848. If a girl is born in October, her marriage will be unhappy ....Negroes

2849. A girl who is born in November will have a mild disposition.

2850. "A swarm of bees in May,
Is worth a ton of hay.
A swarm in June
Is worth a silver spoon.

But a swarm in July
Is not worth a fly."

2851. Birth Flowers:

January—snowdrop	August—poppy
February—primrose	September—morning glory
March—violet	
April—daisy	October—golden rod
May—hawthorn	November—chrysan-
June—honeysuckle	themum
July—water lily	December—holly

2852. Birth Stones:

January—garnet	July—ruby
February—amethyst	August—sardonyx
March—bloodstone	September—sapphire
April—diamond	October—amber, opal
May—emerald	November—topaz
June—moonstone	December—turquoise

2853. Wear your birthstone for luck.

2854. If you let your birthday pass without thinking of it, you will die before the next birthday.

2855. It brings you bad luck to be put under the bed on your birthday.

2856. It brings good luck to receive white flowers on your birthday.

2857. It brings good luck to be born on the eighth of the month ....Mountains

2858. The eighth of the month is a lucky day on which to transact business.

2859. You will be able to get anything that you ask for on the fourteenth of any month.

2860. It is unlucky to be born on either the sixteenth or the seventeenth day of the month......Mountains

2861. At the first of the month say "Rabbits," and you will have good luck through the month..........
..........................Northern Kentucky

2862. When you see in the morning the ground torn up by ants, you will know that summer has begun...
.... Mountains

2863. Snow out of season brings bad luck.

2864. When a general pause comes in the conversation, the time is twenty minutes before or after the hour.

2865. If you blow dandelion balls three times, the number of white seeds left tells the time of day.

CROPS, VEGETABLES, FRUITS, TREES

2866. Crops planted during the first three days of July will be barren.

2867. Do not plant anything on the first three days of May, which are barren days.

2868. Never thank the giver for seeds if you want them to grow.

2869. Slips from plants should be stolen. Only stolen ones grow.

2870. In sowing grain, if you miss a "land," you will have a death in the family.

2871. Plants must be kept in the bed room at night and in the living room in the daytime.

2872. If a row is missed in planting, there will be a death in the family before the year is out.

2873. In planting, bad luck results if you leave a row unfinished.

2874. It brings bad luck not to plant seed after the soil has been prepared for the planting.

2875. Plant in the morning the seed that matures above the ground.................Western Kentucky

2876. Plant in the afternoon the seed that matures underground ....Western Kentucky

2877. If while you are working with someone in a garden your hoes strike together, you will hoe together at the same time next year.

2878. If two men at work on two rows strike hoes, one will die within a year.

2879. If you plant beans in the morning, they will come two weeks sooner than if you plant them in the afternoon....................Western Kentucky

2880. If beans are planted in the afternoon, they will drop the bloom.

2881. If while you are picking beans a leaf sticks on your clothes, you will receive news.........Mountains

2882. It brings good luck to plant beans on the one hundredth day of the year...............Mountains

2883. Plant beans on Good Friday.

2884. When apple trees bloom, plant beans.

2885. Put a yarn string over beans, to prevent frost from having effect on them.

2886. If butterbeans grow downward and send roots upward, the planter will die.

2887. You will have good luck if you carry a horse-chestnut.

2888. It is poisonous to eat horse-chestnuts (also called buck-eyes).

2889. If one eats a buck-eye, his head will turn around.

2890. You must eat carrots, in order to become beautiful .... Mountains

2891. You will have bad luck if you eat celery.

2892. If you find a one-leaved clover, you will get a letter from your sweetheart................Mountains

2893. If you find a two-leaved clover, you will receive a kiss from your sweetheart.

2894. A four-leaved clover brings the finder good luck.

2895. If you find a four-leaved clover, there is always another in its place............Western Kentucky

2896. If you swallow a four-leaved clover whole, you will get whom you wish to marry.

2897. A five-leaved clover must be passed on to other people. Whoever receives it will have good luck if he does not keep it.

2898. If you find a five-leaved clover, give it away; it will bring good luck to the giver and the receiver.

2899. To find a seven-leaved clover brings bad luck.....
.........................Western Kentucky

2900. If locust blooms are heavy, expect a large corn crop.

2901. Plant corn when the dogwood blooms.

2902. When white oak leaves are as big as a squirrel's ear, plant corn.

2903. Plant corn after the woodpecker comes.

2904. Do not plant corn until asparagus tips are high enough above ground to assure a good asparagus crop.

2905. Corn should not be planted on May first, second, or third, as these are barren days.

2906. It is rotten corn that produces the crust of bread...
.... Mountains

2907. If you burn the cobs of your seed corn, you will cause your growing corn to blast......Mountains

2908. If you burn the cobs from seed corn, the fodder will fire the corn......................Mountains

2909. "If it comes, it no comes;
If it no comes, it comes."
The explanation is—
If the crow comes, the corn will not grow.
If the crow does not come, the corn will grow....
..........................Louisville Negroes

2910. If you miss a row in planting corn, one will die in the family before corn-gathering time.

2911. If when you plant a field of corn you miss a row, there will be a death in the family before planting time again.

2912. When white-oak leaves are as large as squirrel ears, plant corn...........General over United States

2913. If you see grains of corn in the road, company will come; if you cover them over, the caller will be a stranger.

2914. In corn-husking, a blue-spotted red ear brings the best luck. It is called in the Kentucky mountains a "skew ball".......................Mountains

2915. If you see a red corn-silk first, you will hear of a wedding before you hear of a death.

2916. If the first corn-silk of the season that you see is white, you will go to a funeral soon.

2917. You will raise one hundred bushels of corn for each white stalk which you find in your field. Mountains

2918. If the first silk that you see on a new ear of corn is white, you will have bad health........Mountains

2919. If you eat corn out of a tomato bowl, you will eat corn cake out of a musk melon the following year.

2920. If a farmer has the brim of his hat turned up in front, he has corn for sale.

2921. If a farmer's hat brim is turned up in the back and

down in front, the farmer wishes to buy corn.....
.............................Western Kentucky

2922. You should plant cabbages on the ninth of May...
.............................Western Kentucky

2923. You must sow cotton seed on the ninth of May....
.............................Western Kentucky

2924. If you plant cotton among your cucumber plants,
insects will not attack your cucumbers..........
.............................Western Kentucky

2925. Plant cucumbers on the fourth of July...Blue Grass

2926. "Plant cucumber seed on the sixth of July;
You will have cucumbers, wet or dry"...........
.............................Western Kentucky

2927. Place cornbread crumbs about your cucumber
plants. They will attract ants, which will destroy
the cucumber insects.........Western Kentucky

2928. If you blow all the seeds off a dandelion ball in two
blows, you will get a new dress.

2929. Plant flax on Good Friday....................
.....................North-eastern Kentucky

2930. If you swallow the first forget-me-not of the season,
you will get a new dress of the same color.

2931. It is bad luck to burn grape vines..............
.............................Western Kentucky

2932. A blade of grass or a leaf a-quiver when all others
are still shows that a fairy is dancing on it.

2933. If you pass a wagonload of fresh hay without seiz-
ing a handful, you will have bad luck...Blue Grass

2934. If you see a hay wagon and say, "Load of hay, load
of hay, Take my wish and go away," you will have
good luck.

2935. To follow a haywagon out of sight with your gaze

will bring good luck. The luck will be better if nothing comes between.

2936. "Where hollyhocks grow,
Beaus never go.".............Central Kentucky

2937. If you plant nasturtiums on St. Patrick's Day, they will grow fast......................Blue Grass

2938. If a nettle points toward you, pick it up, for it means good luck...................Mountains

2939. A nutmeg worn around the neck will bring good luck.

2940. It causes good luck to carry an onion in your pocket .... Mountains

2941. If you swallow the seed of an orange, your best friend is thinking of you.............Mountains

2942. Plant parsley, and you plant sorrow.

2943. It brings bad luck to transplant parsley.

2944. If you accidentally drop peanut shells near your house, you may know that policemen are coming to the house.................Louisville Negroes

2945. It brings good luck to plant peas on the fourteenth of February ....Mountains

2946. Peppers to prosper, must be planted by a red-headed or a hot-tempered person.

2947. If you want peppers to grow, you must be angry when you are planting them...Western Kentucky

2948. You will be poisoned if you eat "pokeberries."

2949. St. Patrick's Day is a good time on which to plant potatoes.

2950. If you plant potatoes on the sixth of April, they will not be attacked by insects.

2951. If you plant potatoes on dark nights, the moles will eat them ....Mountains

2952. An Irish potato is growing until the skin cannot be flipped off with the fingers.

2953. If you see a puff ball (any fungus of the genus Lycoperdon), you will have fever. You can avert the fever by spitting nine times.

2954. The redbud is the tree on which Judas hanged himself.

2955. If you let a rose bloom in the house, a death will follow............................Blue Grass

2956. To plant sage seed will bring death or severe illness to one of the family.

2957. "Where sunflowers grow,
No beaus go."

2958. Plant sweetpeas and garden peas on the fourteenth of February......................Blue Grass

2959. Plant sweetpeas on the twenty-second of February
..........................Central Kentucky

2960. Plant sweetpeas on St. Patrick's Day..Mountains

2961. Plant sweetpeas on Good Friday......Blue Grass

2962. It is bad luck for the dropper of tobacco to get more than one row ahead of the setter.

2963. It is bad luck to buy tobacco at or toward twilight; many stop buying by three o'clock in the afternoon.

2964. It was recently thought unlucky to buy tobacco at exactly six cents a pound. Of late the high price of tobacco has made this superstition obsolete.

2965. Some buyers of tobacco will not bid the even amounts but will skip, for example, from fourteen and three-fourth cents to fifteen and one-fourth cents.

2966. Do not buy tobacco of pawpaw color (motley color); it is called "fool-catcher."

2967. It is bad luck to chew your tobacco twice (that is, bad to tell a story twice).

2968. If one plants a tree by a grave, and the tree dies, the planter of it will die.

2969. "Blossoms out of season,
Trouble out of reason."

2970. It is good luck to find two of any kind of fruit grown together.....................Blue Grass

2971. If you count the fruit on a tree before it is ripe, it will fall off.

2972. If you have a tree that will not bear fruit, drive a peg into it, to make it bear.

2973. To knock on wood will avert disaster—notably disaster that follows boasting.

2974. If you can break an apple in half with your hands, you will always be your own boss.

2975. If you plant a cedar tree in your yard and it lives, you will have good luck.

2976. If you bring in a cedar tree and set it near a building, you will die.

2977. Death will come to the man who transplants a cedar tree, when the lower limbs grow to be the length of his coffin.

2978. If you let a cedar tree grow in your yard large enough to shade a grave, someone in your family will die.

2979. If a cedar tree that you have planted dies in your yard, one of your family will die. Some say that the death will take place within a year.

2980. You will have bad luck if you burn cedar.

2981. It causes bad luck to break a dogwood switch.

2982. You will have bad luck if you ride with a dogwood switch.

2983. It is very unlucky to boom a log upon a log-wagon with a dogwood pole.........Western Kentucky

2984. It is unlucky for a horseback rider to use a hardwood switch.

2985. Locust trees are more often struck by lightning than any others..................Western Kentucky

2986. Mulberries are poisonous during the time of the seventeen-year locust....North-eastern Kentucky

2987. Leaves of the peach in a poultice will cure rheumatism and neuralgia.

2988. If a peach tree blooms before its time, a death will occur in the family soon.

2989. If you can remove the peeling from a pear without breaking it, throw it over your left shoulder for good luck...................Western Kentucky

2990. If you plant a pine tree, you will die when it is large enough to shade your grave......Mountains

2991. As many black pines as you plant in your yard, so many will die in your family.........Mountains

2992. It causes bad luck to burn or haul sassafras wood.

2993. If you burn sassafras wood or leaves, a horse or a mule of yours will die within a week....Mountains

2994. To burn walnut wood brings bad luck..Mountains

2995. Walnut trees often grow near a wooden fence. The reason for this fact is that squirrels plant or drop walnuts for future use and then forget them.

2996. To plant a weeping willow causes bad luck.

2997. If you plant a weeping willow tree, you will be an old maid............North-western Kentucky

2998. "Plant turnips on the twenty-fifth of July, and you'll have turnips, wet or dry."

2999. You must sow turnip seeds on the twenty-fifth of July, wet or dry, and on the twenty-seventh there will be rain........................Blue Grass

3000. Turnips should not be planted on the seventh of August.

3001. Turnips should be planted on the tenth of August .... Mountains

3002. To have good luck with turnips, say as you throw out the handful of seed: "One for the fly, one for the Devil, and one for I."

3003. Plant watermelons one week after apple blossom time ....Blue Grass

3004. Plant watermelons on the first of May before sunrise.

3005. If you plant your watermelons on the first morning of May in your night clothes before the sun is up, the insects will never attack them.

3006. If you plant watermelons on the first day of May and carry the seed out in a washing-tub, the melons will grow as large as the tub.

3007. Plant watermelons on the tenth of May.

3008. Watermelons planted on the nineteenth of May will not grow.

3009. If you point at a watermelon with your first finger, the melon will drop off. You must point with all four fingers.................Central Kentucky

3010. It brings bad luck to have weeds grow about the house......................Western Kentucky

3011. A great deal of snow in winter is a sign of a good wheat crop.

3012. Thunder storms precede a large wheat yield.

3013. You will have good luck if you take a handkerchief, go backward, and throw it over your left shoulder into a wheat field.

MONEY

3014. Carry a coin piece (for example, an old coin) for good luck and to keep from losing money.

3015. If you carry money in two different pockets, you will lose some of it.................Mountains

3016. Falling in love is a sure sign of becoming insolvent ....Blue Grass

3017. It brings good luck to carry three cents.......... ....Northern Kentucky

3018. To find money is lucky..............Mountains

3019. If you find a piece of money, you must keep it, for it will bring money...........Central Kentucky

3020. It brings good luck to wear a coin around your neck ....Mountains

3021. To find a piece of silver will bring you good luck.

3022. To wear a dime in the heel of your shoe will prevent your enemy from putting a "spell" upon you.... .... Mountains

3023. To put money into the foundation of a building brings luck.

3024. A speculator or a traveler will have luck if he borrows money from a woman..........Mountains

3025. If you put the last nickel of your allowance into the church offering, you will get a check within the next few days.

3026. If your initials spell a word, you will become rich.

3027. If you marry a poor man, you will become rich...
.... Mountains
3028. You will have good luck if when you drop a nickel
it sticks up in the floor.............Blue Grass
3029. If you hide a nickel in a hole and never come back.
you will be rich when you are grown...........
........................Louisville Negroes
3030. If you count your profits, you will lose them.
3031. To accept a two-dollar bill is unlucky. This superstition is found frequently among railroad men,
race-track frequenters, saloon-keepers, and waiters
in restaurants.
3032. Avert the disaster of accepting a two-dollar bill by
pinching off a little piece in the middle of a side or
an end.
3033. If you take a teaspoonful of turpentine, you will
be rich...........................Mountains

WALKING FORTH, TRAVEL

3034. It brings bad luck to come to a place in the road
where someone has drawn his foot across the way.
3035. It causes bad luck to run across a bridge. Mountains
3036. If you are walking at night and see a will 'o the
wisp, you must instantly turn your coat wrong
side out and put it on, or you will die.
3037. When you are walking, if you pick up all the burnt
matches you see, you will find money..Blue Grass
3038. It brings good luck to meet the same person on the
way both to and from any place—.............
........................Blue Grass Negroes
3039. It brings good luck to meet the same people two

or three times in the same place on the same day
not by appointment.

3040. If a man or a woman follows you for five blocks
and then turns away, you will lose money........
.... Mountains

3041. When you are going anywhere, it causes bad luck
to meet a woman first, but good luck to meet a
man or boy.

3042. To walk on the opposite side of a post from a companion will bring on a quarrel.

3043. Avert the danger of a quarrel after you have walked
on the opposite side of a post from your companion
by spitting on the post.

3044. To avert the penalty of allowing a post to come between you and a companion, say "Bread and butter."

3045. To avert the penalty of allowing a post to come between you and your companion, join hands.

3046. If two persons who are walking together permit a
third to pass between them, they will have a quarrel.

3047. It causes bad luck to pass between two women.

3048. It causes good luck to pass between two men.

3049. If you do not step on the lines of a concrete or stone
pavement, you will have something good for dinner.

3050. "If you sing on the street,
With displeasure you will meet"....... Mountains

3051. It causes bad luck to cross a street anywhere except
at a crossing.

3052. It causes bad luck to forget something and have to
go back for it.

3053. If you start to go anywhere and then go back three times, you will have trouble.

3054. Avert the bad luck incident to turning back by counting ten.

3055. If you must go back after starting anywhere, avert the bad luck penalty by sitting down.

3056. Avert the ill luck which comes from turning back after starting by spitting over your left shoulder.

3057. You can avert bad luck incident to turning back after once starting, by making a cross and spitting into it.

3058. If you postpone a trip, you will never take it.

3059. To see a red-haired girl in the morning of the day you are going on a journey brings bad luck......
.................................Blue Grass

3060. If the day is clear upon which you start on an ocean voyage you will not be homesick......Blue Grass

3061. If you start anywhere with wet clothes in your trunk, you will have bad luck.

3062. If you watch a person out of sight, you will never see him again.

3063. If you wave a person off or kiss him good-bye a second time, he will never reach his journey's end.

3064. To touch a street-car will bring good luck.

3065. It is an omen of good luck for a red-haired man to run in front of a street car.

3066. It brings good luck for a negro to run and jump on a street-car.

3067. It brings good luck to see an empty street-car.

3068. It causes bad luck for a fuse in a street-car to blow out at the corner of a street.

3069. Bad fortune is invited by the street-car motorman

who scratches his car during his first trip on it; he may expect a violent accident.

3070. It causes bad luck for a street-car to stop in front of a church.

3071. For a wagon to turn from one side to the other before leaving a street-car track means bad luck, for when this happens the motorman's pay will be docked at the end of the week.

3072. If you meet a friend of yours on the train, you will never lose his friendship.............Blue Grass

3073. To count the cars of a passenger train is a sign of death.

3074. It brings bad luck to count freight cars.

3075. Certain rooms in hotels have the name of bad-luck rooms.

3076. To close a hotel register causes bad luck.

3077. If you have a fight with someone in a strange town, you will be defeated.........Western Kentucky

LETTERS

3078. To burn a letter will bring good luck...Mountains

3079. To tear a letter and bury the pieces under a log will bring good luck................Mountains

3080. If you fold a letter in nine folds and put it into a glove, and then sleep on the glove, you will dream how to answer the letter.

3081. To put a stamp on a letter accidentally bottom side upwards means that you will not receive an answer.

3082. It is a sign of great disappointment to get a letter with the stamp turned upside down.

3083. If a stamp is upside down on a letter that you receive, your best friend will leave you.

3084. It brings bad luck to put a one-cent stamp on a letter by mistake.

3085. If a stamp is put on an envelope pointing to the right, it means, "Go quick."

3086. If a stamp is put on an envelope pointing to the left, it means, "I am angry."

3087. If a stamp is put on an envelope upside down, it is a sign of love.

3088. If you wrap a hundred canceled postage stamps in white paper, tie them with a red twine string, and throw them out of the back window, you will find money ....Mountains

3089. If you write the initials of the person from whom you wish a letter on a piece of pie and eat the pie, you will get the letter.

3090. If you find an unopened letter on the street, you will soon have good news.

3091. If you receive a note with one corner folded by mistake, you will have a quarrel with the person who sent it..........................Blue Grass

3092. No news is a sign of good news.

3093. If you pick up a book and turn it upside down, a letter with bad news in it will come to you.

MINES

3094. If a woman comes into a coal mine, there will be an accident to the miners..............Mountains

3095. It causes bad luck for a hole to squib on the right side of the room in a coal mine........Mountains

3096. It causes good luck for a hole to squib on the left side of the room in a coal mine........Mountains

3097. If a woman enter a mine, there will be a death among the miners within six months...Mountains

3098. It causes bad luck to whistle in a coal mine...... .... Mountains

3099. On the day of a death in a camp (even the death of a baby) miners must not work........Mountains

3100. To see a light in a mine is a sign that the death of one or more miners is near...........Mountains

3101. If you go into a mine with a time set for coming out, you will be killed before you are out........ .... Mountains

3102. It will bring bad luck to go down into a mine after dark......................Western Kentucky

3103. If a dog goes inside a coal mine, some one who works in the mine will be killed.......Mountains

3104. If mice run out of a mine, the mine will fall in.... .... Mountains

3105. A white rat in a coal mine is a sign of a cave in.... .... Mountains

3106. To see rats in a mine is a sign that slate will fall.. .... Mountains

3107. It means good luck for a miner to skin his back on an oak board......................Mountains

3108. It means good luck for a miner to get coal dust in his eyes.

3109. It means bad luck for a miner to get slate in his eye ....Mountains

3110. It means bad luck for a miner to strike a sulphur ball with his pick and not strike out fire. Mountains

COLOR

3111. When milk is being churned, the butter will come more quickly if the churn is set on a blue cloth...
............................Blue Grass

3112. If a blue-gummed negro bites you, the wound will poison you.

3113. If a green snake bites you, you will laugh yourself to death.

3114. Peacock colors bring bad luck to the wearer.

3115. To find a red stone is a sign that some one is thinking of you.

3116. You will have good luck if you see a red-haired girl coming up the street.

3117. You will have bad luck if you see a red-haired woman as you leave your home in the morning......
.... Mountains

3118. To meet a red-haired negro brings bad luck.

3119. Actors and musicians consider yellow an unlucky color.

3120. If you see a violet cloud, you will live to old age...
..............................Blue Grass

3121. It brings good luck to see a yellow box-car.

NUMBERS

3122. The third time is for luck. "Three's a charm."

3123. Three is an unlucky number..........Mountains

3124. In fire insurance, one large loss means that there will be three losses.

3125. One suicide or one murder means that there will be two more.

3126. It causes bad luck for a passenger who wishes to

stop a car to ring the bell three times.

3127. It brings bad luck for the last of three people to use a lighted match in smoking.

3128. The third who uses a towel will have bad luck.

3129. The number seven is a good luck number.

3130. The seventh daughter of a seventh daughter, or the seventh son of a seventh son, will be extremely lucky ....Mountains

3131. The seventh son of a seventh son can be a healer, fortune-teller or the like.

3132. The seventh son will always be a preacher, a doctor or a lawyer.

3133. If you stick a knife into the ground eight times, you will have good luck.................Mountains

3134. Nine is a lucky number for travelers.

3135. Eleven is a good number in a crap game (perhaps because it rhymes with seven).

3136. Thirteen is a bad-luck number.

3137. If one is born on the thirteenth day of the month, thirteen is his lucky number.

3138. Those born on the thirteenth will die before they are thirty.

3139. A clock that strikes thirteen prophesies death.

3140. If thirteen people are seated at a table, the first to get up will die before that time next year.

3141. Of thirteen people who sit down to a meal, one will die within a month.

3142. If thirteen people sit at a table, the youngest will die soon.

3143. If you find the number thirteen turned towards you, you will be an old maid.

3144. Put twenty-four canceled postage stamps into an

envelope, and throw them out of a window in the morning. You will find something.

3145. It is a bad-luck sign to have an uneven number of anything.

3146. If you count ninety-nine stars without bowing your head, you will drop dead.

3147. If you try to count one hundred stars without looking down, you will fall dead on the ninety-ninth.

3148. If you count one hundred stars without looking down, your mother will die before the year is out.

3149. If you count one hundred stars, you will drop dead.

3150. Stamp every negro that you meet until you have stamped one hundred; then you will receive a desirable present.

3151. If you stamp one hundred negroes, you will find something.

SPORTS

3152. If you cross bats in playing ball, your luck will change.

3153. In laying baseball bats down, do not cross them.

3154. If the first batter in a baseball game strikes out, the opposing team will win.

3155. If you break your bat, you may expect a batting slump.

3156. It causes bad luck to change bats after you have taken one in your hand.

3157. To change bats after the second strike is unwise.

3158. It causes bad luck for a baseball player to stand on the plate with the large end of the bat down.

3159. If one drops a baseball bat between the home base and the catcher, bad luck will follow.

3160. When one is running toward first base, it brings bad luck to step over a bat.

3161. If on the way to the plate you pass between the home plate and the pitcher, you will be hit by the ball later.

3162. For good luck, spit on the end of the bat before batting.

3163. It is unlucky for the batter to spit on the home plate.

3164. If the pitcher strikes out the first batter, the pitcher will lose.

3165. If a pitcher spits on a ball, the batter will miss it.

3166. If a pitcher finds a toad in the outfield just before he begins the game, he will win.

3167. It brings bad luck for the pitcher to step out of the box after he has thrown the first strike.

3168. It causes bad luck for a pitcher to sleep in the room of a losing pitcher.

3169. A ball team should not have its picture taken before a game.

3170. Some especially bad luck will come to you if you are put out on third base.

3171. To change a baseball locker will bring bad luck.

3172. It brings good luck to pass a hay wagon on the day of a baseball game, if you will tip your hat to it.

3173. It is well for a ball-player to see a load of empty beer barrels while he is on his way to the ball park.

3174. If your hand itches while you are playing baseball, you will catch the next foul ball.

3175. The placing of a black piece of cloth in the dugout of the opposing team, will bring victory to your team.

3176. To use the locker of a great baseball player will bring good luck.

3177. The seventh inning in baseball will be lucky for one of the two opposing baseball teams.

3178. It is bad luck for the batter to try to watch the catcher's signal.

3179. The home team should not permit the visiting team to sit on the bench.

3180. If a towel that you hang up in a dressing room before a ball game remains and is untouched, you will win.

3181. If a baseball player sees a cross-eyed woman in the grandstand, he will not get a hit that day.

3182. The team that loses first blood in football, will lose the game.

3183. To play a game in a new or a clean uniform is unlucky.

3184. A common saying among fishermen is:
"Wind from the south, hook in the mouth,
Wind from the east, bite the least;
Wind from the north, further off;
Wind from the west, bite the best."

3185. Fish bite best when dogwood is in bloom.

3186. Fish will not bite when it is thundering.

3187. When it thunders, the time is favorable to fish for cat fish ....Mountain

3188. Spit on your fishing-bait for luck.

3189. In fishing, you would do well to spit on your bait three times.

3190. Chew sweet enice and spit on your hook for luck at fishing.

3191. It causes good luck when you are fishing to throw

out on dry land a leaf that has been caught in the water.

3192. If you stick your hand with a fish's fin, you will catch nothing more.

3193. To carry a fishing pole into the house will prevent your catching anything.

3194. It is unlucky to change poles, while you are fishing.

3195. If you let the end of a pole touch the water, you will catch no fish.

3196. In fishing, if you step over the fishing pole, you will catch no fish.

3197. If you curse while you are fishing, the fish will not bite ....Mountains

3198. It causes bad luck to change hooks while you are fishing.

3199. If you let another person get fishing bait from your bait can, you will have no luck........Mountains

3200. If you catch a fish in the eye, you will not catch any more that day....................Mountains

3201. If when you go fishing you turn the first fish caught back into the water, you will have bad luck.

3202. It causes bad luck to cross lines in fishing.

3203. If some one steps over your fishing line, you will have bad luck.

3204. It brings bad luck to take a dog with you on a fishing trip, for you will catch no fish.

3205. If when you go fishing a rabbit crosses your path, you will catch no fish.[1]

3206. If in falling weather chickens do not seek shelter but walk about, you may go hunting with assur-

[1] For fishing in connection with the signs of the zodiac, see the chapter on "The Moon and Signs of the Zodiac," numbers 2290-2292.

ance, as birds will also be out...Central Kentucky

3207. When you leave the house on a hunting or fishing expedition, kick off your right shoe. This act will bring good luck.

3208. To have good luck in hunting, you should shoot your gun once before you leave your yard........ ....Blue Grass

3209. A hunter will encounter bad luck if he turns back after he has entered a wood.

3210. If two hunters cross different panels of fence, bad luck will follow.

3211. When you are hunting, you may change your luck by turning the back of your hat to the front.

3212. If you drop a gun, you will have an accident five nights afterward ....Mountains

3213. If you shoot a gun against a tree when the bark is frozen, the shot will come back and kill you.

3214. Do not let your hunting gun be out of your possession over night during the hunting season.

3215. If a horse refuses to drink before a race, he will win ....Blue Grass

3216. To keep a goat in the stall of a race-horse will bring good luck.........................Blue Grass

3217. If a jockey turns his cap around backwards, he will not win.........................Blue Grass

3218. Odd days are lucky for bets on horse-races....... ....Blue Grass

3219. It is disastrous to bet on horse-races on even days.

3220. If you will give a needy person money before you go to the races, you will win your bets.

3221. To touch a hunch-back will bring good luck at horse-races.

3222. It brings bad luck to bet on a gray horse in a horse-race.

3223. If anyone "crosses your luck," as in boys' outdoor games, you will be unsuccessful.

3224. If a prize fighter sees a load of empty barrels on the day of a fight, he will lose.

3225. To spit on one's hands before a fight is lucky.

3226. A girl skipping a rope says:
"Mother, mother, I am sick.
Send for the doctor, quick, quick.
Doctor, doctor, shall I die?
Yes, my child, but don't you cry.
How many carriages shall I have?
One two, three," et cetera until she misses the rope
.... North-eastern Kentucky

3227. If a swing stops before you get out, you will die.

3228. After someone says, "Let the old cat die," it will cause bad luck to quicken the motion of the swing.

LUCK AT CARDS

3229. "Unlucky at cards, lucky at love."

3230. Walk around the table or a chair to change the luck.

3231. You will have good luck if you walk around the table three times during a card game.

3232. To change your luck at cards, turn the back of the chair to the table and sit astride.

3233. For luck at cards, spit into the bottom of your chair upturned.

3234. Break bad luck at cards by sitting on a handkerchief.

3235. For luck at cards, reverse the direction of dealing.

3236. It brings good luck to deal from a deck from which you have cut for deal.

3237. The reverse of the procedure mentioned in 3236 causes bad luck.

3238. For luck at cards, turn back the hem of your skirt.

3239. For luck at cards, turn up the bottom of a trouser leg.

3240. For luck at cards, remove a piece of jewelry.

3241. Change something in your pocket, to change your luck at cards.

3242. It is well for a card-player to carry the wish-bone of a chicken in his pocket.

3243. It is lucky for a card-player to carry the bone of a dead person in his pocket.

3244. For luck at cards, "milk" the deck, that is, deal a card alternately from the top and from the bottom of the deck.

3245. To change luck at cards, change decks.

3246. Kiss a card good-bye for luck.

3247. It brings good luck to pick up your cards with the left hand.

3248. Gamblers have favorite good-luck pairs.

3249. It brings good luck to be the last to take up and look at your cards.

3250. It brings bad luck to have the last card dealt to you.

3251. It brings bad luck to pick up cards one at a time.

3252. If you start in with bad luck, stop, for it will grow worse.

3253. It brings bad luck to play cards any place near where a murder has been committed.

3254. It brings bad luck to play cards across the grain of a table.

3255. In a game of cards if you drop a number of the cards, you will lose so many games.

3256. It brings bad luck to fumble the deal.

3257. Do not cut your opponent's deal when you are winning, as your luck will likely change.

3258. When the ace and the two, three, and four spots make a trick, the winner should kiss the dealer for good luck.

3259. When the ace and the two, three, and four spots make a trick, all should kiss the dealer for good luck.

3260. If in picking up dice you drop one, you will lose, for you have lost your leader.

3261. Never lend a betting opponent money. Never bet against your own money.

ANIMALS, BIRDS, REPTILES, INSECTS

3262. Animals can see haunts or spirits.

3263. Animals can talk on New Year's Eve.

3264. It is a bad omen for an animal to die in one's hand.

3265. If you see a dead animal, spit over your little finger, so that you may avoid bad luck.

3266. All men come back as animals.

3267. To run an animal before you kill it will make the meat tender.

3268. The crossing of a black cat in front of you will bring bad luck.

3269. When a black cat passes in front of you, spit, to avert bad luck.

3270. It brings good luck for a black cat to cross your path to the right....................Blue Grass

3271. It brings bad luck for a black cat to cross your path to the left.....................Blue Grass

3272. Avert the bad luck incident to the crossing of a cat or a rabbit before you by pulling out a thread and throwing it from you—on the left or the right side, according to the animal's position.....Mountains

3273. When a black cat runs in front of you, take off your cap and spit into it, to avert bad luck...Mountains

3274. If a cat crosses your path, you will have bad luck, unless you turn around three times and spit on your little finger.

3275. If a black cat crosses your path, turn around three times to avert bad luck.

3276. It brings good luck to have two cats or two rabbits cross your path at night.......Western Kentucky

3277. It is a bad-luck sign to have a black cat follow you after night.

3278. A black cat seen on the morning of an accident is a sign of warning.

3279. If a black cat takes up its abode at a house, the unmarried daughters will have a good chance to marry.

3280. If a black cat is kept in the family, the girls will never marry................Southern Kentucky

3281. If a yellow cat passing in front of your path turns over, you may expect bad luck........Mountains

3282. If you spit on the floor or the ground and a cat goes near your saliva, you will die...Central Kentucky

3283. It causes bad luck for a cat to sleep with you.....
.... Mountains

3284. A cat on the front porch brings bad luck to the housekeeper.

3285. To kill a cat will bring seven years of bad luck.

3286. If you kill a cat, it will haunt you all your life.

3287. If you kill a black cat, you will see the Devil before you see another black cat.

3288. It brings bad luck for a man with a family to drown cats . . . . Southern Kentucky

3289. A cat you kill in any way except by drowning will not hurt you, but if you drown one, the cat's ghost will come at night and suck your breath . . . .
. . . . Central Kentucky

3290. It causes good luck to kill a cat in a graveyard either at midnight or on a moonlight night.

3291. It causes bad luck to cut off a black cat's tail.

3292. If you step on a black cat's tail, you will be an old maid . . . . Western Kentucky

3293. You will have bad luck if you step on a cat's tail.

3294. It causes bad luck to drive off a cat.

3295. If a cat approaches you kindly, you have a good disposition.

3296. If a cat raises its fur at you, you have a bad disposition.

3297. You will have good luck if a cat or a dog follows you home.

3298. It causes bad luck to move a cat.

3299. It will bring good luck to take a cat to a new house.

3300. If a cat gets on a table, you will have bad luck.

3301. If a street-car runs over a cat, it will also run over a person that day.

3302. If a cat turns over so that its head is away from the fire, someone is coming.

3303. If the cat washes its face in the house, someone is coming.

3304. If a cat washes its face in the door, someone is coming.

3305. The first person that a cat looks toward after washing its face will be the next to marry.

3306. To hear a cat whine at twelve o'clock is a sign of death.

3307. It is a sign of a death in the family for a cat to mew three times at midnight on two or three consecutive nights.

3308. If a cat scratches you, you may look for a disappointment.

3309. If a cat looks into a mirror, there will be a death.

3310. A cat can cause the death of a sleeping person or a sick child by sucking the breath.

3311. A cat has seven lives.

3312. A cat has nine lives.

3313. A cat draws lightning.

3314. If you put cream on your face and let a cat lick it off you will have a heavy beard.......Mountains

3315. If two cats fight for a long time, somebody will have a fight nearby................Central Kentucky

3316. A cat will feed on the flesh of a dead person.

3317. It brings good luck to have a white cat come to your house.

3318. It causes good luck to meet or pass a drove of cattle.

3319. If many of your stock suffer from an epidemic, someone in your family will have an accident or will die ....Mountains

3320. Blood in the cow's milk is a sign of a death in the family.

3321. To shoot a cow brings bad luck.

3322. If a cow falls down, she will die.

3323. If a cow falls down, she will die within a week....
..........................Southern Kentucky

3324. If a cow lows in front of your door, you may expect a death.

3325. If a cow lows over your gate, there will be a death.

3326. A cow's lowing between seven and eight o'clock in the morning is the sign of a death in the family...
........................Northern Kentucky

3327. If a cow's low is heard after dark, there will be a death in the family before the next Wednesday night.

3328. If you move from one city to another and take a cow with you, you will have bad luck.

3329. It is thought that a cow may lose its cud. It does not. Indigestion may prevent the stomach from supplying the cud.

3330. The common belief that cows sometimes have an ailment called hollow horn is a superstition. That is, it is thought that a certain disease will produce hollow horn.

3331. The birth of twin calves is a sign of a death in the family ....North-eastern Kentucky

3332. If you milk a cow on the ground, it will go dry.

3333. If a cow steps over a milk bucket, milk-weed will grow at that place..................Mountains

3334. If you can see the reflection of a calf hoof in a glass of milk, it is pure, that is, free from water.

3335. Butter will come easily all the year if the milk which is milked in April is not mixed with that which is milked in May......................Mountains

3336. When you churn, if the butter does not gather, whip the churn.

3337. If you look into a churn of milk, you will be bald-headed......................Central Kentucky

3338. If a dog points his nose toward you and howls at midnight, you will soon be killed.

3339. When a dog howls without any apparent reason, bad luck may be expected.

3340. There will be a death in the family if a dog howls at night (or some say, at midnight).

3341. The disaster of death presaged by the howl of a dog at night (or according to some, at midnight) may be averted by turning an old shoe upside down.

3342. If a watch dog barks three times when you are pulling it in, you will die.................Blue Grass

3343. If a dog howls twice at night, a woman will die.

3344. If a dog howls three times at night, a man will die.

3345. A dog's howling in a doorway or beneath a window means death.

3346. If a dog howls with his head down, there will be a death. If he howls with his head raised, there will be a fire.

3347. If a dog howls, turn over a shoe; the howling will stop and the danger will be averted.

3348. It causes bad luck, if on your way to a funeral, you meet a dog with hydrophobia.........Mountains

3349. If a dog lies on his back and scratches, expect a death.

3350. If a dog stretches himself out on the ground, he is measuring a grave.

3351. If a dog crawls on his belly and moans, he is measuring his master's grave.

3352. If a dog turns over to scratch his back with his head down hill, there will be a death.

3353. If a dog lies down with his tail toward the house,

and then gets up and shakes, there is a woman coming.

3354. If a dog lies down with his tail toward the house, a man is coming.

3355. If a dog lies down with his head out of a door, some one will leave the family soon (by marriage, death or otherwise) ....Southern Kentucky

3356. When a dog rolls over, gets up, and shakes himself, from the direction that he faces a visitor will come.

3357. Never let a dog see himself in the mirror, for he will die....................Northern Kentucky

3358. You will have bad luck if a stray dog comes to you.

3359. To be followed by a strange dog brings good luck.

3360. If you do not take your clothes from the clothes line and wash them again after a dog has run under them, some one of your family will die........
............................Central Kentucky

3361. If as you start anywhere a dog growls in your path, you will do better to go back, as you will have bad luck on your journey.........Western Kentucky

3362. If you come upon a dog that is attending to a call of nature, you will have bad luck......Mountains

3363. To prevent a dog from causing you bad luck in accordance with the last sign noted, join your two little fingers until you have passed him.

3364. It brings bad luck to sell a dog.

3365. It brings bad luck to kill a young dog.

3366. If you kill a dog, its spirit will haunt you.

3367. To keep a dog at home, cut off the tip of his tail and place it under the doorstep.

3368. If you pull three hairs from a dog's tail and put

them under the doorstep, he will not stray from home.

3369. To keep a dog from running away, measure his tail with a stick, cut off the hair that sticks out at the end, and bury the stick and the hair under the doorstep.

3370. Keep a bird dog from leaving by taking hairs from his tail, splitting a stick, placing the hairs in the cleft, and burying the stick beneath the doorstep.

3371. If you put a piece of meat into your shoe, wear it for a time, and then give it to a dog, he will follow you.

3372. Feed a dog gun-powder and raw meat, to make him savage.

3373. A bob-tailed dog cannot walk a log without falling .... Mountains

3374. A dog with a large posterior part will be a good hunter .... Mountains

3375. If a dog's posterior part is black, he is a good raccoon dog......................... Mountains

3376. If any one steps over a dog, the animal will not grow any more.

3377. If a dog licks the blood of a dead man, he will go mad .... Mountains

3378. A dog with dew-claws will not go mad.

3379. If a dog groans in his sleep, he is dreaming.

3380. If you cut a lock of dog's hair and put it under your pillow, you will dream what the dog has dreamed .... Southern Kentucky

3381. If you slip a hat under the head of a sleeping dog, his dream will come to you the following night....
.... Mountains

3382. If you sleep on the same pillow which a dog has slept on, you will dream the same dream the dog has had................North-eastern Kentucky

3383. When a dog smiles in his sleep, he is dreaming of heaven.

3384. If you see a dog chase a cat up a weeping willow, your sorrows are up a tree, that is, are over......
..................................Blue Grass

3385. A big dog barks but will not bite; a little dog will bite but does not bark much. Hence the stanza of "Sourwood Mountain"—

 Big dog bark an' little un bite you,
  Hey-ho diddle-um-di-ay!'
 Big girl court an' little un slight you,
  Hey-ho diddle-um-di-ay! ....Mountains

3386. Bad dogs are afraid of mean people.....Negroes

3387. Keep goats on a horse farm. If the goats do well, the horses will do well..............Blue Grass

3388. Keep a goat among horses or cattle. Its presence will avert disease...................Blue Grass

3389. If a goat that is kept in a stall with a horse is taken out, something unfortunate will happen to the horse ....Blue Grass

3390. If a ground hog comes to the house, there will be a death.

3391. If a hog is born without a tail, it will require one fewer barrel to become fat on.

3392. It brings bad luck to pass a drove of hogs.

3393. It causes bad luck to give a hog away or to receive one as a gift.......................Mountains

3394. If hogs are fed on beechnuts, the meat will be all fat.......................Western Kentucky

3395. Hogs fed on apples make the sweetest meat......
...........................Western Kentucky

3396. When a hog that has been killed and hung on a tree falls, someone who has taken part in the killing will die soon.

3397. It brings good luck to carry the wisdom tooth of a hog.

3398. Hogs can see the wind.

3399. If when you kill a hog, you put water from his eye into yours, you will be able to see the wind.

3400. If you drink a sow's milk, you will be able to see the wind.

3401. It brings good luck to meet or pass a drove of horses.

3402. If a horse snorts at night, a stranger is near.

3403. The death of a horse is ominous.

3404. If a horse balks at night, he sees a haunt.

3405. A horse can see ghosts. If you place your head between his ears, you may see them also..Blue Grass

3406. It causes bad luck to remove a shoe from the hoof of a dead horse.

3407. It causes bad luck to take the shoes off a dead horse and put them on another horse. He will not live long.

3408. A horse draws lightning.

3409. It brings good luck to change a horse's name after he has changed hands in a trade. Western Kentucky

3410. If a horse in wallowing turns over, he is worth one hundred dollars.

3411. The significance of white feet on horses is thus given:
"One white foot, buy him,

Two white feet, try him,
Three white feet, deny him."

3412. Another version of the significance of white feet on horses is this:
"One white foot, buy him,
Two white feet, try him,
Three white feet, look well about him,
(that is, be suspicious about him)
Four white feet, do without him."

3413. Some horses are moon-eyed, that is, affected by the moon. They become almost blind in the full moon.

3414. A filly cannot win the Kentucky Derby. This tradition was broken in 1915.

3415. If a double-team horse or mule wagon passes you, you will have bad luck.

3416. If you count one hundred white horses, you will find some money. If you stamp one hundred white horses, you will find a bag of gold.

3417. You will have good luck if you stamp one hundred white horses. (To "stamp" is to indicate each unit in counting by wetting one hand with saliva and striking it with the other hand.)

3418. If you count one hundred white horses, someone in the family will die.

3419. If one counts one hundred and fifty horses, he will find something of value.

3420. If you see a white horse, you will get money the same week.

3421. To see a white or gray horse indicates the coming of bad luck.

3422. Spit between two fingers, then you will not have bad luck when you see a white horse.

3423. If you see a white horse, look for a red-headed man.

3424. If you see a white horse, you will meet a red-headed girl.

3425. To see a white horse turning a corner and see a red-headed girl coming up the street, brings good luck.

3426. If you see a white horse and look over your left shoulder, you will see the Devil.

3427. When you see a white horse say,
"Lippity, lippity, white horse;
When you have good luck bring it to me."
You will then have good luck.

3428. A horseshoe hung up inverted, brings good luck.

3429. It brings good luck to find a horseshoe with the points towards you and to hang it up.

3430. For good luck, spit on a horseshoe and throw it away without watching to see where it goes.

3431. If you find a horseshoe, spit through it and throw it over your left shoulder for good luck.

3432. If you spit on one side of a horseshoe, toss it up, and have the side you spit on turn up, you will have good luck.

3433. If you find a horseshoe on a fence, or see one on a fence, it will bring you good luck.

3434. It causes bad luck to pick up a broken horseshoe.

3435. It causes bad luck to pass a horseshoe without picking it up and hanging it up.

3436. He that takes down a horseshoe that has been hung up will be hung up in place of it......Blue Grass

3437. If you count the number of holes in a horseshoe that you have found, you will have so many years of good luck.

3438. One horseshoe under the door-step and one in the

255

fire will keep the hawks away from your chickens.

3439. If you hang a horseshoe on the andiron, the hawks will not catch your chickens.

3440. To keep hawks away from the chickens, have a horseshoe in your stove or in your fireplace.

3441. If you put some shining brass over a horseshoe, you can thus keep off the hawks from your chickens.

3442. Good luck comes from carrying a horseshoe nail in the pocket.

3443. Put horseshoe nails into the cooking stove to keep the hawks from catching the chickens.

3444. Put a horse hair into a bottle of water. After seven (or nine) days it will become a snake.

3445. If you kill a mule, you will have sixteen years of bad luck.

3446. If a mule turns over once, it is worth one hundred dollars.

3447. If a mule turns over twice, it is worth two hundred dollars.

3448. If a mule turns over, it is worth two hundred and fifty dollars.

3449. A mule that cannot turn over is not worth fifty dollars.

3450. To pick up a coin in a mule's track, will bring good luck.

3451. It brings very good luck to stamp all the gray mules you see and all the gray horses.

3452. It causes bad luck to see a gray mule six times.

3453. If you stamp one hundred gray mules, you will have good luck.

3454. If you see a white mule, you will see a red-haired negro.

3455. Mean negroes return after death as mules.

3456. All bricklayers will turn to gray mules when they die.......................Western Kentucky

3457. A muleshoe is a sign of bad luck. Do not keep one.

3458. A white mule will never die.

Whoever saw a dead gray mule or a poacher's grave?

3459. It brings bad luck for a rabbit to cross your path.

3460. To avert the bad luck attending the crossing of his path by a rabbit, the traveler must go back and start over.

3461. It brings bad luck for a rabbit to cross in front of you from right to left.

3462. If a rabbit crosses your path from right to left, be careful not to walk in the dark for three days.

3463. It causes good luck for a rabbit to cross before you from left to right.

3464. If a rabbit crosses the road from right to left in front of you, pull a hair out of your head, to change the bad luck to good.

3465. Avert the bad luck of a rabbit's crossing the road to your left by going to where it crossed, making a cross and spitting into it.

3466. It is well to kill the first rabbit you see in the winter .... Mountains

3467. If you see two white rabbits at night, there will be a death in the family.........Western Kentucky

3468. You will have good luck if you wear the left hind leg of a graveyard rabbit, shot by a red-headed, cross-eyed negro in the dark of the moon.

3469. The good luck rabbit's foot is the left hind foot of

a rabbit, killed in a graveyard at midnight, with a stick ten feet long.

3470. If you kill a rabbit in the light of the new moon and carry its foot around your neck, you will have good luck.

3471. The left hind foot of a rabbit shot in a graveyard at midnight in the dark of the moon with a bullet made out of a quarter found in a horse's track, will bring good luck.

3472. If you will get the left hind foot of a graveyard rabbit on a rainy Friday night, you will have good luck.

3473. You will have bad luck if you touch the left hind foot of a rabbit which has been killed at midnight in a cemetery on Friday, the thirteenth day of the month, by a cross-eyed negro.

3474. If one carries the ear of a jack-rabbit in his pocket, good luck will come.

3475. When you shiver without cause, a rabbit is stepping over your grave.

3476. If a rat cuts your clothes, it brings bad luck to mend the garment yourself.

3477. If a mouse or a rat gnaws your clothes, expect a death or a disaster.

3478. If a mouse eats your clothes, you will never live to wear them out.

3479. When rats increase in great numbers, a war is imminent .... Central Kentucky

3480. If a rat runs up inside the clock, your dog will die.

3481. If you can auctioneer off a rat killed on your place, all the rats will go to the buyer. (You must receive some compensation.)

3482. Singe the hairs of a rat and turn it loose; the rest of the rats will leave................Negroes

3483. If the inmates of a rat-infested house will write the name of some person on a piece of paper, well greased with lard, and put it where the rats will get it, telling them where they will find a better larder, they will forsake this house and go to that mentioned in the paper.......Western Kentucky

3484. To catch two mice in one trap brings bad luck.

3485. Rats abandon a doomed boat or a falling house.

3486. If when you open a drawer a rat runs out, you will have good luck.

3487. It causes bad luck to cross through sheep.........
....................North-eastern Kentucky

3488. To make an old ewe own her lamb, take the lamb by the feet and rub his back against her stomach. She will claim it..............Central Kentucky

3489. You will have good luck if a squirrel crosses the road in front of you.........Southern Kentucky

3490. It causes bad luck for a squirrel to cross your path
......................Western Kentucky

3491. If a ground squirrel that you are looking at goes to the right, you will know your lesson.

3492. If a ground squirrel that a schoolboy or girl is looking at goes to the left, the child will miss his lesson.

3493. A flying squirrel will always bark when he sees a ghost ....Western Kentucky

3494. It brings good luck to have a terrapin or mud turtle in your garden......................Mountain

3495. If you kill a toad, there will be rain.

3496. To kill a toad will bring bad luck.

3497. If you kill a toad, some of your family will die before the year is out.

3498. If you kill a toad, your cow will go dry.

3499. If you kill a toad, your cow will give bloody milk.

3500. By throwing a toad into a pond, you will cause the cows to give bloody milk.

3501. If you kill a toad, you will stump your toe.

3502. If you see a toad, you will stump your toe.

3503. If you do not spit when you see a toad, you will be sure to have a wart.

3504. If you bury a toad alive, you will see spirits......
   ....Mountains
   (Contributed in this form: "If you Beary a frog and hit alive youl see hants.")

3505. At two o'clock on the first Thursday in July, toads turn pink in color. At half past two they regain their natural color.

3506. Carry the jawbone of a tree toad for luck—for example to keep out of jail.............Mountains

3507. Kill a tree toad. Put the head in a snuffbox until ants have eaten the flesh away. Break the lower jawbone into two parts. Put the right half into your clothes and the left half, which has a burr on it, into the hem of a woman's garment. She will not be able to get away from you......Mountains

3508. If you kill a tortoise, it will sleep on your neck the next night ....Mountains

3509. You will have bad luck if a bird lights in your path
   ....Mountains

3510. If birds make nests of your discarded hair, your hair will tangle.

3511. If birds make nests of your discarded hair, you may expect headache.

3512. If birds make nests of your discarded hair, you will die before next spring.

3513. If birds make nests of your discarded hair, you will become insane.

3514. If a bird flies against your window, you will receive a message.

3515. Birds flying against your window bring bad luck.

3516. A bird that flies into a house brings bad luck with it.

3517. If a bird comes into a room in which you happen to be and you speak before you get it out, you will suffer ill luck......................Mountains

3518. The flying of a bird into the house is a sign of death.

3519. When a bird comes into the house and a picture falls down at the same time, a death will occur in the family ....Blue Grass

3520. If a bird of any kind flies into a sick room and lights on the bed post where the sick one is lying, there will be a death in the family in a short time......
..........................Western Kentucky

3521. If a bird in the house injures itself, there will be a death ....North-eastern Kentucky

3522. If a bird comes into the house and lights on the stove, the building will be burned......Mountains

3523. The flying of birds around the house is a sign of visitors ....Western Kentucky

3524. If you put salt on a bird's tail, you may marry any one that you desire.

3525. You will have bad luck if you break a bird's egg.

3526. If you throw a piece of feather over a house, you will find a sack of gold where it falls..Mountains

3527. It brings bad luck to have a blackbird fly across your path. You will have bad luck before you arrive at your destination..............Mountains

3528. To eat chicken feet makes one beautiful.

3529. Go behind the door and eat a chicken foot, to become beautiful.

3530. To become beautiful, eat chicken gizzards.

3531. To become beautiful, swallow a chicken gizzard whole.

3532. To swallow a raw chicken-heart brings good luck.

3533. It brings good luck to have a ten-toed chicken....
................................Blue Grass

3534. Hens will not lay in a field where there are potatoes.

3535. If you set hens in the afternoon, you will have bad luck ....Mountains

3536. If a hen is set after the sun goes down, all the eggs will hatch..................Central Kentucky

3537. It is well to set an odd number of eggs.

3538. If you carry eggs for setting to the nest in a bucket, they will all hatch roosters. If you carry the eggs to the nest in a basket, they will all hatch pullets
.........................Western Kentucky

3539. If you place the eggs under a sitting hen with the left hand, they will hatch hens; with the right hand, roosters.........................Blue Grass

3540. If you set a hen on thirteen eggs, she will not hatch so well as on another number..Western Kentucky

3541. If after the chickens begin to hatch, you put the shells up higher than the chickens can jump, the hawks will not catch the chickens......Mountains

3542. To keep an old hen from sitting, put her head under

her wing and dip her into a tub of water three times.
She will not sit again.........Central Kentucky

3543. If a chicken is hatched in the spring, it will lay only
every second day. If it is hatched in the fall, it
will lay every day...................Mountains

3544. Chickens hatched in June are said to sleep all the
time.

3545. It is unlucky to bring in or take out eggs after dark.

3546. String eggshells on the twigs of trees to keep the
hawks away ....Mountains

3547. Bake eggshells and feed them to chickens to make
them lay.................Southern Kentucky

3548. It causes bad luck to find a soft-shelled egg.

3549. You can avert the bad luck that a soft-shelled egg
brings by throwing it over the house.

3550. The general cackling of hens is a prophecy of bad
luck.............................Blue Grass

3551. A "bullrock," also called a "jackrock" (a small
round rock), in the ashes keeps hawks away from
chickens.

3552. A round rock in the fire will cause a hawk's claws to
draw up to that shape, so that it cannot catch chickens.

3553. Put an Indian arrow into the chimney to keep off
hawks.

3554. Any kind of flint rock in the chimney will keep off
hawks.

3555. To keep a hawk off your chickens, carry a hawk
rock in your pocket.

3556. A bottle half-full of water tied on a pole will keep
away the hawks[1]....................Mountains

[1] For other signs for keeping hawks away, see numbers 3438-3443.

3557. If hawks attack chickens, keep a poker in the fire until it is red hot; then take it out and make a young girl tell you her sweetheart's name. The hawks will vanish.

3558. If a cock crows before the door early in the day, a visitor will arrive.

3559. If a rooster looks in at the door and crows, someone will leave the family............Mountains.

3560. If a rooster looks out of the door, someone is coming into the family.

3561. If a rooster crows before breakfast, someone will come before supper.

3562. If a rooster crows before breakfast, you will have visitors before you sleep.

3563. A cock's crowing in the front door brings a guest.

3564. If a rooster crows while looking in at the door, expect a stranger the next day.

3565. Someone is coming if a rooster crows. He will come from the direction in which the rooster's tail points.

3566. If a rooster crows in the kitchen, a tramp is coming.

3567. If a cock crows before your door, there will be a death in the neighborhood.

3568. If a rooster crows three times in the door, a death will follow.

3569. If a rooster crows on a fence with his head turned toward the house, welcome guests will arrive.... .... Mountains

3570. If a rooster crows on a fence with his head turned away from the house, unwelcome guests may be expected ....Mountains

3571. When a rooster crows with his head turned toward

the door, there will be an increase in the family...
.... Mountains

3572. When a rooster crows with his head from the door, there will be a decrease in the family...Mountains

3573. The presence of chickens on the porch indicates the arrival of a large amount of company.

3574. If your neighbor's rooster whips your rooster, your chickens will not do well.

3575. If a rooster crows in the back-yard, a man will come.

3576. A cock's crowing in the back door brings a servant visitor.

3577. If a rooster jumps upon a fence and crows, someone is coming.

3578. When a rooster crows at night, expect company the next day.

3579. If two roosters fight, a man is coming.

3580. If two hens fight, expect two women. If one hen is dark and the other light, one woman will wear dark and the other light clothes.

3581. If two hens fight in the door, two women are coming.

3582. If two old hens are fighting, two old women are coming soon.

3583. If a rooster crows before ten o'clock at night, bad news may be expected.

3584. When a rooster crows at noon, hasty news in the neighborhood may be expected. Louisville Negroes

3585. If a rooster crows at a certain time in the night, you will hear hurried news.

3586. If a rooster crows about dusk, you will hear unexpected news.

3587. It is a sign of bad luck when a rooster goes crowing to roost.

3588. If a cock crows on the roost, someone in the family will die.

3589. If the cocks crow on the roost, you will hear bad news of some one of your relatives.

3590. If a rooster begins to crow about nine o'clock at night, it will turn cold.

3591. If a rooster crows before midnight, there will be a fire.

3592. A rooster's crowing at night, except at Christmas time, is a sign of bad luck.

3593. There will be bad luck in the family if a rooster crows on the steps on Sunday, unless he is killed at once ....Mountains

3594. Should you find a feather in your hair in the morning, you will get a whipping..........Blue Grass

3595. "A whistling woman or a crowing hen, never comes to a very good end."

3596. "A woman that whistles or a hen that crows, has her way wherever she goes."

3597. When a hen crows in the door, someone in the family will die.

3598. A crowing hen must be put to death; otherwise death in the family or other bad luck will follow.

3599. It is a very bad omen for a chicken to die in one's hand.

3600. It is disastrous to let the chicken head die in your hand when a chicken is killed.

3601. If you pull a bunch of feathers from the back of a chicken's head before you wring its neck, it will not flop............................Mountains

3602. To make a chicken die quietly after you have wrung its neck, pluck three feathers from its breast......
.... Mountains

3603. After wringing a chicken's neck, pull some feathers from its back and put them on its breast, to make it die quietly.

3604. A black chicken's meat is coarser than that of other chickens.

3605. The scratching of a gray chicken under a window means bad luck.

3606. If on your way to a funeral, you meet a white chicken, you will have bad luck.

3607. A turtle-dove's cry on the first day of the year means a good crop year....... Western Kentucky

3608. The flying of a turtle-dove over a house portends death in the family.

3609. If a turtle-dove comes into the room, there will be a death before the week is out........ Mountains

3610. If you hear a turtle-dove call as you are going up a hill, you will have bad luck the rest of the year....
.... Southern Kentucky

3611. If you kill a turtle-dove, you will have a boil, carbuncle, or other skin eruption.

3612. It is a sign of death to see two turtle-doves in a tree .... Blue Grass

3613. If you see a white turtle-dove before breakfast, your father will die very soon............. Mountains

3614. If a duck comes into your kitchen, you will never starve .... Blue Grass

3615. Wild geese flying south make the initials of each state through which they pass........... Negroes

3616. It brings good luck to pass a flock of geese.

3617. If an owl hoots, someone will die.

3618. If an owl hoots on the top of a house, there will be a death in that household.

3619. It brings bad luck to imitate the hoot of an owl...
...................................Blue Grass

3620. If an owl hoots at the door for three successive nights, the sound foretells a death in the house.

3621. An owl's hoot about midnight is a sign that a member of the family will meet with an accident.

3622. Tie a knot in your dress or skirt to stop an owl's hoot.

3623. Avert the disaster of an owl's hooting by turning an old shoe upside down.

3624. To make an owl stop hooting, take off your left shoe and turn it over.

3625. An owl will stop hooting if you pull your shoes off and cross them.

3626. To stop an owl from hooting, turn the toes of your shoes to touch the wall.

3627. To avert the disaster that follows the hoot of an owl, heat a poker until it is red hot.

3628. If you eat the lights of a partridge, you will have success in love.

3629. To hear a peacock cry or to see a peacock means bad luck.

3630. A peacock feather brought into a house will surely cause death.

3631. Do not put your hand into a pigeon's nest, for the pigeon will not come back.

3632. If a pigeon flies against the window, there will be a death in the household.

3633. The cooing of pigeons is a sign of death in the family to which they belong..........Blue Grass

3634. It causes bad luck to kill a raincrow.

3635. It brings bad luck to have a redbird fly across the road when you are out riding.

3636. You can avert the ill luck which the flying of a redbird across your path brings by turning the lap-apron over.................Southern Kentucky

3637. If a redbird flies across the road in front of you, you will get a letter.

3638. If a redbird crosses your path, going to the right, good luck will follow.

3639. If a redbird crosses your path, going to the left, bad luck will follow.

3640. If you see a redbird, you will get a letter.

3641. If a redbird comes into your house, the house will be burned ....Mountains

3642. It brings good luck to see a Kentucky Cardinal.

3643. If a redbird or a Kentucky Cardinal flies in front of your door, someone unexpected is coming.

3644. If you see a redbird in the morning, you will see one of your cousins before night......Mountains

3645. If you see a redbird on Saturday, your sweetheart is coming.

3646. The sight of a robin means that someone is coming.

3647. To kill a robin will bring bad luck.

3648. When you see a robin, spit on your fingers and stamp them with your fist; if you go through this operation a hundred times, you will find something ....Blue Grass

3649. If you put salt on a sparrow's tail, you may catch it.

3650. If a lone turkey-buzzard flies over the house, some-one is coming.

3651. If a turkey-buzzard flies close to the house, some-one will die........................Blue Grass

3652. If a turkey-buzzard is killed with a gun, the gun will soon burst and will never be of any more value ....Western Kentucky

3653. If a whippoorwill sings in a tree near the house, a death will follow.

3654. You will have bad luck if you kill a whippoorwill.. .... Mountains

3655. If a woodpecker picks on a tree in the immediate neighborhood of your house, expect a caller..... ....Blue Grass

3656. If a woodpecker is heard on or near the house, there will be a death.

3657. If a woodpecker pecks on the roof of a house, a person will die there soon.

3658. It brings bad luck to kill a wren.

3659. A wren building near a house brings good luck.

3660. If a bat flies into a house at night, there will be someone missing the next night.

3661. If a bat lights on one's head, it will stay there until there is thunder.

3662. You will have bad luck if you kill a bat.

3663. If a honey-bee flies before you, you will get a letter.

3664. A yellow honey-bee is a sign of good luck.

3665. A black honey-bee is a sign of death.

3666. It brings bad luck to sell a beehive; if you sell one, the contents of two hives will die.

3667. All of your bees will die if you count your bee hives.

3668. If you ring a bell while bees are swarming, you can

drown the orders of the kingbee or the lieutenants.

3669. When the head of the house dies, someone must go out to whisper his death to the bees; unless this precaution is taken, they will leave or die.......
.... Negroes

3670. If a butterfly comes into the house, a lady will call wearing a dress of the same color.

3671. If a butterfly comes into the porch, somebody is coming.

3672. If you bite a butterfly's head off, you will have a dress the color of its wings, or, as some believe, the color of the butterfly.

3673. It causes bad luck to pull a butterfly's wing off..
.... Mountains

3674. If a butterfly lights on you, you will get a new suit of clothes.

3675. It is a sign of good luck to have a butterfly light on your shoulder.

3676. Put some green pennyroyal in your pocket, to keep away chiggers .... Mountains

3677. When a crab bites one, it will not let go until there is thunder.

3678. If a crawfish catches your toes, it will hold on until there is thunder.

3679. To kill a cricket will cause bad luck.

3680. If you kill a cricket, the rest of the crickets will eat your clothes.

3681. If a cricket is killed, its mate will come and cut the socks or stockings of the killer.

3682. A cricket brings luck into a house.

3683. It brings bad luck for a cricket to crawl over a hoe
.... Mountains

3684. It brings good luck to hear a cricket singing after you go to bed at night.

3685. A doodle-bug will obey the following rhymed command, spoken at its hole:
"Doodle-bug, doodle-bug, come out of your hole,
If you don't I'll beat you as black as a mole."

3686. If you speak the following words at a doodle-bug's hole it will come up:
"Doodle-bug, doodle-bug, doodle-bug,
Jim fire's burning up."

3687. If after catching an eel you draw a circle around it, it cannot get out of the circle.

3688. If you put your initials on a terrapin's shell he will never leave your farm.

3689. If a firefly comes into the house, there will be one person more or one fewer the next day, that is, someone will go or someone will come.

3690. In firefly season, toads will eat fire.

3691. If you cut a fishing worm into pieces, each piece becomes a complete worm.

3692. If you kill a fly, ten flies will come to the funeral.

3693. If a fly flies around your face continually, a stranger wishes to meet you.

3694. If you kill a daddy-long-legs, the cows will go dry.

3695. If you kill a daddy-long legs, you will lose all your cows .... Mountains

3696. A white shell-shaped bone from the head of a fish brings good luck. In particular it prevents loss of money, if it is carried in the purse.

3697. If you speak the following couplet to a grasshopper, he will obey you:

"Spit tobacco-juice,
And I'll turn you loose."

3698. It brings bad luck to kill a lady-bug.

3699. A lady-bug will obey the following piece of advice, if it is whispered into its hole:
"Lady bug, lady bug,
Fly away home.
Your house is on fire;
Your children will burn."

3700. If you kill a spring lizard, your spring will go dry.

3701. Locusts come every seventeen years; if they have a W on the wing, it means, woe, war and want...
..........................Southern Kentucky

3702. The first louse found in a child's head, if cracked on a tin cup, will make a dancer of the child; on a song-book, a singer; on the Bible, a reader; on the child's head, a simpleton!...........Mountains

3703. To dream of head lice will bring money.

3704. A white moth flying is the spirit of a grandparent hovering near.

3705. If you knock down a mud-dauber's nest, you will break your dishes............Western Kentucky

3706. If you carry a piece of oyster shell in your pocket-book, you will have good luck always in the way of riches.................North-eastern Kentucky

3707. When you kill a snake, it will not die until sundown.

3708. If you put a coal on a snake's stomach, while it is awaiting sundown to die, its legs will come out, and it will walk.

3709. If a snake dies before sundown, there will be bad luck.

3710. If you spit into a snake's trail, the snake will die..
....................................Western Kentucky

3711. If you step on a dead snake, there will be sores on
your feet ....Mountains

3712. If you do not kill the first snake you see every year,
you will not overcome your enemies.

3713. If you find the first snake that you see in the spring
dead, your enemies are all conquered.

3714. If you kill a snake at mating time, its mate will
come to the body.

3715. If you kill a snake and hang it over a fence, you
will not see any more snakes that day..Blue Grass

3716. If you cut a snake into pieces and leave them together, the fragments will unite and crawl away.

3717. Snakes are blind in August.

3718. Snakes will not come about a garden where gourds
grow ....Western Kentucky

3719. Snakes may be kept off by the carrying of snake-
root.

3720. Black snakes suck cows.

3721. Keep a black snake with you, to drive away bad
luck ....Mountains

3722. If you kill a snake that has sucked a cow, the cow
will go dry.

3723. It causes bad luck to touch a rattlesnake skin.

3724. The rattles of a rattlesnake kept in a violin bring
good luck to the owner.......Western Kentucky

3725. If you receive rattle-snake rattles from someone,
you will come to no harm while that person is near
.... Mountains

3726. Snake dust (that is, the dust made by pulverizing

a dried snake), shaken into one's shoes, will poison one ....Negroes

3727. A "snake-doctor" (that is, a dragon-fly) warns snakes of danger and shows them the whereabouts of food.

3728. It causes bad luck to kill a dragon-fly.

3729. If a dragon-fly lights on your line while you are fishing, the fish will not bite.

3730. The crawling of a spider on you brings good luck.

3731. It causes bad luck to kill a spider found crawling on you.

3732. A spider at night brings good luck. Do not kill it.

3733. If a spider comes down in front of your face, you will get a letter. But if you kill the spider, you will not get the letter.

3734. If you catch a spider weaving its web downward, catch it in the palm of your hand and kill it. You will receive a letter.

3735. If a spider crawls on your head, a letter will come from the direction it is moving.

3736. If a spider weaves a web over your head, you will get a letter.

3737. If a spider lets a web down on your shoulder, you will get a letter.

3738. If a spider spins its thread in the doorway or in front of one's face, a welcome visitor may be expected.

3739. The crawling of a spider on your bed foretells the coming of a stranger.

3740. By killing a spider on your bed, you prevent the coming of a stranger.

3741. When a spider swings down from a web in front of

you, you will see a good friend whom you are not expecting.

3742. If a spider crawls up the door, a stranger is coming.

3743. "Where the spider-webs grow,
The beaus don't go."

3744. If a spider gets on your dress, you will have a new one.

3745. It is lucky to find a spider on your clothes. It spins your wealth.

3746. If a spider is hanging over your head, you will receive money.

3747. Carry a dead spider in your shoe for good luck.

3748. If you catch a spider on you, wrap it up and put it into your stocking for luck.

3749. If a spider spins a web in front of you, take it and put it into your pocket-book alive. It is supposed to bring you money.................Mountains

3750. It brings bad luck to kill a black spider..Blue Grass

3751. If there is a black spider on you, you will get a letter from a black-headed person.

3752. With every spider that you kill, you kill an enemy,

3753. A spider on a bride's trousseau brings good luck.

3754. It causes good luck to go through a spider-web.

3755. It is unlucky to see a spider spin his web from the ceiling at night.

3756. It brings good luck to see a spider spin his web from the ceiling in the morning.

3757. If you run into a cobweb, you will get a letter.....
.................................Blue Grass

3758. Brightly-colored spiders, lizards, snakes, and the like are poisonous...................Mountains

3759. All spiders and tarantulas are poisonous.

3760. It is firmly believed by the people of Leslie County, a mountain county, that President McKinley's name was written by spiders in their webs as a prophecy of his death................Mountains

3761. If you cut a tick's head off and bury its body with its back down, there will be rain........Mountains

3762. If you kill a turtle, it will not die until sundown.

3763. When a turtle bites, it will hold on until there is thunder.

3764. If a wasp flies into the house, it brings good luck for the family......................Mountains

3765. If you see a fever worm, you must spit on it over your left shoulder; otherwise you will have typhoid fever.

3766. When you see a fever worm, you must, to avert a fever, spit three times.

3767. It brings bad luck to kill a fever worm.

3768. If you sit in the sun and look at a yellow caterpillar, you will have a chill..........Western Kentucky

3769. If a measuring worm measures your whole length, you will die.

3770. If you find a measuring worm on your dress, suit, or hat, you will have a new one.

3771. If you see a thousand-legged worm, you will die, unless you spit or stamp your feet.....Mountains

3772. If a thousand-legged worm counts your teeth, you will die. Therefore close your mouth in the presence of one ....Mountains

WITCHES

3773. To become a witch, go to a mountain top at dawn, shoot through a handkerchief at the rising sun, curse Jehovah three times, and own the Devil as master. When you shoot through the handkerchief, blood will fall from it.........Mountains

3774. To become a witch: the candidate goes with the Devil to the top of the highest hill at sunrise nine successive days and curses God; the Devil then places one hand on the candidate's head and one on his feet, and receives the promise that all between his hands shall be devoted to his service. Mountains

3775. To become a witch, you shoot at the moon nine times with a silver bullet, cursing God each time .... Mountains

3776. You can become a witch by taking a spinning-wheel to the top of a hill, giving yourself up to the Devil, and waiting until the wheel begins to turn. The witches will then come to instruct you.. Mountains

3777. One who teaches witchcraft to more than three people will herself lose the power.........Mountains

3778. If a witch goes to church, she will sit with her back toward the minister.........Northern Kentucky

3779. If an old woman has but one tooth in her mouth, she is a witch......................Mountains

3780. A witch frequently takes the form of a black cat.

3781. When a witch is at her mischief, she is invisible to everybody except the person bewitched. Mountains

3782. A witch can kill a person or animal with a witch or hair ball, which is made by rolling a small bunch of hair from a squirrel, horse, or cow into a hard, round ball ....Mountains

3783. By rubbing a hand over a gun, a witch can put a "spell" on it, so that its shot will not hit anything .... Mountains

3784. A witch can put a "spell" on a dog, and thus make him back-track on a deer's trail. She rubs her hand over the dog........................Mountains

3785. If you find a small egg in a hen's nest, you will have trouble, for it is a witch-egg.............
...........................Northern Kentucky

3786. If a horse's mane is matted in the morning, the witches have ridden him during the night.

3787. If you ride your horse on the same day that you have found witch stirrups in his mane, he will throw you.

3788. Tie strands of a horse's mane or tail together, to keep off witches.

3789. Plait your horse's mane with corn shucks, to prevent witches from riding him..Western Kentucky

3790. Witches transfer milk from the victim's cow to their own cows ....Mountains

3791. A witch can obtain butter by merely squeezing the handle of an ordinary table fork.

3792. If you burn the wisp of the bushy part of a cow's tail, the animal will cease to be bewitched........
.... Mountains

3793. A bewitched cow is cured by the witch-doctor's taking some hair from the sick cow's back and boiling some of her milk over the fire into which the hair had been thrown....................Mountains

3794. If your cow is bewitched, shut the door, do not let her have anything to eat, and then milk her in silence without looking up............Mountains

3795. To free butter from a witch's control, put a horse-bridle over the churn........Blue Grass Negroes

3796. If the butter will not come, drop a red hot horseshoe into the milk to kill the witches; then the butter will come......................Mountains

3797. For bewitched milk, heat the filings from a horseshoe and put them into the milk. The butter will then come, and by next day something disastrous will happen to the witch that will establish her identity ....Mountains

3798. To avert a witch charm, put a spindle into the churn ....Mountains

3799. If butter will not come, put a hot poker into the churn. You will thus drive away witches.......
.... Mountains

3800. If the butter will not gather, put a dime into the bottom of the churn.................Mountains

3801. Money should be put into the churn to keep away witches ....Mountains

3802. To keep witches off, let some drops of the cow's milk fall on a piece of silver.........Mountains

3803. To keep witches off, keep a piece of silver in a glass of water and sprinkle the cow's back with the water every few days.........Western Kentucky

3804. When a cow is bewitched, the charm may be broken by cutting her tongue with a silver coin sharpened on a grindstone.....................Mountains

3805. Never go to bed with your shoes higher than your head, for if you do, the witches will be after you for three months....................Mountains

3806. If you are awake at eleven, you will see witches and black cats at twelve.................Mountains

3807. If a fire that you are attempting to make goes out three times, you are bewitched..Central Kentucky

3808. If a spider is consumed through falling into a lamp, witches are near....................Blue Grass

3809. The twitching of the eye is a sign that one is bewitched.

3810. If you step on a crack in a sidewalk, a witch will appear and seize you.

3811. It is unwise to keep egg shells because witches go to sea in them. Burn the shells.

3812. The witch-hazel leaf should not be plucked and carried about you. Witches conjure with it.

3813. A person that does not believe in witches cannot be bewitched.

3814. Witches cannot cross running water.

3815. Take a chew of tobacco to keep off the witches.... .... Mountains

3816. A piece of rattlesnake skin worn in the clothing keeps witches away..................Mountains

3817. One penny will prevent the witches from riding you ....Western Kentucky

3818. If you put a silver dollar under your head, the witches cannot trouble you...........Mountains

3819. A piece of silver in the pocket or a silver ring on the finger or on the horse's bridle will keep the witches away ....Mountains

3820. To keep off witches and evil spirits, you must take off your hat and turn it around.

3821. A negro with a rabbit foot, mounted on a white horse in the dark of the moon in a cemetery, will break a witch spell..................Mountains

3822. If a jack-o'-lantern gets on your back, it will ride you until morning. Avert this fate by turning your coat wrong side out.

3823. When you lie on the ground, draw circles around you with a willow fork, to keep off the witches.

3824. If when you see a bunch of hair near the door you fail to pick it up, the witches will overtake you before midnight .... Mountains

3825. A witch cannot step over a broom.

3826. Witches will not trouble you at night, if you sleep with a Bible under your head......... Mountains

3827. If you are troubled by witches, it is a good plan to sleep with a meal sifter over the face. When the witches come to worry you, they are compelled to pass back and forth through every mesh. By this time you will have had sufficient sleep and can get up..................... Western Kentucky

3828. If you han ga bread sifter on a door-knob at night, you will find witches in it the next morning....... .... Louisville Negroes

3829. Draw a picture of a witch that is tormenting you and shoot through it with a silver bullet.

3830. Get rid of a witch by shooting her picture over running water .... Mountains

3831. You may kill a witch by shooting at her picture over running water. If you shoot the picture under other conditions, you may break the charm but may not hurt the witch.............. Mountains

3832. If you are about to break a witch's charm by shooting her picture with a silver bullet, she can break the charm, provided she or a member of her family borrows anything from you or your family....... .... Mountains

3833. You can remove a witch's charm and also kill her by driving a nail through her picture near the heart,

and then by striking it once each day for nine days
.... Mountains

3834. You can break a witch's hold on you by boiling
ragweed in a pot, beating it all the time. She can
break the charm by borrowing from you or having
any of her family do so..............Mountains

3835. You can cure a bewitched person by removing daily
one twig from a bundle of nine willow twigs which
you have gathered...................Mountains

3836. If you are afflicted with witches, a hoodoo ball made
of gum and purchased with a piece of silver will
scare away the witches...North-eastern Kentucky

3837. To break the charm of a witch, spit on the brush end
of a broom, once for the witch and once for each
member of her family. Brush it down the rear of
the fireplace; then place the broom across the front
door. Finally send for her. She can do you no
further harm unless you give or lend her salt or
something else......................Mountains

3838. To drive off a witch, place a dime under the hearth
.... Mountains

3839. To remove a witch's hold on a person, cut the witch
out of the victim's leg...............Mountains

HOODOOS

3840. Hoodoo a person by putting a shoe with a dead rat
in it on his door step.........Western Kentucky

3841. To hoodoo a person, shake down dust on him
through a crack in the ceiling..Blue Grass Negroes

3842. To hoodoo anyone, put snake dust (that is, the dust
made by pulverizing a dried snake) into his shoes
.........................Blue Grass Negroes

3843. To hoodoo a person, put an old shoe full of red pepper under his house..North-eastern Kentucky

3844. To do harm to a person, take a lock of his hair, burn a part, throw a part to the wind, and bury a part.

3845. A hoodoo bag is a red flannel bag about six by four inches in size, containing a pinch of salt, a pod of red pepper, a rabbit's foot, a chicken spur, and some ashes. It must be "made in dead o' night, widout a spec' o' light." Central Kentucky Negroes

3846. A blue-gummed negro is dangerous. He has the hoodoo power.

3847. To keep a person from hoodooing you, wear red pepper in the heel of your shoe..................
............................Blue Grass Negroes

3848. Put red pepper in your shoe, to keep off a conjurer's work..........Central Kentucky Negroes

3849. If you wear a silver dime in your shoe, you cannot be hoodooed.................Louisville Negroes

3850. Wear a piece of silver about each ankle to keep from coming under the power of the hoodoo.....
....................Central Kentucky Negroes

3851. Negroes keep chickens with the feathers turned back the wrong way, to keep away the hoodoos...
.... Negroes

3852. Hoodoos can often be warded off by a change of the victim's home or room....................
....................Western Kentucky Negroes

3853. The victim of a hoodoo may break the charm by giving up a sweetheart or a lover.............
...................Western Kentucky Negroes

3854. To overcome a hoodoo, kill a scorpion, dry it by

smoking it, beat it to a powder, mix the powder with whiskey, and drink the mixture...........
.....................Central Kentucky Negroes

3855. Hoodoo doctors, as they are commonly called, are considered able to break hoodoo charms and also to cure illness ....Negroes

3856. A certain arrangement of sticks in a path that leads to a house may cause a hoodoo. A hoodoo doctor sometimes has all the sticks in such a path removed before he attempts to treat an illness that is due to a hoodoo..........Central Kentucky Negroes

3857. If anything is placed in a so-called conjuration hand, the hand will move in such a way as to indicate whether good or bad luck will follow........
...........................Louisville Negroes

3858. Negroes are said to be able to find "hoodoo tracks" in ashes of the fire, which show that some kind of disaster is coming to the house..........Negroes

HAUNTED HOUSES, GHOSTS, EVIL SPIRITS

3859. Almost every community has a house which the credulous believe to be haunted.

3860. If a picture falls off the wall, the house is haunted
....................Central Kentucky Negroes

3861. If a snake runs across your foot in front of a house which you are about to enter, the house is haunted
.......................North-eastern Kentucky

3862. If a door closes or moves without any wind or other visible cause, the house is haunted..............
.......................North-eastern Kentucky

3863. If you bury anything alive, it will haunt you.....
.... Mountains

3864. If a murder or suicide is committed in a house and a drop of blood falls on the floor, the house will be haunted and the blood can never be washed out or painted over.

3865. If you have killed a person and are troubled over the fact, go to his grave at midnight, face the north, step forward over the grave and then backward over it. You will be troubled no more..........
................Central Kentucky Negroes

3866. A seventh son is able to see ghosts or spirits......
......................Louisville colored

3867. One child in each family is able to raise knocking spirits ....Mountains

3868. There is a legend in Kentucky that the shades of departed Indians return from the Happy Hunting Ground annually in the dark of the moon in October and silently tread again the old trails.

3869. "Rappen," a spirit of the other world, knocks on the wall when one in the house is sure to die......
..............................Blue Grass

3870. A deaf and dumb supper is prepared as follows. While preparing this supper the participants must neither speak or be spoken to by any one. All the work must be done backwards, that is, they walk backwards and hold their hands behind them while doing the work. When all is ready for eating, some supernatural sign appears to them. Sometimes it is two men carrying a corpse; or a large white dog may appear. Whatever it may be, it is always very alarming in appearance.

3871. A much feared animal, called the dog-eater, occasionally appears in folk superstition. He is thought to devour dogs and even other animals. He also terrorizes people.

3872. Soldiers at the front usually have a "call" or "vision" before death................Blue Grass

3873. Ghosts are the spirits of people who died and were not satisfied........................Blue Grass

3874. A sudden warm breeze means the passing of a ghost ....Negroes

3875. If one asks a ghost what it desires, it will tell him ....Blue Grass

3876. Negroes wear matches in their hair to keep evil spirits away ....Negroes

3877. You can frighten evil spirits away by burning rubber ....Mountains

3878. To keep away ghosts, put a feather duster in the doorway....................Western Kentucky

3879. If a spirit or a ghost pursues you, stop in the middle of a stream and make the sign of the cross with your fingers.......................Mountains

3880. To frighten ghosts away when you meet them in a lonely lane on a dark night, cross the left thumb over the index finger, draw a long breath and exclaim in a sepulchral voice: "Skip-i-to!" No ghost can withstand this process, especially if the words are repeated..........Western Kentucky

3881. If one shoots at a ghost with a silver bullet, he will kill it.............................Blue Grass

3882. If you think you hear your name called, you will probably die if you answer before you are sure; for it may be that the ghosts are calling your spirit... ....Blue Grass

MISCELLANEOUS

3883. To change a will is unlucky.

3884. It brings bad luck for a boat to be christened with anything but champagne.

3885. "Laughing's catching," that is, if you laugh at another's bad luck, you will have bad luck yourself.

3886. To leave a book unfinished that you have begun to read is unlucky.............Western Kentucky

3887. It causes bad luck to break a piece of candy or the like in anybody else's hand.

3888. It is unlucky to throw a gift away.

3889. Never walk under a ladder, especially if there is someone on the top of it, for bad luck will follow.

3890. If one jumps from a window, someone in the person's family will pass away.

3891. To go through a window brings bad luck.

3892. If you forget anything, you will see a cross.

3893. It brings good luck to bury a pencil....Mountains

3894. If you start to say something and do not finish it, you will be disappointed..North-eastern Kentucky

3895. If you measure a person while he is lying down, he will soon die.

3896. It brings death to answer a mysterious voice...... .... Negroes

3897. If you think that you hear someone call your name when no one has done so, something bad will happen to the person whom you thought you heard calling you.

3898. If you hear your name called, some soul in purgatory is calling for your prayers................ ....North-eastern Kentucky

3899. If you slip on a banana peeling, you will have bad luck.

3900. It brings bad luck to boast (unless you knock on wood) of immunity from any trouble or illness.

3901. Billikens bring good luck.

3902. After making a call, you must leave the room through the same door by which you entered it.

3903. Leave any room by the door through which you entered; otherwise you will have bad luck.

3904. If you give something away that is given you, it will smell bad......................Blue Grass

3905. Misfortunes never come singly.

3906. If a person's given name is changed, he will die.

3907. Never whistle in a dressing room of a theatre. This superstition is held by actors.

3908. It brings very bad luck to step over a hole.

3909. It brings bad luck to ring a bell upside down......
..........................Central Kentucky

3910. It brings bad luck to give away or spend anything you find.

3911. If you sing secular music, you will come to grief..
.... Mountains

3912. You will have good luck if you rub coal oil on your neck ....Mountains

3913. It causes good luck to meet a gypsy fortune-teller.

3914. It is a sign of good luck if, upon opening the Bible, your finger accidentally falls on the words, "Verily, verily."............................Blue Grass

3915. Upon the first visit to the source of a spring, put a pebble from the brook into the hem of your skirt. Then lose it without being conscious of the loss. You will have good luck.....Southern Kentucky

3916. If you smoke a cigarette with a gold band on it, you will have good luck.

3917. A whistling girl and a bleating sheep, will always come to the top of the heap....Western Kentucky

3918. To pick up gravel under the right foot and sleep on it will bring good luck..............Mountains

3919. If you have hiccoughs, someone will tell a story on you ....Mountains

3920. If you have hiccoughs, you have told a lie........ ....Blue Grass

3921. If you once get your feet wet in the Cumberland river, you will always return to the Kentucky mountains ....Mountains

3922. Human vitality is always lowest between midnight and morning.

3923. Human vitality is lowest at three o'clock in the morning.

3924. If you cross your fingers when you see a one-legged negro, you will remove the ill luck that follows the sight of such a person..............Blue Grass

3925. Smoke follows beauty.

3926. Smoke from an out-of-door fire drifts to the most beautiful person within range.

3927. If you go through an unfinished building, you will see someone whom you are not expecting to see.

3928. If you use the same towel with another, you will certainly quarrel with that person.

3929. The negroes think that when they "get religion," the Lord speaks to them directly. For instance, one said that the Lord told him to crawl on a log .... Negroes

3930. Poison oak will not affect a really black negro.....
........................Central Kentucky

3931. A sandman who sprinkles sand in the eyes is responsible for sleepiness.

3932. If you wish to learn to pick a banjo, take the banjo to the forks of the road on a dark night and try it
....................Central Kentucky Negroes

3933. Engineers have a premonition that they should avoid a certain run.

3934. If you curse God and shoot at the sun, you will be able to see the wind.................Mountains

3935. If you start to tell a thing and forget it, what you were planning to tell is not so........Mountains

3936. If the dews are heavy in August, tobacco will weigh heavy.

3937. Jews will not kill a chicken.

3938. In talking to someone if you call him by someone else's name, the one named is thinking of you.

3939. "Come easy, go easy," that is, something that comes without effort will be lost.

3940. A sudden silence in the midst of a conversation means that an angel is passing through the room. Human voices are hushed in reverence.

3941. If two persons collide at work, they will work together another year.

3942. If two people in bending over knock their heads together, they will sleep together that night.....
........................Southern Kentucky

3943. A comet is a sign of war.

3944. If three persons in conversation say the same word simultaneously, a fool is coming.

3945. "If you speak of an angel, you will hear the rustle

of his wings," that is, if you speak of anyone, you will find him near.

3946. "If you speak of the Devil, he will appear." This saying has the same meaning as the preceding one.

3947. Keep a seat for the unexpected guest. You will some day entertain an angel in disguise. Blue Grass

3948. You will have good luck if you find a rusty nail. You should not pick it up, but you should reverse the ends just where the nail lies.......Mountains

3949. You will have bad luck if you follow the light of a jack-o'-lantern ....Blue Grass Negroes

3950. A stone with a hole through the middle is a good talisman....................Central Kentucky

3951. You will have bad luck if you find a stone with a hole in it, unless it contains a crack from the outer edge to the hole..............Central Kentucky

3952. To have iron or steel about you during a thunder storm will bring good luck.

3953. A fool for luck.

3954. Some people have the power of finding underground water with the use of a forked peach or hazel switch. When the water-witch, as such a person is called, walks above the water, the fork or divining rod turns downward.[1]

---

[1] The divining rod is considered by some folk-lore students to have been originally a symbol of forked lightning. See, for example, John Fiske: *Myths and Mythmakers*, pp. 41-44, 64, 66-67.

INDEX

INDEX

Bridesmaid, 700.

Bridle, 427, 3795, 3819.

British Lady, 238.

Bronchitis, 1126.

Broom, 239, 240, 565, 566, 1285, 1522, 1524, 1588-1628, 1722, 2014,
    2770, 3825, 3837.

Brother, 1912, 2216, 2326.

Brown, 629, 904, 907, 1223, 1421, 2352.

Buckeye, See Horse-chestnut.

Buggy-riding, 403, 2029.

Bullet, 734, 2177, 3471, 3775, 3829, 3832, 3881.

"Bullrock," 3551.

Bumble-bee, 1300.

Burdock Root, 1384.

Burn, 235, 237, 331, 332, 345, 348, 413, 415, 544, 567, 785, 799-805,
    1007, 1106, 1108-1113, 1147, 1554, 1555, 1572, 1735, 1781,
    1805, 1806, 1819, 1838-1843, 1853, 1855, 1871, 2119, 2160,
    2337, 2693, 2711, 2712, 2737, 2770, 2907, 2908, 2931, 2980,
    2992, 2993, 2994, 3037, 3078, 3522, 3641, 3686, 3699, 3792,
    3811, 3844, 3877.

Burning, 544, 807, 808, 1221, 1557, 1558, 1559, 1829, 2036.

Bury, 367, 468, 772, 774, 778, 779, 781, 880, 981, 1007, 1059, 1076,
    1194, 1214, 1251, 1340, 1354, 1399, 1409, 1430, 1433, 1434,
    1437, 1441, 1444, 1447, 1462, 1470, 1472, 1474, 1479, 1492,
    1518, 1523, 1524, 1527, 1532, 1533, 1539, 1676, 1703, 2176,
    2178, 3079, 3369, 3370, 3504, 3761, 3844, 3863, 3893.

Bush, 410, 532, 1034, 1154, 1530, 2275.

Business, 1001, 2760, 2858.

Butter, 241, 1245, 1671, 1672, 1852, 3044, 3111, 3335-3337, 3791,
    3795-3801.

Butter-beans, 2254, 2886.

Butterfly, 242, 290, 1141, 2339, 2488, 3670-3675.

Buttermilk, 1204, 2375, 2987.

Buttons, 243, 693, 2064-2071, 2141.

Buzzard (turkey-buzzard), 139, 591, 592, 3650-3652.

INDEX

C

Cabbage, 1365, 1804, 2237, 2256, 2257, 2793, 2922.

Cake, 241, 244, 246, 263, 693, 1258, 1837, 1846, 1853-1858, 2776.

Calendar, 1685.

Calf, 1635, 1660, 2277-2279, 2281, 2340, 2773, 3331, 3334.

Camphor, 2341-2343.

Cancer, 1114, 1115.

Candle, 245-247, 396, 1735-1741.

Candy, 1435, 2344, 3887.

Canebrush, 2217, 2326.

Cap, 248, 508, 2093, 3217, 3273.

Car, 166, 765, 2223, 3064-3067, 3069-3071, 3073, 3074, 3121, 3126, 3301.

Carbon, 1301.

Carbuncles, 1116, 3611.

Cards, 42, 249, 250, 1628, 3229-3261 (luck).

Cat, 144, 251-253, 478, 479, 480, 686, 762, 1117, 1183, 1332, 1333, 1353, 1442, 1443, 1584, 1913, 1914, 1915, 2346-2351, 3228, 3268-3317, 3384, 3780, 3806.

Caterpillar, 2352, 3768.

Catfish, 3187.

Cattle, 1251, 1487, 3318, 3319, 3388.

Caul, 12.

Cedar, 254, 2975-2980.

Ceiling, 207, 1386, 3755, 3756, 3841.

Cellar, 255, 380.

Cemetery, See Graveyard.

Chair, 239, 256-259, 400, 1630-1642, 3231, 3233, 3234.

Champagne, 3884.

Change of Garments, 185, 1257, 2114-2118.

Charcoal, 260, 1077.

Charm, 516, 614, 910, 1018, 1030, 1113, 1430, 1520, 3122, 3798, 3804, 3831-3833, 3834, 3837, 3853, 3855.

Cheek, 261, 1001.

Chest, 1290, 1420.

Chestnut, 262, 2826.

D

Daddy-Long-Legs, 106, 3694, 3695.

Daisy, 300, 2851.

Dance, 301, 699, 1003, 2538, 2671, 2932, 3702.

Dandelion, 86, 87, 302-304, 1460, 2865, 2928.

Danger, 1037, 2059, 2689, 2690, 2816, 3043, 3347, 3727, 3846.

Dark-haired, 904, 1843, 3721.

Daughter, 99, 436, 1375, 3130, 3279.

Day, 87, 114, 281, 420, 422, 425, 426, 427, 428, 429, 441, 473, 475, 503, 529, 537, 575, 625-627, 644, 647, 650, 651-653, 655, 657, 698, 701, 762, 781, 834, 930, 1038, 1044, 1146, 1148, 1203, 1208, 1212, 1231, 1296, 1369, 1379, 1433, 1434, 1437, 1493, 1504, 1631, 1677, 1800, 1858, 1860, 1861, 1948, 2023, 2025, 2029, 2030, 2085, 2183, 2234, 2264, 2334, 2338, 2339, 2357, 2361, 2371, 2383, 2385, 2388-2390, 2392, 2393, 2400, 2401, 2403, 2405, 2406, 2408, 2410, 2412, 2418, 2424, 2430, 2431, 2435, 2439, 2440, 2442, 2445, 2454, 2457, 2461, 2462, 2465, 2477, 2479, 2485, 2486, 2488, 2515, 2521, 2538, 2557, 2567, 2577-2581, 2592, 2596, 2615, 2616, 2627, 2629, 2647, 2648, 2652-2654, 2657, 2658, 2678, 2681, 2696, 2699, 2700-2865, 2866, 2867, 2871, 2905, 3006, 3025, 3039, 3060, 3099, 3137, 3172, 3181, 3200, 3218, 3219, 3222, 3301, 3444, 3462, 3473, 3543, 3558, 3564, 3578, 3607, 3689, 3715, 3774, 3797, 3803, 3833, 3947.

Days and Seasons, 2700-2865.

Dealing (cards), 3236, 3237, 3244, 3250, 3256-3259.

Death, 77, 80, 164, 265, 289, 305, 313, 316, 365, 412, 421, 425, 428, 478, 524, 636, 676, 685, 706, 708-782, 811, 874-876, 878, 882, 889, 958, 973, 980, 998, 1028, 1040, 1047-1050, 1059, 1067. 1152, 1180, 1218, 1328, 1352, 1461, 1471, 1545, 1565, 1568, 1572, 1574-1577, 1581, 1612, 1622, 1635, 1640, 1643-1647, 1649, 1651, 1652, 1658-1660, 1666, 1681, 1682, 1703, 1704, 1729, 1735, 1738, 1743, 1747, 1750, 1764, 1824, 1877, 1888, 1904, 1905, 1912, 1918-1921, 1927, 1928, 1953, 1956, 1964, 1966, 1967, 1971, 1981, 1991, 1992, 1994, 1998, 2002, 2005, 2013, 2015, 2016, 2020, 2022, 2024, 2078, 2103, 2119, 2120, 2136, 2165, 2167-2169, 2171, 2172, 2175, 2184, 2188, 2189, 2191, 2193, 2194,

Frostbite, 1193-1197, 2506, 3213.

Fruit, 594, 1950, 1951, 1952, 2237, 2262, 2264, 2315, 2325, 2399, 2421, 2513, 2526, 2572, 2835, 2970-2972.

Funeral, 80, 289, 524, 708, 754, 757-764, 777, 782, 1059, 1764, 1953, 2168, 2916, 3348, 3606, 3692.

Fur, 678, 1195, 2327, 3296.

Furniture, 75, 1626-1651.

G

Garment, 185, 579, 1355, 1565, 2043, 2071, 2103-2105, 2107, 2111, 2112, 2115, 2116, 2119, 2774, 3476, 3507. See also Clothes.

Garter, 607, 2130, 2131.

Ghost, 3289, 3405, 3493, 3859-3882.

Gift, 3888, 3904.

Ginseng, 1249.

Glass, 458, 504, 756, 1695, 1867, 1869, 1870, 2175, 2221, 2489, 3334, 3803.

Goat, 1251, 3216, 3387-3389.

God, 506, 3773-3775, 3929, 3934.

Goitre, 1214-1218.

Gold, 117, 333, 504, 691, 859, 861, 942, 1216, 1355, 1468, 2695, 3416, 3526, 3916.

Good Luck, 20, 30, 97, 99, 100, 115, 357, 386, 619, 621, 626, 630, 634, 641, 646, 652, 653, 655, 656, 661-666, 670, 678, 681, 686-688, 695-697, 771, 823, 863, 864, 867, 892, 988, 1000, 1001, 1021, 1032, 1045, 1578, 1580, 1582, 1583, 1585, 1590, 1592, 1602, 1608, 1636, 1676, 1730, 1751, 1753, 1845, 1907, 1916, 1929, 1937, 1945, 1947, 1948, 1950, 1951, 1955, 1957, 1960, 1962, 1963, 1975, 1977-1979, 2010, 2011, 2018, 2025, 2026, 2037, 2040, 2054, 2060, 2063, 2064, 2070, 2074, 2075, 2080, 2087, 2093, 2113, 2114, 2116, 2118, 2128, 2130, 2131, 2159, 2203, 2207, 2213, 2219, 2224, 2233, 2298, 2704, 2709, 2713, 2714, 2716, 2730, 2745, 2749, 2755, 2758-2760, 2764, 2765, 2784-2786, 2796, 2805, 2830, 2853, 2856, 2857, 2858, 2861, 2882, 2887, 2894, 2897, 2898, 2934, 2935, 2938-2940, 2945, 2970, 2975, 3002, 3013, 3014, 3017-3021, 3023, 3024, 3028, 3038, 3039, 3041, 3048, 3064-3067, 3078, 3079, 3096, 3107, 3108,

K

2583 (around moon), 2586, 2590, 2655, 3126 (bell), 3668, 3819, 3909.

Ring-worm, 1328, 1329, 1330.

Robin, 232, 513, 2364, 3646-3648.

Rock, see Stone.

Rocking-chair, 1639-1641.

Roof, 487, 1898, 3657.

Rooster, 1451, 1454, 2358, 2361-2367, 2795, 2808, 3538, 3539, 3558-3572, 3574-3579, 3583-3593. See also Chicken.

Rose, 515, 623, 692, 1946, 2955.

Rubber, 2161, 3877.

Rug, 678, 1516, 1686, 1687, 2624.

S

Sage, 1373 (buds), 1374, 2956.

Sailor, 740, 2480, 2481, 2549, 2611, 2627.

Saliva, see Spit.

Salt, 1, 333, 517-519, 663, 1137, 1140, 1243, 1254 (of steel), 1345, 1508, 1566, 1585-1587, 1806-1818, 2323, 2625, 3524, 3649, 3837, 3845.

Sand, 2330, 2762, 3931.

Sassafras, 1115, 1509, 1510, 1781, 2322, 2992, 2993.

Saturday, 446, 453, 539, 591, 625, 626, 1035, 1894, 1895, 2233, 2234, 2289, 2466, 2473, 2700, 2702, 2703, 2772-2779, 3645.

"Scarify," 1240.

School Book, 89-94.

Scissors, 186, 1167, 1761, 2723.

Season, 289, 290, 311, 1890, 1952, 2329, 2370, 2393, 2513, 2680, 2683, 2700-2865, 2916, 2930, 2969, 3214, 3690.

Second Sight, 12.

Seeds, 87, 302-304, 580, 581, 1396, 1454 (wart), 2210, 2211, 2260, 2865, 2868, 2874, 2875, 2876, 2907, 2908 (corn), 2923, 2926, 2928, 2941, 2956, 2999, 3002, 3006.

September, 617, 2399, 2847, 2851, 2852.

Seven, 114, 295, 389, 481, 482, 553, 554, 555, 561, 604, 675, 1042, 1065, 1105, 1212, 1375, 1449, 1455, 1468, 1493, 1512, 1515, 2179, 2426, 2474, 2475, 2582, 2678, 2899, 3000, 3129, 3135,

Thorn, 1154, 1530.

Thousand-legged Worm, 3771, 3772.

Thread, 113, 577-579, 1476, 1513, 1531, 1532, 1681, 3272.

Three, 225, 270, 311, 339, 427, 433, 455, 458, 514, 523, 539, 541, 552, 603, 762, 869, 899, 930, 1040, 1045, 1054, 1055, 1111, 1112, 1114, 1146, 1148, 1155, 1176, 1211, 1218, 1240, 1241, 1257, 1275, 1351, 1362, 1363, 1367, 1369, 1374, 1377, 1436, 1441, 1472, 1474, 1482, 1494, 1497, 1507, 1516, 1524, 1534, 1540, 1584, 1721, 1741, 1746, 1901, 2025, 2172, 2376, 2388, 2392, 2393, 2435, 2462, 2473, 2477, 2485, 2488, 2520, 2523, 2538, 2557, 2629, 2696, 2865, 2866, 2905, 2963, 2965, 3017, 3039, 3046, 3053, 3122-3128, 3189, 3226, 3232, 3258, 3259, 3274, 3275, 3307, 3342, 3344, 3368, 3411, 3412, 3462, 3542, 3568, 3620, 3766, 3773, 3777, 3805, 3807, 3923, 3944.

Throat, 1132-1137, 1170, 1181.

Thrush, 1369-1380.

Thumb, 152, 338, 384, 585, 937-942, 966, 990, 1086, 1237, 1297, 1368, 3880.

Thunder, 782, 1669, 1799, 2394, 2395, 2404, 2407-2413, 2449, 2489, 2564, 2697, 2698, 2717, 3186, 3187, 3661, 3677, 3678, 3763.

Thunder-storm, 648, 764, 2329, 2689, 2690, 3012, 3952.

Thursday, 625, 626, 1035, 1039, 2464, 2700-2703, 2706, 2760, 2761, 3505.

Tickle, 71.

Toad, 582, 583, 1214, 1215, 1325, 1352, 1415, 2660, 3166, 3495-3507, 3690.

Tobacco, 862, 1064, 1116, 1138, 1429, 1535, 2626, 2732, 2962-2967, 3697, 3815.

Toe, 584-588, 985, 989, 990, 991, 993, 1002, 1004, 1005, 1059, 1149, 1163, 1255, 1281, 1320, 1346, 1377, 1416, 2147, 2150, 3501, 3502, 3533, 3626, 3678.

Toe-nail, 1132, 2707.

Tongue, 78, 84, 854, 855, 859, 860, 1291, 3804.

Tooth, see Teeth.

Tooth-ache, 1395, 1398-1414, 2134, 2707.

Toothpick, 1536, 1538.

Towel, 563, 1730, 1731, 1793 (tea), 3128, 3180, 3928.